AN ANATOMY OF AMERICAN POLITICS

An Anatomy of American Politics

Innovation versus Conservatism

by

ARTHUR BERNON TOURTELLOT

GREENWOOD PRESS, PUBLISHERS
WESTPORT, CONNECTICUT

For

JONATHAN BERNON

And in today already walks tomorrow.
—SAMUEL TAYLOR COLERIDGE

Contents

Part One: The Idea

Political Institutions in America

Part Two: The Reality
Political Experience in America

Part Three: The Mechanics
Political Methods in America

Part One

THE IDEA:

POLITICAL INSTITUTIONS IN AMERICA

For politics is a business of interpretation . . .
—WOODROW WILSON

Chapter One

The Beginnings

ON WHY THE YOUNGEST RACE ON THIS PLANET, MAN, DEVISED
THE STATE IN THE FIRST PLACE, WHAT HE HOPED TO ACHIEVE
THEREBY, AND HOW, DESPITE SOME GREAT ADVANCES, THESE
HOPES WENT AWRY BUT WERE RESTORED BY A LITTLE GROUP OF
MEN IN PHILADELPHIA WHO GOT BACK TO FIRST PRINCIPLES

I

OF ALL the forms of animal life that have been dominant on this planet, the rule of mammals (including
the youngest and a weaker variety—man) has thus
far been astonishingly brief. And man himself has been the
ruling mammal for only a tiny fraction of that short time. Such
venerable animals as the horse, the rhinoceros and the bat have
been on earth forty times as long as man or forty million years
to man's one million. Reptiles, currently treated with some
disdain, have been here a hundred and sixty-one times as long
as man and, immediately preceding the rise of mammals, ruled
the earth with crawling persistence for over a hundred million
years. Before that, fish, which took over in 475,000,000 B.C., were
dominant for over three hundred million years. For a billion
years before that, the utterly placid and spongelike jellyfish and
later the no more inspired shellfish were the dominant forms of
life. Indeed, if the rise of animal life on earth were represented
by its ascent up the earth's highest mountain, the 29,141-foot
Mount Everest, the ascendancy of man would not begin until a
scant twenty feet from the top; and his political experience, from
prehistoric times to the present, would begin scarcely an inch

and a half from the top. In fact, if you stuck an ordinary paper match vertically on the very summit of Everest, you would have the chronological relationship of man's political experience to the whole span of all animal life on this planet. Yet that political nature of man, which has got him where he is and won him domination over much stronger and larger and fleeter mammals, has in that short time become a necessary condition of his existence, his primary agency of progress and also perhaps the greatest single threat to his continued dominance.

Consider the young race of man in his primitive phase. He arrived on the face of the earth the very latest of all animals. He was weaker than the tiger, smaller than the elephant, slower than the horse. His hide was relatively thin, his hairy covering sparse. He reproduced infinitely more slowly than the insects, lacked the ready adaptability of the amphibians. But he had two intangible assets that outweighed all these limitations. He shared the ape's curiosity about his environment, and he had a faculty previously as unknown on earth as animals with legs had been some hundred and eleven million years earlier: he had reason. He could figure out cause and effect. He knew that one condition could give rise to another, that certain conditions that produced undesirable effects could be changed, or eliminated, that some could be turned from liabilities to assets, that still others could be controlled to serve his ends or at least to cease hampering them. Reason taught him, after a considerable amount of trial and error, that he could kill a tiger in spite of his relative lack of strength by throwing a stone and that he could be as fleet as the horse by riding it. His reason was compensation at once for his comparative weakness and his comparative slowness.

Yet although his reason insured his survival through his first critical centuries on earth, it did not of itself get him very far so long as he employed it only within the area of his individual existence. He had to spend too much time outsmarting other animals and others of his own kind to progress very fast. It was, indeed, roughly four hundred thousand years before he came to the elementary conclusion that a handleless weapon could be made by pounding one end of a chunk of flint into a sharp edge, and it took him another fifty thousand years to make the discovery that the weapon would be more useful and easier to employ if a piece of wood were attached as a handle. Living in an interglacial period, when the earth was warm and pleasant, he did not exercise his mental faculties to the extent of devising shelter or using fire until the descent of the last glacier, which occurred at a point about 95 per cent along man's path from his beginning to the present.

In view of this limited use of his reason, man remained an extraordinarily vulnerable animal. With his innate curiosity he noticed that he was the only animal whose young was totally helpless for a long period. The issue of other mammals could walk shortly after birth and could take care of themselves within weeks. The issue of man could not even turn over for months and could not take care of themselves for years.

Moreover, in addition to the constant threats of nature, intensified by the new problem of coldness brought by the last glacier and the resulting sharpening of the struggle of other and stronger mammals to get the remaining food, man noticed that he was having more troubles with his own kind. As soon as he found himself a suitable cave, another man came along to threaten his security; and, if the interloper was stronger, he took the cave for himself. With less opulent fruit trees after the glacier, he had difficulty getting enough food without fighting another man for access to a tree which had enough for both of them. His flint ax thrown at a beast to secure a fur covering for himself was frequently matched with one thrown at him by another man who wanted the same fur. He had not come very far in his million years on earth, and he was already on the brink of extinction.

And then—somewhere around ten thousand to eight thousand years before Christ—he hit upon what proved to be at once his salvation and the greatest acceleration to progress in his history: he began to evolve a political life.

II

Man's decision to enter upon a political life, his origin of the state, was purposive: he originated it for a purpose, which was to promote his own welfare and, therefore, the welfare of his kind. And he devised government as a means of giving the state effective expression. Today, after all these ages, a state is headed for trouble and its government for collapse as soon as it forgets or ignores that ancient reason for its existence. For if it does not from time to time renew itself with a realization of its aim and the aim of its people in having created it, its purpose becomes distorted, its usefulness over and its downfall, from either revolution within or crusade without, inevitable. Conversely, a state is healthy and its government good according to its awareness of those original aims and its genuine effort to meet them.

As early Neolithic (that is, of the New Stone Age, when rough stone tools were gradually replaced by polished stone tools) man groped about to begin his political life, he was primarily concerned with filling his physical wants, insuring his safety and furthering his freedom. He had discovered a staggering thing in his long, slow experimentation with life on a jungle level, and that was the terrifying injustice of Nature. The strongest who needed it least got the most food, and the weakest who needed it most got the least or none at all. Even when there was no overwhelming difference in strength but the interests of two men clashed at a banana tree, the best fighter claimed and usually got all the bananas, the loser none. Similarly, a man could lose both his life and his mate if an intruder decided to appropriate the mate by clubbing the man while he slept. Consequently, no man had any real freedom; for if he was not on the prowl for food, he was on guard for his life—and he had no assurance of either. And so ultimately—after the desperation of a million years—he sought, in a word that remains the highest aspiration of good men everywhere, simple justice, the ideal and the goal of his political life.

Man's discovery of the concept of justice, his fumbling creation of the state to set a stage for its entrance into human affairs and his discovery of the device of governments to insure its dispensation together form the greatest single step in his advancement. Compare only the last five hundred thousand years of his existence (no more than half of his whole history) to a climb up the 102-story Empire State Building, and it would take him up to the eighty-second story to get to the point of using a crude, handleless flint ax and another fifteen stories to get to the discovery of fire. But since the institution of his political life, it would take him only half a story to cover the time from the enslaving reigns of the pharaohs of Egypt to the drafting of the United States Constitution. Considering the biologic history of mankind, then, the race's progress under political living has been amazingly fast.

Nevertheless, men would do well to ponder occasionally a predecessor of theirs on this planet—the dinosaur, who represented the flowering of the Age of Reptiles as man does the flowering of the Age of Mammals. The thing that gave the dinosaur its ascendancy and rule over animal life and the thing that brought about its destruction were the same: its great size, the agency of its salvation when size counted most in the pristine struggle for life and the agency of its dissolution when the glaciers descended and it could not move fast enough to get food for its great bulk. And this instrument of man's salvation, this political genius, could conceivably, if its original purpose ever be sufficiently forgotten, lead him to a similarly gloomy end. Before this chapter is done, we shall see how from time to time some steps in that melancholy direction have been taken and how, on the positive side, some very great steps were taken along the opposite and infinitely more hopeful way.

III

Essentially the state was originally evolved, as has been indicated, to resolve the conflicting interest of individuals. Where there were such conflicts, there were physical strife, hunger, uncertainty, fear. These clashes were unquestionably highly localized at the beginning—as, for example, the perpetual conflict over the local banana tree, when two men fought for the fruit and a third probably appeared to make away with it while their backs were turned, only to be waylaid himself on his route home. The older and wiser heads of the community eventually concluded that under this anarchy no one really won, everyone lost and that the fruit tree was sufficient to nourish them all if its use were regulated. Elders were chosen to prescribe such regulations, which sooner or later involved not only the relationship of men to their environment but to one another. And the area of concern was gradually widened so that such regulation grew from an application only to one family or tribe to a whole geographic area which ultimately came to be called a state or nation. The first elders outlawed modes of conduct, such as killing and stealing, that might be harmful to their tribe or community or state, and encouraged conduct that might be helpful, such as trade, which permitted some men to stay away from the fruit tree altogether and remain at home making awls of bone which could later be swapped for fruit.

Now obviously this overly simplified primitive state would not have worked at all if it had not been a reflection of the will of most of its members. When the elders chose a chief to carry out their prescriptions he would have been promptly ignored or more probably stoned to death if the majority had wanted to go right on stealing and killing and had considered such conduct prudent and desirable and to their own best interests. Moreover, regulations or laws made would have been similarly treated; for to be effective, indeed to exist at all, they had to be nothing more than a codification, a formal enactment, of the moral judgment of the community. And this is a condition of statehood and lawmaking which, despite the transitory success of some aberrations, survives after some ten thousand years. World government—a world state—has thus far failed in the approaches of both the League of Nations and the United Nations because it did not really reflect in sufficient strength the will of the majority of its members, who were either still too blinded or too shortsighted to see its desirability or who had its purposes distorted for them by powerful and evil men. In equal degree any law that is not in effect a statement of the verdict of the majority of the community will not work. A classic example was America's prohibition law, which no amount of money or preachments could enforce in the absence of any strong general conviction that liquor traffic was in fact as well as in law a crime. Political institutions among men, therefore, whether the framework which is the state or the documentation of principles of conduct which is the law, came into existence and remain as implements for man's serving himself.

Although the state was originated, at the volition of men, to administer justice among them, it gradually took on a personality of its own. It had life, could make decisions and could act— always, theoretically, for the purpose of advancing the interests of its people. Soon, however, it became apparent that, just as the

interests of individuals had conflicted and given rise to the introduction and development of political life, so the interests of
states were conflicting. If the human race had decided then and
there that there would have to be a government and a body of
law among nations, if indeed it had prescribed the same course
that it had adopted to cure conflicts among individuals, nearly
all the great woes of history would have been averted. But it
had taken a million years of struggle among individuals to institute the state among men, and it is probably not unreasonable
now to have to know that ten thousand years of struggle among
nations have not been enough to demonstrate the need for a
larger accomplishment. At any rate, in spite of man's experience that physical force led only to disaster when used as an
instrument to settle conflicts among individuals, he very early
adopted it as an instrument to settle conflicts between states.
Too soon for his own good, he saw the use of such force become the chronic and exclusive occupation of specialized bodies
known as armies and navies, and occasionally some leaders even
lost sight of the reason for the existence of armed might and set
off world disasters by regarding it as an end in itself.

The association of armed forces with political institutions
coupled a great evil with a great good. Not only did armies fail
ever to cure permanently conflicts among nations (often they
have in fact created them), but they also confused political leaders so that they soon forgot their primary business of administering justice and began to fancy themselves as potentates or men
of power but not necessarily of responsibility. They threw their
weight around, forced people into their armies and finally imposed their personal wills on the people whose own will their
appropriate role should have been to determine and execute.
These rulers were soon visited with the notion that not only
was their will paramount but that their favored positions should
be perpetuated by the business of their holding office for life

and then passing it on to their sons and the sons of their sons. The first thing the somewhat baffled race of man knew, he had kings and emperors on his hands. He began then to accept the idea that he was born to execute the will of the state or the monarch, having lost sight completely of the fact that the state was founded for the express purpose of executing his will.

With two conspicuous exceptions, this distortion, coming so soon after the founding of the state, persisted in general among men for nearly five thousand years, and man never entirely corrected it everywhere. (The American Indians apparently did not forget the major functions of their political institutions. The Pueblos, for example, had a high form of council rule that lasted from prehistoric times to their dislodgment by white settlers. This political consistency was probably due to the fact that the Indians had small states in a large area and did not encounter the complications of the crowded European areas.) Their purpose distorted or lost, political institutions often sponsored rather than alleviated injustice, suppressed rather than promoted freedom, instilled rather than mitigated fear. The ancient and absolute rulers of Egypt enslaved hundreds to build the great pyramids—a project of tremendous proportions that had no relationship to the true functions of the state. Kings became intrigued with a singularly useful but utterly fantastic theory that they ruled not because men willed governments into existence to protect the general welfare of the people but because they, the kings, were appointed by the gods and were *ex officio* in some cases gods themselves. This conceit of the "divine right" of kings was no mere transitory illusion. It persisted in England until the reign of James II two hundred and sixty years ago, and it extended from the courts of Europe to the island of Japan, where it lasted until the defeat of Hirohito in 1945. With the spread of the theory of monarchy, armies were soon being raised less for protection than for proud display. Trade, devised by ancient man to expedite the distribution of food and clothing, was enriching small groups and impoverishing large groups. With succeeding ages, these distortions of the state with their abnormalities of governments have assumed different forms but none have endured permanently—not the dynasties of Europe, the Roman emperors, the feudal monarchs, the absolute kings, the czars of Russia or the dictators of later days. We do not need to inquire here into the circumstances of the rise and fall of these political monstrosities, but it should be remembered that all had this in common: they had very little to do with the protection and advancement of the interests of their peoples and no pure concept of the function of the state.

But two great concepts arose among ancient states which have endured for centuries and which were profoundly expressive of the true political purpose of humankind: the Athenian concept of liberty and the Roman concept of law. Upon these two foundations nearly all that has been politically good in Western civilization has been built. And the political leaders, over some two thousand years and more, who have done most to advance the lot of mankind through political action have been those who were quick to see and willing to explore new frontiers of human liberty and who have conceived of laws among men not as rigid principles for controlling the members of the state but as an itemization, as it were, of a voluntary compact entered into by the citizens for their own protection. And those men whose public lives have been most disastrous have been those whose view of liberty has been least imaginative and narrowest and who have limited their concept of the law to a weapon for the maintenance of order.

So firmly rooted, indeed, are the ideas of liberty and law in Western political life that few men have ever announced bluntly that they were against either one or both ideas. Most essential conflicts in modern politics (including the present major partisan phases of American and of English politics) can be ultimately reduced to differences about the nature of individual liberty, the appropriate role of the law and the desirable extent of both. Thus, to most enlightened citizens (of whose views the development of major political parties are an expression) the prospect of a state that is pointless because it does not care at all about the welfare of the people is more repugnant or less repugnant than the prospect of one that is equally erring because it suffers from the delusion that the function of the state is to take care of its members rather than to help them to take care of themselves. For this reason extreme charges and countercharges fly back and forth in election years which are quite natural but which no one takes too seriously.

The Athenian concept of liberty assumed that the individual could live his life most richly and best develop his particular gifts for self-expression and self-fulfillment only if he was assured of two things: that there was no physical restraint upon his person and that there was no moral restraint upon his actions, so long as he did not violate or infringe these same rights in others. The state existed to insure him of these liberties so far as it was possible. Consequently it behooved the citizen to take intelligent and active interest in the affairs of the state—especially in its lawmaking, since he was thereby concerning himself with his own destiny, which was, of course, simply to make the most of himself. But the ancient Greeks took a high view of the capacities of man, and came to believe that there was inevitably a great number of people whose potentialities were so limited that, not only would they never under the best conditions make much of themselves, but their limitations would seriously hamper the more promising members of the community. This was a half-truth which permitted the liberty-loving Athenians to tolerate slavery within their states and the denial of civic freedom to conquered peoples without. And to this paradox of prizing liberty for themselves and yet refusing it to others (which actually revealed a basic lack of faith in the ability of the mass of people to rule themselves) may be traced the downfall of Athenian democracy.

Before its decline, however, Athens had set mankind on its path of government by law, and this was itself the direct product of the Athenian insistence on the preservation of liberty as the first business of the state. As far back as the seventh century before Christ, the body of Athenian citizens began to doubt the adequacy of the unwritten laws of tradition and custom which formed the standards of reference for their magistrates in dispensing justice. They were aware that social and economic changes often made the ways of one generation inappropriate to another. They saw, too, that the magistrates, who were usually drawn from the wealthy class because they received no salaries, were frequently disposed, even if unknowingly, to favor the rich against the poor. In response to public demand, a literal-minded advocate named Draco was called on to substitute for the mass of inherited tradition a code of written laws by which the judges would be bound to render decisions. Draco did not get the idea of what was wanted too clearly and came up with a legal catalogue which listed every known offense in singular detail and prescribed the death penalty for nearly all of them, from petty larceny to murder.

The result of this stringent legalizing was an even greater public clamor which resulted in the commissioning of the worldly scholar, Solon, to rewrite the laws. Solon, whose name has since become a nickname for all lawmakers, threw out all Draco's laws except the one against homicide and proceeded on a program of economic and constitutional reform that has never been surpassed by any legislative event for the importance of its effect on political history. The most epochal of his constitutional reforms was the introduction of a jury system, which provided for laymen to return verdicts on questions of fact in court cases and limited magistrates (who had previously been both judge and jury) to finding on questions of law. Solon also devised a council of four hundred as a top governmental advisory committee, which was a great and long step towards Western representative government.

Economically the laws of Solon instituted reforms and practices to which neither the Republican Party in America nor the Conservative Party in England are yet reconciled. He conceived it to be a function of the state to enact laws to eradicate economic inequities and to control, if necessary, certain aspects of the economy. With a startling similarity to Democratic legislative programs in the United States and similar liberal programs in England, Solon introduced laws to limit the acquisition of properties affecting the public interest, to control the rates of interest, the planting of figs and the cutting of olive trees and even to force all heirs to learn useful trades.

From this body of specific laws, bringing new freedom and new responsibility to the citizens of the state, Athens moved to its Periclean golden age, perhaps the most magnificent civilization this planet has ever known.

The Roman concept of law, to which Western political institutions are no less indebted than to the Athenian ideal of liberty, was broader and politically more mature than that entertained by the Greeks. This very breadth and maturity made Roman law in general as applicable to the complex, industrial society of today as it was to the ancient Roman world, and it expressed itself in two important and still-living legal principles which the Greeks had never appreciated: compromise and universality. One of the troubles encountered by the Greeks in their democratic experience was the rise of conflicts between groups, such as patricians and plebeians, within the state whenever the law was not equally pleasing to both. Now to institute a new law to please only one faction, whether the largest or the most important to the health of the state, although superficially it might appear a democratic solution, could lead only to constant bitterness and eventual insurrection from the losing faction. The Romans, averting this error, regarded the law as necessarily the guardian of the major interests of all groups and presupposed the willingness of all to sacrifice minor factional interests in order to protect and advance the major interests of all. The prudent practice of this art of legislative compromise has been the primary achievement of great legislators and statesmen ever since, while those who have insisted on all or nothing in the name of one group, however enlightened, have been voices crying in the wilderness, the advance agents of false hopes and the dispensers of alternatives of extremes.

The Romans also saw the necessity for extending the benefits of the law to all people whose allegiance was desired by the state. Unlike the Greeks, they offered citizenship to peoples outside the city-state and set up the foundation for the later *res publica,* the commonwealth or republic. This extension of the law to insure protection to all, to see that the peoples of other communities had legal rights and recourse to the law, was the greatest advance in politics since Solon. As a result of its realism and maturity, Roman law not only tended to eliminate conflicts between groups within the state but also welded together the states that formed the Roman Republic and brought, for the first time on the face of the earth, a brotherhood among nations and a universal devotion to a common interest.

The race of man was to see much agony before the principles of ancient Greece and Rome were again asserted once Rome had declined. The dark days of feudalism were still to come, and the rise of tyrants and absolute monarchs. All such political distortions arose not so much from overwhelming new complications in society as from the diverting of the attention of members of the state from the fundamental truism that the state existed solely for their welfare and that when it claimed existence for any other reason it might better not exist at all. Fortunately, in 1215 A.D., when the purpose of the state had been all but lost in the web of trappings, superstitions and mumbo jumbo incidental to the rise of kings and princes, the barons of England gathered at Runnymede and forced King John to recognize that the state did not exist for the sole purpose of supporting a king and to sign a great charter (Magna Charta), which specified the limits of royal powers and the extent of baronial privileges. In the same century, after the crusades had left the monarchs impoverished, the kings found it prudent to gather together representatives of the common people, eventually Houses of Commons, to talk about raising money. From these parliaments was derived the policy of taxation by representation, a departure from which by George III some five centuries later cost the British their American colonies. Meanwhile, the bloodless revolution of 1688 in England, which substituted the enlightened rule of William and Mary for the divine-right persuasions of James II, accomplished the final defeat of absolute monarchy in Britain and marked the supremacy of parliamentary processes in the West.

Both the barons of Runnymede and the deposers of James II, however, failed to press the matter back to first principles. That was the accomplishment of the philosophers first and then of the statesmen of the New World.

IV

It took the race of man perhaps a million years from his appearance on this planet to learn that he could make more progress with political organization than he could without it. It then took him from the decline of the Roman Republic in the second century before Christ to the end of the seventeenth century after Christ to get back again on any very large front to his original reason for founding the state. The reminder came most forcibly from a restless British philosopher, a product of the Puritan revolt against kings and later a rebel against the Puritan authoritarians, John Locke, who said that the purpose of the state was to serve the people and that the people had a right to revolt when the state ceased to serve them. He further pointed out that a government was a conditional moral trust and not an absolute power and that the people had both the right and the obligation to throw it out if it failed or violated the trust imposed on it.

Locke's re-examination of the origin of the state was carried somewhat further by the much less disciplined thinker, Jean Jacques Rousseau. Writing *The Social Contract* thirteen years before the outbreak of the American Revolution, he stated that men were better off in a state of nature without any government at all—a hypothesis that there is little reason for accepting— but that since conditions of insecurity required the setting up of governments, government existed only at the pleasure of the governed and with their consent to its actions. With characteristic zest, Rousseau went on to say that all governments in which the people did not have the right to participate were impostors.

In the little stretch of colonies along the eastern seacoast of the vast American wilderness, Rousseau's views and those of the earlier Locke found a well-disposed audience, for here was an environment where men had perforce got back to an appreciation of why the state existed in the first place. And after they had proclaimed themselves done with the maldeveloped governments of the Old World by turning out their British rulers, they sat down to devise a state and a government which would do what, those fifty thousand years earlier, the groping, ascending human race had originated politics to do: establish justice, insure domestic tranquillity, provide for the common defense, promote the general welfare and secure the blessings of a liberty which had proved meaningless when men in the raw state of nature were at liberty also to kill and steal.

The fifty-five men who met through the hot Philadelphia summer of 1787 to draft the first written constitution in the long history of man's political experience began by restating these objectives. And they finished, as the summer drew to its close, by drawing a pattern for self-government which had both sufficient flexibility and sufficient form to endure through the most violent economic and political upheavals the world has ever known. According to the pattern, they created a machinery for government which had three major and balanced parts: the executive, the legislative and the judiciary. Of these the most original and, in many ways, the most remarkable was the executive, which was called the Presidency.

Chapter Two

The Presidency

A CHAPTER NECESSARILY HISTORICAL FOR IT SHOWS HOW, IN
THE ABSENCE OF A FULL AND SPECIFIC DEFINITION OF THE
AMERICAN PRESIDENCY IN THE CONSTITUTION, THAT OFFICE
HAS BEEN THE CREATION OF THE MEN WHO HELD IT, AND
HOW SOME OF THESE WERE GREAT, SOME GOOD, SOME INDIF-
FERENT AND SOME BAD—AND WHY

I

THE American Presidency, a unique political institution, is also a young one compared to the extent of its growth. Any man who was seventy-three years old in April 1945 was born closer to the death of George Washington than to that of Franklin Roosevelt, and those who were forty at that time were born closer to the end of the administration of Lincoln, the sixteenth President, than to that of Roosevelt, the thirty-first. Yet in the relatively short time from Washington to the present, no more than the life span of two octogenarians, the Presidency of the United States has become the most powerful and effective elective office in the world. And its present strength is almost entirely the product of its own growth. For the Constitution did not create the Presidency: it merely launched it. The creation of the office was the work of not more than sixteen, or half, of the thirty-two men who have held it.

The language of the Constitution was purposely general about the functions of the Presidency. The founding fathers implied rather than stated its powers, partly because everyone attending the Constitutional Convention of 1787 was sure that Washington, who presided over its deliberations, would be the first President and they wanted to leave the specific nature of the office to his shaping, and partly because the "cipher" governors of most of the colonial states made the delegates fearful of rendering the office impotent by restricting its powers and duties by too specific language. Even the language of the prescribed Presidential oath was vague, requiring only that the incoming President "will faithfully execute the office of President of the United States" and "to the best of my ability preserve, protect and defend the Constitution of the United States." There was not a word of what he should refrain from doing nor was there any literal pledge that he would even obey, much less enforce, the laws. As a matter of fact, shortly after his first inauguration, Abraham Lincoln violated an article of the Constitution itself and said afterward that he did so in order to "preserve, protect and defend the Constitution."

Indeed on only three points was the language of the Constitution specific with regard to the Presidency. First, it fixed the term definitely at four years; but it did not restrict the number of terms, so Jefferson could write of the office, "This President seems a bad edition of a Polish king. He may be elected from four years to four years to life." Secondly, it empowered the President to grant pardons or reprieves for any Federal offenses, excluding only cases of impeachment; but it put no qualification on the power, and any President so minded could empty every Federal prison by a stroke of his pen. Thirdly, it made the President "Commander-in-Chief of the Army and Navy of the United States" but did nothing to hinder him from going out to lead the army in the field or the fleet at sea.

At the same time, the drafters of the Constitution, after a good deal of discussion, were careful to plant in that document the seeds of the implied powers of the Presidency, and it is from these that the leading Presidents have nurtured the office along

three major courses of development: as the nation's instrument
for the conduct of foreign relations, as its central agency for the
administration of domestic affairs and as its leader in legislative
action. These great functions have all been developed from
superficially minor provisions of the Constitution. The President shall "appoint ambassadors, other public ministers and consuls" and receive those from other countries and make treaties
with the consent of the Senate is all that the Constitution says of
the Presidency and foreign relations. "He may require the opinion in writing of the principal officer in each of the executive
departments," shall appoint all "officers of the United States" for
whose appointments the Constitution does not otherwise provide and "he shall take care that the laws be properly executed"
is all that it says of the Presidency as an administrative agency.
Finally, his specified power to report to the Congress on the state
of the Union, to recommend measures, to convene the Congress
and adjourn it if the two houses disagree about adjournment and
to disapprove enacted bills (which disapproval the Congress
could ignore by enlisting two thirds of its own members to
ignore it) is all the Constitution provides the Presidency as legislative influence.

In none of these particulars does the Constitution do any more
than present an opportunity to the President. And that opportunity has been as frequently rejected by men holding the office
as it has been welcomed. Consequently the growth of the Presidency has not been a steady one but subject to leaps and bounds.
At times it has not grown at all. It has yielded to judicial
supremacy, as in the early days of the Republic, and to Congressional supremacy, as during the long years before Lincoln
and the longer ones between Lincoln and Cleveland. Sometimes it has yielded to anything at all and become almost empty
and admittedly powerless, as it did between Woodrow Wilson
and the second Roosevelt. In nearly all cases, the limitations of

the office and its periods of retrogression were not the results of external pressures upon the incumbent but rather of the attitudes of those incumbents themselves. No overwhelming pressures were exerted on Taft, for example, that required him to make less of the Presidency than his predecessor and sponsor, Theodore Roosevelt: they were of the same time, of the same party and, for some years at least, of the same governmental team. Nor again have great demands on the office been the measure of the incumbent's conception of it: as much was required of James Buchanan as of Lincoln, but the former allowed the conditions encountered by him to survive for Lincoln to master; and similarly the conditions unalleviated by Herbert Hoover were left for Franklin Roosevelt to allay.

The Constitution has, then, left the American Presidency open to its incumbent's appraisal of the office. In a very literal sense and to an extent true of no other office, therefore, a Presidential election is a vote for or against the man who aspires to it, even when partisan philosophies of the role of the Presidency are considered. Wrote Woodrow Wilson long before he held office: "The President is at liberty, both in law and in conscience, to be as big a man as he can. His capacity will set the limit . . ." The variety of that capacity is the substance of the history of the American Presidency and has almost alone determined its dimensions.

II

What is that capacity which has raised some men of little earlier distinction to undisputed greatness and that has bitterly frustrated other men whose earlier careers were full of promise?

Consider the hundred-and-sixty-year history of the Presidency. Of the thirty-two men who have held the office, these seven achieved a very real degree of greatness, in this order: Abraham Lincoln, George Washington, Franklin Roosevelt, Woodrow Wilson, Thomas Jefferson, Andrew Jackson and James K. Polk—all of whose terms combine to cover about a third, or fifty-two years, of our national history. These were the leaders, the men who took the office and through vision and courage used it to advance the interests of the nation and of humanity. All of them were men who were strong in purpose and whose purpose was closely attuned to their times. Each of them knew where he was going, even if all of them did not know all the time how they were going to get there. Each of them was equipped by gifts of insight and perception to see the needs of his times and by gifts of leadership to respond to them. But each of them had also a more precise quality, and this is the thing that has governed the capacity of any man to grow great in the office: an active moral awareness of the responsibility of the Presidency—that thing which the good Calvinist political scientist Wilson meant by conscience.

In all these men that sense of Presidential responsibility was so strong that they considered it the only moral, if not the only legal, check upon Presidential powers. Consequently, under each of them the powers of the Presidency were greatly expanded. Sometimes this was done by Presidentially inspired act of Congress, as in the first administration of Franklin Roosevelt, to meet an emergency. Occasionally it was done by extralegal steps, as when Lincoln decided two months after taking office to increase the size of the Army and to tell the Congress about it afterward. But most often it was done by a liberal interpretation and strong application of the existent but previously narrowly confined Constitutional powers of the office, as in the case of Jefferson and Polk. Thus there emerge, as a corollary to that active moral awareness of the responsibility of the Presidential office, two principles of Presidential action that the seven great Presidents shared: first, that to meet his responsibility a

President had to take the broadest and not the narrowest view of his Constitutional powers; and, secondly, that it is his duty to suggest and shepherd through the Congress temporary legislation to broaden those powers, if no reasonable interpretation of them is sufficient to meet the requirements of the situation that confronts him and that critically affects the public interest. In short, therefore, the great Presidents have been men who welcomed rather than evaded responsibility and who found some way of meeting it.

Now consider briefly the men who were good but not great Presidents: Theodore Roosevelt, Cleveland, the two Adamses, Monroe, Hayes, Madison, Van Buren and Arthur—perhaps in that order, although they are much less easily graded than the great Presidents. With the exception of Theodore Roosevelt, whose theatrical manner and shrill speeches confuse his real record, most of these men had a less inclusive view of the responsibility of the Presidency to the people than Franklin Roosevelt had, or to the destiny of his nation than Polk had, or to the whole race of man than Lincoln or Wilson had. They missed greatness because their sense of the office, while far from narrow, was more limited than that of the seven leaders. Indeed, some achieved a record of being "good" Presidents only because they had enough breadth in their concept of Presidential powers to accomplish their immediate objectives.

Thus, Cleveland, who went to the White House equipped with the best administrative temperament of any President, succeeded in rescuing the nation temporarily from some of the strange values that had obtained from the end of the Civil War to his first inauguration, but he had insufficient sense of responsibility to the coming industrialized society, whose problems fermented in the 1894 Pullman strike, to handle the strike without using Federal troops in a state which had made no request for such coercive assistance. On the other hand, the imposing

Chester A. Arthur, the worst-equipped man to become President, who had been nothing more than an elegant New York machine politician before he was nominated to the Vice-Presidency strictly as a political manipulation, astonished the people and everlastingly alienated his own party on Garfield's death by vigorously supporting Civil Service reform, prosecuting grafters of his own party and reorganizing the cabinet; for Arthur, despite his hack spoilsman background, had a high concept of the responsibility of the Presidency, and neither adherence to his party machine nor hopes of winning a nomination of his own to the Presidency could swerve him from his stubborn loyalty to that concept. Yet Arthur was no more than a good President and quite far from a great one; he confined that sense of responsibility to much too limited an area.

If we turn to the indifferent Presidents—the men who were neither good nor bad as Presidents—we find in all of them not only a restricted sense of Presidential responsibility but also either an ineptness in carrying out whatever responsibilities they did recognize or such a restrained idea of the powers of the Presidency that they attempted little. It is not insignificant that of the ten indifferent Presidents (headed by Tyler and including in declining order McKinley, Johnson, Taft, Hoover, Benjamin Harrison, Fillmore, Taylor, Pierce and Coolidge), no fewer than four succeeded to the Presidency from the Vice-Presidency, and of these four only one was elected to a term of his own.

Tyler, at the top of the list, was a very special case and a man probably of Presidential caliber who was badly limited by the circumstances of his administration: never elected to the Presidency, he nevertheless served all but thirty days of a full four-year term after the aged William Henry Harrison died of pneumonia contracted at his own inauguration; he was the first Vice-President to succeed to office and had no precedent to follow for guidance; finally, he was a Democrat on a Whig ticket whom the Whigs had nominated as Harrison's running mate in the hopes of capturing a few anti-Van Buren Democratic votes. Tyler, a man of principle, consequently was a virtually powerless President, without a mandate from the people, without a party and without a Congressional following.

Herbert Hoover, on the other hand, had such a confined notion of Presidential responsibility that he was seriously convinced that the President of the United States had no alternative to sitting impotently by while the nation skidded to economic ruin, though he labored long and hard within the rigid limits of the office as he saw it.

The worst of the indifferent Presidents, Calvin Coolidge, simply gave up and thought the office relatively meaningless: "I suppose I am the most powerful man in the world, but great power doesn't mean much except great limitations." If Jefferson and Polk had shared that persuasion, the United States would have remained a thin strip of colonies along the Atlantic seaboard. Presiding over the most amoral period in America's economic history, Coolidge had an ice-bound concept not only of the Presidency but of the whole Federal Government: "It does not at all follow because abuses exist that it is the concern of the federal government to attempt their reform," and the query suggests itself, Why else than to correct and prevent abuses were governments instituted among men at all? And Coolidge lived to see the abuses that he had in mind result in the most desperate plight of this nation since the dark day of Fort Sumter.

Coolidge did, however, have one string on his lute, which he plucked from time to time with a brittle snap: economy. Even if it turned out to be penny-wise and pound-foolish, it stood in some contrast to the three completely disastrous men who occupied the White House: Buchanan, too timid and irresolute to face the problem of secession; Grant, too confused and imperceptive to see the corruption that invaded his own office; and Harding, too weak and undiscriminating even to form an administration. What these three men uniformly lacked was the remotest sense of what the Presidency was all about. Whether they could ever have got anything constructive done remains a completely academic question since none of them showed any signs of knowing what should have been attempted. And the only rewarding aspect they present to the democracy is their relatively low number—less than one in ten of American Presidents—and the brevity of their combined tenure: fourteen years, or less than a tenth of the span of our national history.

III

We have seen above how the Constitution, without going into details or even proposing an executive machinery, launched the Presidency by implication along three great and critical courses: as the head of foreign affairs, as the chief administrator of domestic affairs and as the leading influence in legislative affairs. To the first of these powers, since the days of Washington, the executive has clung more consistently than to either of the other two, and with regard to this function he has been less challenged, with certain conspicuous exceptions, by the other two divisions of the government.

The reason for this is that there is actually in the United States no agency for the conduct of our relations with foreign nations other than the Presidency. The Congress has no Constitutional authority to participate directly in foreign affairs and has been limited to such indirect participation as the Senate's power to approve treaties and the House's authorization to appropriate money. Consequently Congress has had to amplify and sometimes to distort these powers in order to nullify the intent of the executive, without necessarily presenting an alternative and equally constructive program of its own. The Supreme Court has virtually nothing to do with foreign affairs at all, since they are seldom the subject of laws but more often of diplomatic conversations, negotiations and the personal skill of the President, his ambassadors and his special advisers. Moreover, when such negotiations conclude in a treaty, that treaty becomes, in the language of the Constitution, "the supreme law of the land"— which means that it is on a level with the Constitution itself and no more subject to judicial review by the Supreme Court than are the articles establishing the Presidency or the Court itself. As a matter of fact, the Supreme Court has largely limited its concern with foreign affairs to the review of the occasional attempts of individual states to deal directly with foreign powers on such minor matters as the extradition of fugitives—of which attempts the Court has always taken a negative view.

The Congress, which has never been afflicted with the same chronic sense of restraint as the judiciary, has frequently resisted the power of the Presidency in foreign affairs. It began with Washington and hasn't given up yet. Some reasons for this are suggested in the next chapter, which considers the Congress; but for the present it is our purpose only to see what happened from time to time to strengthen the executive as the nation's implement for the conduct of our foreign relations, how various Presidents have contributed to that strengthening process, and what constitutes the awesome world powers of the President of the United States today.

The whole process began with Washington, a man of singular genius in government. Washington saw very clearly that nothing could be more disastrous to this infant republic than having the foreign correspondence of the nation carried on simultaneously by two or three independent agencies of the government, with no one sure what the other was saying. Among the first principles that he established, therefore, was that the Presidency was the only official agency in the United States with which foreign governments could communicate. Seven months after his inauguration he made this obvious, with dramatic sternness, when King Louis XVI of France communicated to "The President and Members of the General Congress of the United States" the news that his son, the heir apparent, had died. Washington did not send the letter or a copy of it to the Congress but merely informed the two houses of its receipt, telling them that he would send the King an answer, which began with the unmistakable information, for the King's benefit, that the President alone should receive and answer communications from foreign governments.

In that same month of October 1789 he also made it abundantly clear that the President had the right to conduct the mechanics of foreign relations as he saw fit and to use extraconstitutional and extrastatutory methods if he wished. He, therefore, started a custom which was often and notably revived in American government, particularly in the twentieth century by Woodrow Wilson and Franklin Roosevelt: that of sending private emissaries, without official position and therefore not subject to Senate approval, to deal on his behalf with foreign governments. Washington did this, in the first year of his first administration, when he asked a private United States citizen, Gouverneur Morris, to talk with British leaders about the terms of a possible treaty of commerce and other matters. His letter to Morris stating, "I desire you . . . on the authority and Credit of this Matter, to converse with His Brittanic Majesty's Ministers on these Points" bears a striking resemblance to the manner in which Franklin Roosevelt empowered Harry Hopkins to conduct top-level diplomatic negotiations: "I am asking you to convey a communication . . . to His Majesty King George VI."

In addition to indicating the unlimited powers of the President in using private agents on fact-finding missions to foreign countries, Washington also assumed the right to recognize other governments. After the French monarchy was turned out in 1792, Washington received an envoy from the new French Republic, Edmond Genêt—an act which in itself constituted recognition of the new republic. Similarly, in the Franco-British War of 1793, Washington issued a proclamation of neutrality, which led to a storm of protest from adherents to the concept of Congressional supremacy (briefly, that since Congress had the sole right to declare war it had also the sole right to declare neutrality). The fury that the proclamation aroused resulted in Congress passing its own Neutrality Act of 1794, but Washington's action succeeded in establishing the principle that the President had all powers involved in foreign relations that were not specifically reserved to the Congress by the Constitution.

Among these few exceptions was the Senate's right of "advice and consent" on the making of treaties, a phrase which Washington was inclined at the beginning to take quite literally. During his first year in office, he proposed to the Senate that they "advise" him on a treaty to be made with some Indian tribes. He visited the Senate in person for such advice, but the Senators turned the whole matter over to a committee and asked the President to come back next week for their advice and consent. Washington never repeated the experiment and afterward started the long tradition of presenting the Senate with a treaty as a *fait accompli* for its approval or disapproval.

As his terms progressed, it became increasingly obvious to Washington that the executive should be in effect the sole agency not only for the conduct of foreign relations but also for the determination and definition of foreign policy. Moreover, Washington concluded that the machinery set up to carry out the policy or to arrive at it was the business only of the executive.

The first major treaty in United States history was arrived at, not through the ordinary channels of the Department of State or the regular executive establishment, but by the Chief Justice of the United States, John Jay, whom Washington sent to London in 1794, when relations between the United States and England had so deteriorated that war appeared to be inevitable. (In the autumn of 1948, when relations between Russia and the United States had also deteriorated to approach the prelude to war, President Truman proposed publicly to send another Chief Justice, Fred Vinson, to Moscow to arrive at a settlement. Truman's action was leaped on as the most revolutionary and strangest proposal in the history of American diplomacy. Actually, had Vinson gone on the mission, he could not have had a more parallel precedent than that of his predecessor Jay's mission for Washington.) To put the Jay Treaty in effect, the House of Representatives was required to make an appropriation and, before doing so, requested from the President all papers to and from the President and Jay that led to the treaty. In a sharp reprimand Washington told the House that he had no intention of furnishing any such papers, and the House has never thereafter ventured a similar request from the President. Although approved by the Senate without a single vote to spare (20-10), Jay's Treaty was greeted by the public with the chronic unpopularity with which Americans are inclined to regard all treaties, despite the fact that it rescued the country's national existence when it was too weak and too loosely united to defend it.

The present world status of the American Presidency is ultimately traceable to Washington's handling of the office. Without his dignity, his competence, his persistent adherence to the theory of a strong executive, the office might well have wallowed in a sea of impotence in foreign affairs. Moreover, his example was readily seized on by the more constructive of American Presidents for a century and a half afterward.

Of the chief executives succeeding Washington (excluding Mr. Truman, whose record is in this respect promising but not yet complete), only nine distinguished themselves in the area of foreign relations: John Adams, Jefferson, Tyler, Polk, Lincoln, Cleveland, Theodore Roosevelt, Wilson and Franklin Roosevelt. Each of these leaned heavily on the precedents set by Washington, especially on his insistence on the Presidency as not merely the servant of the Congress in foreign relations but the sole and, to a considerable extent, independent agency of the government for the conduct of foreign affairs and for the right to initiate treaties. It is easy to oversimplify the "ifs" of history, but it seems obvious that without the development of the Presidency as a strong agency in international affairs, the United States would have been not one or two but at least three and possibly four small nations. For the Congress has always been so sectional in its interests and viewpoints that each Congressional delegation saw its own proportionate strength lessened with the addition of new states and therefore of more Representatives and Senators. Thus, Jefferson, Tyler and Polk (the latter two, up until recent years, greatly underestimated as Presidents), through the broad use of Presidential powers and sometimes virtually in spite of Congress, increased the original area of the United States by some 227 per cent, or more than tripled its original area. The Louisiana Purchase was entirely an executive operation in which Jefferson, there being neither Constitutional provision nor precedent for the acquisition of new territory, arranged the purchase and then called Congress into special session. Anticipating trouble with the Northeast representation, which had no desire to have its strength counterbalanced by new Western and Southern territory, he had a Senator from Kentucky round up Western Senators and Representatives for the first day of the session, thus forcing the ratification and appropriation through in spite of New England opposition.

Tyler, first of the Vice-Presidents to succeed to the Presidency and with no sure following in the Congress, acquired Texas by depending on a joint resolution of the House and Senate, which required a simple majority, rather than by drafting a treaty, which would have required a two-thirds vote of approval by the Senate—of which he had slim hopes. Polk, when his single term began in 1845, set out to re-establish the independent Treasury (as a good Jacksonian should), to reduce the tariff, which oppressed everyone to protect the manufacturers, to settle the Oregon boundary dispute and to acquire California. He toiled without ceasing and accomplished all four purposes, renounced any ambition for re-election, and died from overwork three months after the end of his term, as what George Bancroft called "one of the very best and most honest and successful Presidents the country ever had." It was Polk's arduous, farsighted labors, indeed, that resulted in the United States spanning the continent, and he stands, with Jackson, as the only exception in that long succession of nonentities between John Quincy Adams and Lincoln; for, like Jackson, he succeeded in placing the Union above sectional interests and in averting civil war at least until the nation was sufficiently strong to survive.

If the normal diplomatic responsibility of the Presidency is to maintain peaceful and mutually beneficial relations with other countries or, when war is inevitable, to maintain as successful alliances as possible, then those men who as Presidents refused to drift and who had sufficient insight and skill to give direction and purpose to our foreign policy were obviously those who best realized the potentialities of their office: John Adams, who despite the belligerence of Congress and his own party, avoided war with France (in contrast to Madison and, later, McKinley, both of whom yielded to pressures and fought wars which they did not really think necessary, with England and Spain, respectively); Lincoln, who used all his immense wisdom in dealing with people to prevent Britain and France from recognizing the

Confederacy (in contrast to Grant, who simply turned over all foreign relations to his providentially able Secretary of State, Hamilton Fish); Cleveland and Theodore Roosevelt, both of whom so reaffirmed the Monroe Doctrine that it was never successfully challenged; and the two world statesmen America has produced, Wilson and Franklin Roosevelt, both of whom saw, in the words of Wilson, that "what affects mankind is inevitably our affair" and the "principle of public right must henceforth take precedence over the individual interests of nations."

Now, all these men who were at the top among United States Presidents as conductors of our foreign affairs were in one way or another challenged by the Congress. For under them, and to a lesser extent under some of the other executives, the role of the American Presidency evolved from the beginning as a creative one, while the role of the Congress, also from the beginning, evolved as a critical one, in the field of foreign relations. And because the leading Presidents have created new foreign policies, often without either direct or collateral precedent, they have also—as has already been noted—had to create from time to time new methods to put those policies in effective operation. This has been the more necessary because the Congress, in its traditional critical role, has almost always been suspicious of anything new and has frequently been outrightly hostile. Indeed, perhaps too often the Congress has been moved to assume that Presidents have been guilty in their conduct of foreign affairs until proved innocent and that the appropriate function of the Congress has been to use all legal devices at its disposal to impede them in the execution of their respective policies. As a result, the three great methods evolved by the Presidents in order to carry out their foreign policies have all been devised as methods also of reducing Congressional impedimenta.

First of these was the appointment of "personal" agents or representatives, who have occasionally been in effect, and some-

times in actual name, ambassadors at large, and almost all of
whom have superseded in Presidentially delegated authority the
regularly constituted ambassadors in the places to which the
former have been sent. Washington so appointed Gouverneur
Morris to handle conversations with the British on the execution
of our Treaty of Peace with them in 1791, because he felt that
a special personal agent of the President would make this nation
"less committed" if the talks were conducted by "a private
rather than a public person." Probably what Washington really
sought to avoid was any accountability to the Congress for the
mission's commitments until he was sure they would work out;
and since Morris was not theoretically appointed to a public
office and thus not liable to Senate confirmation, Washington
regarded the whole affair as a "private" one of the President.

Other Presidents, less attached to the quality of privacy, have
used the same method to avoid conflict with the Senate on confirmation of the personal representative or, since 1855, to avoid
the necessity of asking the Congress to create a public office.
Thus, Madison sent two special representatives to Europe in
1813 to work with his minister, John Quincy Adams, in nego-
tiating a treaty to end the War of 1812, and later supplemented
this "commission" with two more representatives. He appointed
these without confirmation by the Senate and without consulting it. Similarly, Jackson sent special representatives, without
consulting the Senate, to Turkey in 1831; Cleveland sent J. H.
Blount to Hawaii as a special agent while the shenanigans incidental to annexation were going on in 1893; Wilson sent Elihu
Root to Russia in 1917, and Franklin Roosevelt sent Myron
Taylor to the Vatican in 1940—all these and many more such
special emissaries were usually named to accomplish or inquire
into some specific course of action determined solely by the
President. Usually, too, their appointments were related to a
conscious effort on the part of the President to avoid involving

the Congress in any way. With the appointment of Colonel House by Wilson in 1914 as a kind of "roving" ambassador (a rather poor choice for a badly confused and vaguely defined mission) and of Harry L. Hopkins by Franklin Roosevelt in 1941 to go to London and Moscow (a rather good choice for a very clearly defined mission), the fundamental propriety of such special agents of the President has come to be accepted.

What is more important, they appear on the whole to have been of peculiar usefulness not only in strengthening the Presidency as the agency for carrying on our relations with the rest of the world, but also in eliminating much of the slowness and ponderousness that governmental processes too often involve to the point where the end is no longer pressing or desirable by the time the methods to reach it have been effectively employed. Moreover, without involving the Department of State and ordinary diplomatic channels, special agents permit the President, who cannot himself be long absent from Washington, to acquire information and responses vital to the construction of sound policy. For whether or not the Congress has ever been totally reconciled to it, the conduct of foreign affairs was left by the Constitution as so much more a personal function of the President than any other of his great duties that it would take major changes in the Constitution itself ever to change it. It is significant that the Commission on Organization of the Executive Branch of the Government, headed by Herbert Hoover, in all its scores of reports of 1949, nowhere suggests intervention into the President's personal command of our foreign relations or advocates the establishment of any executive procedure that would make such command less personal.

The second major and an extraconstitutional method evolved by the Presidency to control and expedite the conduct of foreign affairs is the executive agreement, a device which has frequently replaced a formal treaty when the President was certain that he could not count on the support of the two thirds of the Senate Constitutionally required for a treaty's ratification or when there was no time to seek it. In some cases such agreements have been reached and put into effect without any Congressional participation whatsoever. McKinley, who tended to be a much more decisive President when he was acting independently than when he was worrying about the pressure from others, did not even advise let alone enlist the support of the Congress when he entered into the Boxer Indemnity Protocol of 1901, which provided for the payment of damages and the punishment of Chinese officials after the Boxer Rebellion against foreign legations in Peking.

It was McKinley's successor, however, the impatient, assertive Theodore Roosevelt, who brought the executive agreement to real stature as a vigorous weapon of the Presidency in concluding terms with foreign powers without bothering with the formality and delay of going to the Senate for its approval. In 1904 the little Caribbean republic of Santo Domingo feared that European creditors might force the intervention of European powers. To protect the collecting of Santo Dominican customs, Roosevelt agreed, through a special emissary and the American minister to Santo Domingo, to put the collectors under United States control, to turn over 45 per cent of the collections to the Dominican Government and to dole out the rest to its creditors. Mindful of the dangers that might result if any of the European creditor nations decided to intervene in the little republic in the absence of United States protection, Roosevelt did not propose to see his project bogged down in the Senate and put it into immediate effect as an executive agreement without Senate approval.

Of his action, Roosevelt later said: "The Constitution did not explicitly give me power to bring out the necessary agreement with Santo Domingo. But the Constitution did not forbid my doing what I did. I put the agreement into effect, and I continued its execution for two years before the Senate acted; and I would have continued it until the end of my term, if necessary, without any action by Congress." Roosevelt went on to point out that he would have preferred a treaty confirmed by the Senators (but "all that they had really done was to shirk their duty. Somebody had to do that duty, and accordingly, I did it.") on the grounds that a treaty would be the law of the land while an executive agreement would terminate, as he thought, with the end of his term. He might have been relieved perhaps to know that thirty-three years later in 1937 the Supreme Court, in considering the force of Franklin Roosevelt's agreement of 1933 embodying the terms of our recognizing Russia, maintained that such executive agreements were as much the law of the land as a treaty. Franklin Roosevelt unquestionably found comfort in this decision in September 1940 after the fall of France when he agreed to turn over fifty destroyers to Great Britain without asking Congress to ratify his action.

More numerous in our diplomatic history than solely Presidential executive agreements, entered into without any sort of Congressional participation, are those which have been arrived at by the President and then submitted to the Congress for confirmation by joint resolution. The obvious advantage of this procedure over a treaty is that it is easier to secure a simple majority vote of assent than the Senatorial two thirds required by a treaty. In recent years, culminating in the reciprocal trade and Lend-Lease agreements of Franklin Roosevelt, an increasing volume of United States foreign affairs has been conducted through this device of joint resolution, which was first applied to a major problem by John Tyler. It was one of Tyler's winning battles, during a term that lasted all but one month of a full four years.

By April 1844, three years after Tyler had succeeded to the

Presidency on Harrison's death, Sam Houston, President of the Texas Republic, had three times offered to join the United States and had been twice rejected for internal, sectional reasons within the United States. Tyler, in 1844, was determined to see the annexation through. In April he sent a treaty of annexation to the Senate, which that body rejected by the two-thirds rule after two months' delay. In the fall, during the Polk-Clay campaign of 1844, the annexation was a major issue, and Polk, outspokenly in favor, won. Tyler interpreted this as popular endorsement of his policy and reproposed annexation—this time by joint resolution of both the Senate and the House. With the one-third veto power of the Senate thus by-passed, the resolution, requiring only a simple majority in both houses, carried easily three days before Tyler was to leave office. Texas was annexed, and the Presidency had introduced, for permanent use, a method of wiping out a basically undemocratic technique for obstructing its foreign policies.

Once Tyler had introduced executive agreements under joint resolution, succeeding Presidents of both parties resorted to the device: McKinley used it to annex Hawaii in 1898; Harding, Coolidge and Hoover all used it in agreements involving World War I debts; and it was the usual instrument of Franklin Roosevelt's administrations both before and during the war; finally, in contrast to the fate of the League of Nations at the hands of twenty-three Senators in rejecting the Treaty of Versailles without reservations in 1919, United States backing of the United Nations was assured in the Participation Act of 1945, a joint Congressional Act which required only a majority in each house.

The steady growth of the use of joint resolutions in authorizing executive agreements is one of the most rewarding aspects of the evolution of democratic processes in this country. For in effect the treaty-making power of the Senate, with its two-thirds rule for ratification, actually merely subjected the will of the

President, elected by all the people, and frequently the will of a majority of the Senate, to a strangling veto by one third of the Senate. Indeed, it is mathematically possible under the two-thirds rule for the Senatorial representation of 11,668,033 of the nation's 132,000,000 people to defeat completely the will of the Senatorial representation of the remaining 119,338,151. If all ninety-six Senators were present, ratification of a treaty would require sixty-four votes. Thus, the votes of thirty-three Senators could defeat it. If those thirty-three came from the States of Arizona, Colorado, Connecticut, Delaware, Idaho, Maine, Nebraska, Nevada, New Hampshire, New Mexico, North Dakota, Oregon, Rhode Island, South Dakota, Utah, Vermont and Wyoming—less than one tenth of the nation's population could stop dead in its tracks the will of the other nine tenths of the nation. In view of such possibilities as this, it is difficult now—except among Senators themselves—to work up much popular resentment or to present any logical arguments against the increasingly employed system of confirming executive agreements with other countries by joint Congressional resolution. The allocation of Senators was originally designed to protect the regional interests of an agricultural nation and bears no proper relationship to the democratic conduct of our foreign affairs.

Of this, the first Committee on Foreign Relations of the Senate itself was appropriately and wisely aware when it reported in 1816: "The President is the Constitutional representative of the United States with regard to foreign nations. He manages our concern with foreign nations and must necessarily be most competent to determine when, how, and upon what subject negotiations may be urged with the greatest prospect of success. For his conduct he is responsible to the Constitution. The committee considers this responsibility the surest pledge for the faithful discharge of his duties. They think the interference of the Senate in the direction of foreign negotiations [is] calculated to diminish that responsibility and thereby to impair the best security for the national safety. The nature of transactions with foreign nations, moreover, requires caution and unity of design."

Since answerability of the leadership to the people is the *sine qua non* of a democracy, foreign commitments entered into with confirmation of an executive agreement by a majority of both houses of Congress are unquestionably more expeditiously referred to the electorate than a ratification by two thirds of the Senate would be. Senators who might ratify an unpopular treaty can be charged with their actions at the polls only once in six years, while a President who made a foreign agreement unacceptable to the people can be held answerable once in four years, and the entire membership of the House which confirmed it could be turned out of office to a man in two years at most. There is consequently less to fear, by way of answerability to the people, in executive agreements confirmed by Congressional act than by formal treaties ratified by the Senate.

In general, moreover, the diplomatic history of the United States has tended to justify the evolution of the Presidency as the agency for both the determination and the conduct of our foreign policy. The nation's hundred-and-sixty-year history has seen three major divisions, in all of which Presidential rather than Congressional determination of policy has worked most advantageously: the first period, lasting from 1789 to 1825, was one of consolidating before the world the independence and status of the new republic, and it was highlighted by Jefferson's masterly purchase of the Louisiana Territory and by Monroe's long-famous doctrine; the second period, from 1825 to 1900, was one largely of continental expansion and integration, distinguished by Tyler's annexation of Texas, Polk's acquisitions in the Far West, the arbitrations in the Northwest with Great Britain, and Lincoln's skilled averting of a foreign war during the Rebellion; the third period, beginning shortly after the turn

of the century and continuing now is one of American moral
leadership in world affairs, summarized best by Woodrow Wilson before America entered the First World War: "We are participants, whether we would or not, in the life of the world. The
interests of all nations are our own also. We are partners with
the rest. What affects mankind is inevitably our affair as well
as the affair of the nations of Europe and Asia."

In each of these great phases of our diplomatic history the
interests of the nation and of mankind have always been best
served by those American Presidents who have had a very high
sense of the responsibility of their office before the world and
posterity. Conversely, those Presidents, like Madison and Mc-
Kinley, who yielded easily to the pressure of Congressional
groups or to the more inflammatory elements of the press or who
never even attempted to exert leadership in foreign affairs because of personal inadequacies, have very frequently done less
than little to vindicate their ever having held the office.

IV

A logical extension of the power of the Presidency in foreign
affairs is its role as supreme command of the military forces
of the United States. The Constitution would appear on the
surface to be very specific on this executive function: "The President shall be Commander-in-Chief of the Army and Navy of the
United States, and of the militia of the several States when
called into the actual service of the United States." Actually,
however, the extent of this command and its application to such
attendant problems as direct control over civil affairs affecting
the strength, supplying and supporting of the Army and Navy
have long been of controversial interest to students of the Presidency. It is not without significance that Lincoln, Wilson and

Franklin Roosevelt, our great wartime Presidents, have invited the most extreme appraisals—have been denounced as dictators by some and revered as saviors by others.

Except for routine affairs of the services, employment of the powers of commander in chief has been exercised by only six Presidents: Madison in the War of 1812; Polk in the Mexican War; Lincoln in the Civil War; McKinley in the Spanish-American War; and Wilson and Franklin Roosevelt in the two World Wars.

Madison, whose greatness as a political theorist was compromised by his weakness as a President, was the worst wartime commander in chief ever visited upon the republic, and his War of 1812 was a hodgepodge of mismanagement, bad appointments, disastrous reverses, embarrassing retreats and home-front disunity. We did not win the war: the British simply lost it. And the ultimate outcome was in spite of rather than because of Madison's employment of the command powers of the Presidency.

In the Mexican War, Polk, on the other hand, exhibited a firm grasp on military problems and planning, actively and successfully concerning himself with the major campaigns, even though Congress would not create a new general rank so that he could name his own top field commander: "My situation is most embarrassing. I am held responsible for the war, and I am required to entrust the chief command of the army to a general in whom I have no confidence."

Half a century later, McKinley faced a war of the same dimensions but one to which he yielded only to keep "the war party" happy. Once the war was on, however, he had to run it himself, for he had accumulated one of the saddest war Cabinets ever to sit together, with the War Department headed by Russell A. Alger, one of the most stupendously incapable men ever to hold that Secretaryship in war or peace, and the Navy Department by John D. Long, who felt himself to be less the head of the Navy than the people's representative in the Department. McKinley, who did not even have a general staff worth the name, showed no brilliance in conducting a war that he never wanted anyhow, and only the absence of an enemy of any proportions brought it to an early end. Primarily from the nature of all three of these conflicts, Madison, Polk and McKinley had no occasion to develop the command power of the Presidency or to touch on its implications.

Abraham Lincoln had a far different problem, complicated by the fact that, as commander in chief, he was required to head the military forces in war operations and also, as executor of the laws of the United States, he was charged with putting down an insurrection. Inevitably there was to be an overlapping of these two Presidential duties and also, therefore, an intermingling of Presidential powers. Moreover, Lincoln was also the ranking leader in an actual theater of war, for the Confederacy had invaded Northern territory. It furnished a rare occasion for a literal-minded man to be so preoccupied by hairsplitting and rigid adherences to legal points that the war would be hopelessly lost. But Lincoln was neither a literal nor a rigid man. His remarkably lucid sense of values convinced him at the outset that a literal observance of the Constitution might cost him the nation and consequently the Constitution itself: "I did understand, however, that my oath to preserve the Constitution to the best of my ability impressed upon me the duty of preserving by every indispensable means, that government—that nation, of which that Constitution was the organic law. Was it possible to lose the nation and yet preserve the Constitution? By general law, life and limb must be protected, yet often a limb must be amputated to save a life; but a life is never wisely given to save a limb. I felt that measures otherwise unconstitutional might become lawful by becoming indispensable to the preservation of the Constitution through the preservation of the nation. Right or wrong, I assumed this ground and now avow it."

Uncongenial as it was, therefore, to the American political temperament, Lincoln assumed a kind of absolute power that no President in war or peace assumed before or since. What Lincoln did in effect was to suspend the Constitutional limitations on the powers of the Presidency and interpret the "Commander-in-Chief" clause so broadly that it superseded all such limitations: "I conceive that I may in an emergency do things on military grounds which cannot constitutionally be done by the Congress," and again "as Commander-in-Chief of the Army and Navy, in time of war I suppose I have a right to take any measure which may best subdue the enemy."

Lincoln did, in fact, take any measure that appeared to him necessary, and some of these were patently not only extraconstitutional but unconstitutional. Some he first put into effect and then, presenting the Congress with a *fait accompli,* applied for legislative authorization. Some he did not even communicate to Congress at all. Distrustful of the slow and often trivial processes of the Congress, Lincoln did not call the houses into special session when the emergency of Fort Sumter and civil war first came. Instead he acted directly and extraordinarily: he increased the size of the Army and Navy, called for volunteers, paid out unauthorized and unappropriated public funds to unauthorized people, proclaimed a blockade, suspended the writ of habeas corpus. In some of the most remarkably rational if legally elastic documents in our history, Lincoln justified all these courses to the satisfaction of his wisest contemporaries and to the admiration of posterity. Moreover, still acting as commander in chief, he proclaimed the slaves free in his Emancipation Proclamation—an action he meant solely as a war measure to expedite the crushing of the Rebellion.

It is high tribute to the genius of Lincoln that in the employment of these powers he strengthened both the Presidency and the Constitution. For there is no serious student of American history who doubts that the Union would have been lost had Lincoln permitted government by Congress during the war, that the effectiveness of the Presidential office in time of grave emergency would never have been established if he had not filled it with wisdom and rare insight, and that the Constitution itself would have survived only as an interesting and ephemeral document had he not acted beyond its literal limitations to preserve it.

Lincoln presided over the republic and conducted a great war in a day of bleeding division. Both Wilson and Roosevelt presided over the republic and conducted great wars in days of strong union. Consequently neither of the latter two was required to appropriate to himself the kind of power over civil affairs that Lincoln needed. Moreover, since both the World Wars involved military operations outside our continental limits and since there was no immediate threat of direct assault, Wilson and Roosevelt did not have to *assume* extraordinary powers but could solicit from Congress a carefully weighed scale of *delegated* war powers. In many ways, because of the economic intricacies and vast military establishments of modern warfare, the powers, though less dramatic, were far more penetrating than those assumed by Lincoln.

Wilson's wartime powers, in general, were derived from Congress, while those of Lincoln were interpreted by him to be logical adjuncts of his Constitutional role as commander in chief. Thus, with Congressional authorization, Wilson exercised a greater control over the natural resources, industry, commerce, transportation and communications of the nation than Lincoln did. He was empowered to create and direct vast administrative agencies touching on every aspect of national life. Many of the activities of these agencies and also many of Wilson's direct acts as commander in chief touched sensitively on the status of Constitutional provisions in wartime. And again, as in the Civil

War, the consensus of judicial and lay minds tended to bolster the theory that certain otherwise inviolate principles of the Constitution have to be compromised in wartime for the greater good—as Lincoln clearly saw—of preserving the nation of which the Constitution is the organic law.

When World War II came and even before, during the Lend-Lease days, only the legal academicians and the querulous were inclined to view with alarm the passing of exceptional powers to the President and his assumption of others as inherent in the office. For the most part, the actual war powers followed the same pattern as those of World War I, with a more far-reaching scope that was no more than proportionate to the greater challenge of events.

To those legislators who might have been inclined to waste desperately needed time, Franklin Roosevelt addressed himself in a manner indicating that the lessons of Lincoln had not been lost on him: "In the event that Congress shall fail to act, and act adequately, I shall accept the responsibility, and I will act. . . . The American people can be sure that I will use my powers with a full sense of my responsibility to the Constitution and my country. The American people can also be sure that I shall not hesitate to use every power vested in me to accomplish the defeat of our enemies. . . . When the war is won, the powers under which I act automatically revert to the people—to whom they belong."

Critics of governmental processes in America who like to look at the Presidency in a Constitutional vacuum have pounced on that last sentence, implying that no very strong and particular relationship of the Presidency to the people has developed in American politics. Actually, the major evolution of the Presidency has been as an independent agency of the Federal Government that directly represents and is directly answerable to all the people—not to those of one state or of one Congressional district or of one party, but to all of them. And no restraint will ever be imposed on the office comparable to a national election.

V

By the mid-twentieth century, with the exception of the isolationist press and its small and fast disappearing group of followers in Congress, the powers of the Presidency in foreign affairs are no longer seriously challenged, nor are they viewed with alarm by any considerable body of public opinion. The apparently increasing powers of the Presidency in domestic affairs are, on the other hand, the subject of continuing controversy, with men of good will and of motives to be respected divided on the implications of this growth. Much of the controversy, however, is caused by both sides overlooking some very important basic factors.

Foremost among these is that the fundamental and Constitutional powers of the Presidency have not been altered or augmented in any of the amendments to the Constitution from the beginning. Presidential powers have actually been expanded very little. What has happened (and this has been going on since Washington's first administration, although sometimes the process has been accelerated by critical events such as those of the Civil War and the Depression of the 1930's, or by strong Presidents such as Jackson and both Roosevelts) is that the area of national affairs over which the President has been able and required to exercise his powers has expanded immensely. And in general the expansion of this area has been commensurate with the growth in industrial, social, and economic intricacy of the society to the preservation of whose interests the President must apply his powers.

The second factor to be remembered is that the real complaint is probably less against the growth of the Presidency in power than the growth of the government in scope, for every new administrative function of the Presidency has had its root in the acts of the Congress. It is consequently as baseless to indict the Presidency for usurping powers because it executes those acts, which is a Constitutional duty, as it would be to indict the Congress for usurping power because it passed them, which is a Constitutional function.

This leads to the third factor, which is that what both the Presidency and the Congress do are subject to judicial review by the courts and to popular review at the polls, and can be annulled in the absence of adequate enabling legislation or repudiated if such legislation is held by the courts to be contrary to the Constitution or by the people at the polls to be hostile to their best interests.

It is necessary, therefore, at the outset of any appraisal of the domestic powers of the Presidency to realize that the area of national affairs subject to executive powers has grown immeasurably, but that this is due primarily to the accumulated convictions of several Congresses that the growth of the nation has required more and more legislation to keep the government an effective instrument for serving the interests of the people. As a result, the President has had more and more laws to execute. And as a result of that, he has had to have more and more administrative bureaus (some of them added to the Executive Department and some independent of it, but all authorized by Congress) to execute them.

It is important to remember constantly that all of these have been established by Congress, and not by Presidential fiat, and that they were set up to enforce Congressional acts and not, except insofar as these are made to aid such enforcement, executive orders. These orders have themselves been the subject of wide misunderstanding, for actually an executive order has its root in the Congress and not in the Presidency: an executive order is nothing but a Congressional authorization of the President to make such regulations as are necessary to give effective expression to legislative acts of the Congress. Reference to such orders as a "lawmaking" power of the Presidency is a distortion, for they reflect in the President no such implied legislative power at all. They constitute only a regulatory power within the referential framework of a specific act of Congress.

Nor are such authorizations of executive orders casually given by the Congress. Ordinarily executive orders have been authorized when an act could be adequately enforced only if the fulfillment of the intent of the act varied with where or when it was applied, as in the case of conservation laws; when the act was designed to meet emergency situations as they arose without recourse to Congressional action on each development, such as the War Powers Acts; or when the Congress was able as a matter of sound common judgment to fix a policy (incorporated in and expressed by the act) but was unequipped technically to formulate the detailed regulations necessary to bring about the desired end, as in the Pure Food and Drug Acts. Because, in such cases, the Congress has authorized the President, or a Commission appointed by him, to draft as occasion may require the regulatory measures needed to give its act meaning and effectiveness, it does not thereby delegate any of its own basic legislative functions, nor does it abrogate them.

It is not insignificant that nearly all such regulatory powers vested in bureaus of the Executive Department or in independent, quasi-legislative and quasi-judicial agencies, like the Interstate Commerce Commission and the National Labor Relations Board, are largely related to the economic life of the nation. Alarmists over the increased power of the Federal Government are likely to forget that the Federal Government does not intrude itself any more upon the political or religious lives, for example, of the people than it ever did. Moreover, in that area in which it does intrude itself more conspicuously than in the past, the pace of growth of the nation itself has been amazingly fast. For in this country the major remaining frontier has been and continues to be an economic one. And just as in the last century, when physical frontiers were important, the government legislated broadly concerning the land, so in this century must it legislate broadly in economic terms. Such legislation inevitably involves the President, who not only has to execute the new laws but must also recommend to the Congress those measures which he thinks desirable to the national welfare and veto those which he thinks undesirable. An energetic President is apt to take an active role in the formulation of such legislation and to recommend measures with such vigor that the people will respond by themselves exerting pressure upon the Congress to pass them. But that is a Constitutional function of the Presidency which has from time to time lapsed into such disuse by passive Presidents that it seemed strangely new when fully exercised by the more active ones. Much of this legislation has necessarily resulted in augmenting the statutory powers of the President, largely because it would otherwise be impossible to enforce new acts at all. The question is constantly suggested whether such increased statutory powers represent any real menace to our institutions.

A sound answer to this question cannot be found in a legal vacuum but must be related to the main course of American history. In general, the incumbents of the White House have adhered, more or less closely, to two opposite views of the essential nature of their office. The old Whig theory, inherited by a majority but not all of the Republican Presidents, holds that the Presidency is limited strictly to following the Congress and adhering to the letter of the Constitution, that it could reasonably suggest fields in which legislation was required but no legislative program itself, that the veto power should be used sparingly and mainly on the question of an act's Constitutionality rather than its desirability.

This view was reduced to an absurdity by the ancient and ill-fated William Henry Harrison, at his inauguration in 1841, in the finest tribute to the impotence of the American Presidency that we have. Harrison even viewed the veto power with alarm and obviously thought of the President as a kind of office manager of the nation, not capable of determining or even of suggesting policy and certainly not constitutionally competent to exercise any kind of leadership. Dying three weeks following this strange inauguration, Harrison had no time to put his feeble appraisal of his office into practice and left the office to John Tyler for nearly a full term. Not until another aging warrior, Zachary Taylor, went into office in 1848 was the Whig ideal of a weak Presidency restored, but it lasted only until his Vice-President, Fillmore, finished his term for him. The two succeeding Democrats, Pierce and Buchanan, had such startling personal inadequacies that they expected at best merely to act as conciliators of opposing elements of the Congress and, without formally subscribing to the Whig theory of Presidential incompetence, nevertheless left the country without any executive leadership at all. The Whig theory did not again gain Presidential support until Ulysses S. Grant was inaugurated, and Grant went the first Harrison one better by indicating that the President was merely the office boy not only of the Congress but also of any private body that had an interest in national affairs.

Grant indeed so upheld the view that the Presidency is a hopelessly weak office that the next three Presidents—Hayes, Garfield and Arthur—all of them from the Republican Party, which had taken over the Whig theory, refused to regard the office as so weak and fought vigorously to exercise its inherent powers. Garfield, like both his predecessor and successor, set out, as he said, to determine "whether the President is registering clerk

of the Senate or the Executive of the United States." Grover
Cleveland had come and gone before the Whig theory again
asserted itself in the White House with Benjamin Harrison
(who received nearly 100,000 less popular votes than the defeated candidate in 1888), who was inclined, however, to take
a less constricted attitude towards the office than his grandfather.
Cleveland had served a second Presidential term before the
Whig theory was again restored with McKinley, and it endured,
with two major interruptions and with varying narrowness,
down through Taft, Harding, Coolidge and Hoover. But all
these regarded the major responsibility for the destiny of the
nation as resting with Congress, to which they were necessarily
subservient.

Out of the thirty-two Presidents of the United States, then, ten
(William H. Harrison, Taylor, Fillmore, Grant, Benjamin Harrison, McKinley, Taft, Harding, Coolidge and Hoover) were
formally devoted to the Whig concept of a weak executive, and
two others (Pierce and Buchanan) were so devoted in practice
if not in theory. Together their administrations cover only
forty-four years or little more than a fourth of the nation's history. On the whole, theirs were the least distinguished administrations in the history of the Presidency, periods of national
drifting through most of their terms and of outright and tragic
floundering through at least four, those of Pierce, Buchanan,
Grant and Hoover. Only one sixth of them were elected to
more than one term, whereas a third of all the Presidents were
re-elected. None of them was able to meet an emergency and
steer the nation through it, though some of them steered the
nation right into it. What then is the effect of an executive
whose powers are so narrowly interpreted that its Constitutional
definition serves only as a catalogue of limitations? In practice
it has been demonstrated repeatedly in our history that, under
such a pilot, the nation is a ship without a rudder, sometimes

coming through safely, sometimes quite shattered from the passage and sometimes dangerously near to cracking up on the rocks.

VI

Opposed to the Whig theory of the Presidency, which was actually a segment of a party philosophy conceived by the Whigs and seized on by the more passive of Republican Presidents, is the Jacksonian concept, which had its root in Alexander Hamilton, its historic application by Andrew Jackson and its broadest interpretation by Abraham Lincoln. Its development has been bipartisan and its usage has also been bipartisan. With the exception of the twenty-year succession of Madison, Monroe and John Quincy Adams and of the Whig intervals from Harrison to Hoover already noted, it has grown steadily until it became at its best, long before Franklin Roosevelt, an independent agency of the people to furnish leadership to the nation. The most successful Presidents have accepted the leadership challenge from the beginning and have pressed the office to its Constitutional and statutory limits and, in the cases of two Republicans, Lincoln and Theodore Roosevelt, and one Democrat, Franklin Roosevelt, beyond them, to meet the needs of their times.

The Jacksonian revolution, coming after the twenty years of Presidential subservience to Congress from Madison through John Quincy Adams, was essentially the product of Congressional ineptness. Its acceptance by the people was to no small extent the acceptance of the lesser of two evils, for there was in the American character almost as much wariness of a strong executive as there was impatience of a fumbling legislature. But the strong executives were more sensitive on the whole to the spirit of their times. They acted with courage and they did not drift; moreover, the risks were covered by their being subject to dislodgment every four years. Consequently, the cries of tyrant and dictator, which the Whigs first shouted at Jackson and which reached a mighty chorus with Lincoln and a persistent but by then familiar antiphon with Franklin Roosevelt, never really frightened the people. It has, therefore, been very difficult for either the Congress or elements within either major political party to convince the people—or, for that matter, for anyone at all to convince the Supreme Court even at its most conservative periods—that the Jacksonian concept of the Presidency was irreconcilable with the letter or spirit of the Constitution.

Briefly, in direct opposition to the Whig theory, the Jacksonian concept holds that the Presidency is equally with the Congress and the Supreme Court an independent branch of the Federal Government; that it has inherent powers not catalogued in the Constitution but embraced in the inclusive and unqualified language of Article Two: "The Executive power shall be vested in a President"; that the President is responsible directly to the people and not to the Congress; that he also derives his mandate from the people and not from the unwieldy sum of their representatives; that he should furnish a leadership for the nation's legislative processes and not, as Herbert Hoover insisted, limit himself to pointing out where legislation is needed, which is to say that he should direct the fire engines at the fire and not just ring the alarm; that the office is an opportunity for service rather than an exercise in restraint.

Historically, the Presidency as a strong and independent agency of the people was first asserted by Andrew Jackson in his fight to destroy the private control over the nation's moneys vested in Nicholas Biddle's Bank of the United States (in which he succeeded by withdrawing the government's funds, despite a resolution of confidence in the bank passed by the House), and in his direct action to prevent South Carolina from declaring a law of the nation null and void (in which he succeeded by issuing a Presidential Proclamation that sent the nullifiers into a hasty convention to nullify their own nullification). Both Tyler, in annexing Texas, and Polk, in shaping the final continental integration of the United States, depended heavily on the Jacksonian precedent of broad use of the Presidential office, on a leadership independent of the Congress and on direct answerability to the people. Wrote Polk: "The President represents in the executive department the whole people of the United States, as each member of the legislative department represents portions of them."

But it was the Republicans, Lincoln and Theodore Roosevelt, who pressed the Jacksonian theory even farther. As we have already noted, Lincoln held that there were not even any Constitutional limits on the office when it was functioning to "preserve, protect and defend" that Constitution: "... would not the official oath be broken if the government should be overthrown when it was believed that disregarding the single law would tend to preserve it?" So the first Republican President took the view that no limitations on the powers of the President existed if they tended to inhibit his execution of his oath. Lincoln therefore stretched the Jacksonian concept farther than it had ever been before or since—and, so doing, saved the Union. (The only occasion when the extremeness of Lincoln's view was duplicated was in 1933 when Al Smith, with characteristic impatience at listening to pleas that the Constitution permitted no action against the downward-spiraling Depression, starkly observed that it might be a good thing to put the Constitution "on the shelf" and save the country.)

Granting that Lincoln faced peculiar problems and that his particular genius gave in retrospect comforting reassurance for his acknowledged disregard for the Constitutional limitations on the Presidency, we have to proceed to another Republican to find the broadest interpretation of the powers of the office in more or less normal times: Theodore Roosevelt, whose administration certainly faced no major crisis. To a considerable extent, Roosevelt took advantage of the strides made by Grover Cleveland in his two separated administrations. Cleveland used the influence of the Presidential office to carry out Presidential policies which often conflicted with Congressional policy. He reduced the tariff and repealed the Silver Purchase Act and the Tenure of Office Act, which had limited the power of the President in removing officeholders within the Executive Department. Contesting successfully the Whig doctrine of Thaddeus Stevens that the President "is the servant of the people *as they shall speak through Congress,*" he echoed Jackson and Polk when he insisted that the President represented the people directly: "The Presidency is pre-eminently the people's office."

Theodore Roosevelt, though of the opposite party, used nearly the same words: ". . . The Executive is or ought to be peculiarly representative of the people as a whole." In intervening in the hard-coal strike of 1902, Roosevelt set a pattern for the extension of the Presidential office to the settling of labor disputes that has since become an implied extraconstitutional duty of the office, and today even the stoutest adherent to the old Whig theory would be horrified if the President of the United States sat idly by as the economic life of the nation was paralyzed by a general strike in a basic industry. In 1902, the mining of anthracite stopped entirely, and Roosevelt prepared for action on two fronts: he would have the strike arbitrated under Presidential auspices or, if this failed, he would send in the Army to mine the coal. Arbitration finally worked; but until it did, Roosevelt was busy perfecting his operational plans for the Army with a customary energy never yet equaled for Presidential boldness of action outside of war.

Theodore Roosevelt's theory of the Presidency came to be known as the "stewardship theory," because he held that he was charged with the welfare of the country by the people and that in carrying out that charge the President was limited by nothing which was not specified in the Constitution or the statutes. Thus, the President not only could do everything the Constitution empowered him to do but could also do everything that it did not forbid him to do. More than any other man, including Wilson and Franklin Roosevelt, the effectiveness of the Presidency today is the product of Theodore Roosevelt. Moreover, he was responsible for the injection of the Federal Government into the economic life of the nation, both in a regulatory and a creative role: he policed the great corporations, he regulated the meat packers, he split up the railroads and coal mines, he used the influence of the Presidency to indict before the public "malefactors of great wealth," and he set a prototype of TVA by having the government build and operate a public utility, the Panama Canal.

A man of direct and often impetuous action rather than a theorist, he nevertheless saw clearly that a weak executive in a society of increasing intricacy could never fully perform his general Constitutional functions: "I declined to adopt the view that what was imperatively necessary for the nation could not be done by the President unless he could find some specific authorization to do it. My belief was that it was not only his right but his duty to do anything that the needs of the nation demanded unless such action was forbidden by the Constitution or by the laws. Under this interpretation of executive power I did and caused to be done many things not previously done by the President and the heads of the Departments."

Nor was his strengthening of the Presidency merely for his own sake or for his own time: "I have used every ounce of power there was in the office, and I have not cared a rap for the criticisms of those who spoke of my 'usurpation of power'; for I knew the talk was all nonsense and that there was no usurpation. I believe that the efficiency of this government depends upon its possessing a strong, central executive, and whenever I could establish a precedent for strength in the Executive ... as I did in internal affairs in settling the anthracite coal strike, in keeping order in Nevada this year when the Federation of Miners threatened anarchy, or as I have done in bringing the big corporations to book—why in all three actions I have felt, not merely my action was right in itself, but that in showing the strength of, or in giving strength to, the executive office, I was establishing a precedent of value."

It was a precedent nevertheless to be ignored blandly by his successors of his own party—Taft, Harding, Coolidge and Hoover—but to be grasped eagerly by Woodrow Wilson and Franklin Roosevelt. Both Wilson and the second Roosevelt, however, associated the strength of the Presidency with two collateral roles, party leadership and legislative leadership, while Theodore Roosevelt seemed to prefer to act independently. In this respect, they guided the evolution of the Presidency along safer democratic channels and made it, both in theory and in fact, much less government by one man. Theodore Roosevelt derived his strength, and seemed also to derive his satisfaction, from a vigorous and independent course of individual action. Both Wilson and Franklin Roosevelt acted in concert with their party and the Congress and appealed to the people in cases of discord instead of using the "big stick" that Theodore Roosevelt loved to brandish. Indeed, since Franklin Roosevelt's administration was historically only the resumption and extension of Woodrow Wilson's, Wilson might—next only to Washington—be called the most creative statesman to sit in the White House, for he—interested in Constitutional processes all his life—depended not on the direct action of Lincoln or the thunder of the first Roosevelt but on the building of the Presidency as a legislative influence.

This had in fact been a goal of Theodore Roosevelt: "As often as not the action of the Executive offers the only means by which the people can get the legislation they demand and ought to have. Therefore a good executive under the present conditions of American political life must take a very active interest in getting the right kind of legislation. ...." But he was too devoted to the dramatic action and had come toward the end of too long a period of Congressional supremacy to get very far.

Wilson worked in quieter and more informed ways with a predominantly new kind of Congress. Moreover, Wilson had, in addition to immense erudition in political science, a practical political skill of a high order. When he delivered a message in person to the Congress, it was for the first time in a hundred and twelve years, ending a practice—as he put it—of the President "hailing the Congress from some isolated island of jealous power." His reform program passed both houses with a speed unparalleled in our legislative history until 1933, and for five years he was the guiding genius of Congress, primarily because he understood the appropriate role of an extraconstitutional institution, the political party, in strictly Constitutional legislative processes. His acquaintance with the evolutionary character of the Congress led him to depend less on floor leaders than on committee chairmen. Wilson thus established at once the party and legislative leadership of the Presidency and, going beyond this, established it also as an office of moral leadership. In fact, after the Congressional elections of 1918 resulted in revolt of the Congress, he relied solely on the moral strength of the Presidency and lost the fight only after his physical collapse.

Despite his high sense of the responsibility of his office and his awareness of its powers, Wilson was not inclined to set aside the Congress. He preferred joint Presidential and Congressional action and, far from deriving satisfaction from unilateral action as President, was always disturbed when it was necessary, as it was in arming American merchant vessels before our entry into World War I. His vast war powers were not assumed, as Lincoln had assumed them, but granted by the Congress. And when it came time to make the peace and to decide on the extent of American participation in the League of Nations, Wilson still stuck to Constitutional processes and spent his last able days attempting to rally public opinion to influence two thirds of a hostile Senate to ratify the treaty. This very devotion to the Constitution no doubt accounted for the failure of the United States to join the League. Had Wilson followed in Tyler's footsteps and presented the question of American participation as the subject of a joint resolution, it would not have failed, for on two test votes in the Senate it received a majority in favor. The Constitutional flaw of subjecting treaties to death if sixty-three Senators favor them and thirty-three oppose them killed the League and was an ironic reward indeed to the one "strong" President in our history who sought to avoid compromising the power of the Congress.

No two more radically different personalities, unless they were Harding and Coolidge, ever shared closely the same view of the Presidency than Wilson and Franklin Roosevelt. The latter, a much less profound mind than Wilson and a much more genial nature, reverted *in toto* to the values and the methods of the Chief he had known in his youth. Franklin Roosevelt was not one of the great innovators among American Presidents but essentially an imitator. However, he brought the gifts of a very great and effective political personality—perhaps the greatest in our history—to the office. And as both the domestic and foreign situations with which he had to cope were more extensive repetitions of those Wilson faced, so Roosevelt's meeting of those situations was an extension of methods already employed by Wilson. The New Deal had its prototype in Wilson's New Freedom; the war powers of World War II had their prototype in the war powers of World War I; and the United Nations had its prototype in the League of Nations. In fact, Franklin Roosevelt's main contribution to the growth of the Presidency was the stamp of his personality, particularly in respect to the Wilsonian functions of assuming party and legislative leadership.

But his lasting achievement was that he proved the office, without Constitutional alteration although with statutory enlargement, equal to the most desperate domestic and foreign crises. His historic significance is that he used with prompt and exceptional vigor the influence and fullest powers of the Presidency to rescue capitalism in this country at a time when its real interests had been so badly and so casually served that not only did it invite, but actually had the nation on the verge of, economic ruin. In this sense, Roosevelt, who could in 1933 have rallied the nation to the support of a violent and basic change, proved himself the greatest conservative, in its true sense, of our history—for he showed not only that our political institutions are capable of survival through the kind of upheaval that could swamp those in other lands, but also that a free and justly regulated capitalism and a degree of security for the individual were not mutually exclusive.

Franklin Roosevelt left the American Presidency vastly strengthened, but it remained, ironically, to his cautious predecessor, Herbert Hoover, to preside over the most exhaustive study of the Executive Department ever made and to submit to the Congress a vast bill of particulars that would strengthen the Executive mechanically far beyond its present status. Mr. Hoover reported that his commission found "that the President and his department heads do not have authority commensurate with the responsibility they must assume"; that "the President lacks authority to organize the agencies of the Executive branch for the most effective discharge of his executive duties"; that the "tendency to create by statute interdepartmental committees . . . has limited the President's authority to choose his advisors"; that the granting of statutory powers to subordinate officers has denied "authority in certain areas to the President"; and, among many other complaints, that "where executive duties are assigned to the independent regulatory commissions (*e.g.,* the Federal Trade or Maritime Commission) the President's authority is also weakened." If all this seems strange coming from a commission bearing the name of a man who two decades earlier had taken a very narrow view of the powers of the Executive, it should be remembered that the commission studied the Presidency in antiseptic detachment from partisan philosophies.

<h2 style="text-align:center">VII</h2>

What then has in fact happened to the American Presidency? Briefly, the Constitutional powers of the office haven't changed since the establishment of the Republic. The area to which Presidential powers have been applied has expanded greatly. In general, this broadened application has been with authorization by the Congress, has been sustained by the Supreme Court and has been endorsed by the people. The affected area has been almost entirely economic, which is to say that the extension of Presidential power to that area has been logical rather than arbitrary or sinister, because it is the one area in which the nation has so grown that chaos and anarchy therein would pull all our other institutions down with it. The surprising factors in the political history of the United States are that all the leading Presidents have found their office sufficient to the needs of their times, that the welfare of the nation has always been preserved and frequently rescued by the strong Presidents who made use of their powers and that, conversely, it has been allowed to drift and sometimes to verge on stark ruin by the weak ones. When the mild and totally inadequate Warren Harding tragically said, "I am not fit for this office and should never have been here," he left a far more frightening message to responsible citizens than Jefferson, Lincoln or Theodore Roosevelt ever left. For danger has come closer to the republic in the past through default in the White House than through strength there. None of the strong Presidents has abused the powers of the office, however extraordinary at some times they have been, for none of them has used such extraordinary powers in a spirit or toward an end inconsistent with the purpose for which they were granted.

Nevertheless, the Constitutional and inherent powers of the President in the United States are so very great that a very real danger is attached to the office, the only cure for which is the sense of responsibility of the individual voter, who must in turn labor to keep the political parties and their candidates responsible. For despite those who long for a return to the Congressional rule of the nineteenth century, there is little sound reason to be extracted from a serious inquiry into our history or a serious appraisal of our present problems ever to expect such a return. The history of American business alone has taught our people that much less intricate organizations than a great nation can fail without leadership, and it is unlikely now that the people would read virtues into such leaderless periods as the administrations of Franklin Pierce or James Buchanan, to name two Democrats, who abrogated the office, or of Grant or Coolidge, to name Republicans.

The great lesson to be derived from all this, and particularly in the face of the fact that both major parties' Presidential candidates in the last three elections have stood for a strong Presidency, is that the man and the office are inseparably associated; and there are few directions in which the nation can advance its interests more than by scrupulously watching the men who aspire to the office. In no other place on the face of the earth is a man, rather than a party nominee, the real subject of an election.

Chapter Three

The Congress

HOW THE CONGRESS, GREATEST HOPE OF THE FOUNDING
FATHERS, HAS BEEN THE VICTIM OF ITS OWN PAROCHIAL
NATURE, AND SUGGESTING THE CAUSES AND EFFECTS OF ITS
ARCHAIC RULES AND HOW, BY DEFAULT, IT HAS CONTRIBUTED
TO THE GROWTH OF THE PRESIDENCY WITHOUT
BEING RESIGNED TO IT

I

IN GENERAL, periods of strong Presidential leadership in
the United States have been periods of government by
progressive action; and periods of strong Congressional
dominance have been periods of government by strategic compromise.

In the absence of a strong President and given luminaries of
a high order in the Congress, such compromise can, at worst,
stave off disorder and, at best, advance the political maturity of
the nation. The historic example, of course, is that extraordinary
thirty-first Congress that sat for three hundred and two days,
from December 3, 1849, to September 30, 1850, in its first session.
The tired old Whig general, Zachary Taylor, having served sixteen months of his term, died in the White House midway
through the session; and his successor, the suave and mild Mil-
lard Fillmore, left affairs to the Congress. And a great Congress
it was—one that under the masterful insight of Henry Clay fore-
stalled for a decade a war to settle the issue of secession, a war
which would have been even more disastrous in 1850 than ten
years later. Indeed, in all the hundred years of Congress since

then, no group of Congressional names equals that composed of Henry Clay and Daniel Webster, Jefferson Davis and Salmon P. Chase, Stephen Douglas and John Calhoun, William Seward and Thomas Hart Benton. No speeches in the Congress have ever reached the eloquence of Webster's; no defiance the thunder of Calhoun's; no politics the expediency of Seward's; no conscience the tenacity of Benton's; and no strategy the brilliance of Clay's. If ever the Congress flowered it was that one which fashioned the Compromise of 1850 to avert the war. Yet even in so averting war, it advanced it; for like all compromises which do not pursue to ultimate justice the issues that inspire them, it solved nothing permanently. It merely gave the nation time, which it needed badly; and then at last the essence of the problem was left to be met for all time to come by a solitary man in the White House, for all during those grim years of Pierce and Buchanan the Congress floundered about helplessly.

Since in times of emergency compromise is very apt to be both costly in delay and ineffective in result, the people have been inclined to depend more on the Presidency in times calling for creative statesmanship and to gravitate towards Congressional rule only in times which seem to be safe but which very often have been merely intervals between great storms. Consequently, the Congress has become associated historically in America with periods that should have been devoted to positive preventive legislation but have instead been characterized by shortsighted compromise or almost complete inaction, as, for example, during the years before the Civil War, the years between Andrew Johnson and Grover Cleveland and the years between World War I and the Depression. All of these were periods that called for clear and positive Congressional action; all were periods of weak Presidents by whom the Congress was in no way inhibited; and yet all were periods at the end of which the Congress found itself indicted by the people for either neglecting or abusing its powers to guide the nation.

Nevertheless, the Founding Fathers, drafting their remarkable Constitution of 1787, had great hopes for the Congress—greater hopes than for either the Presidency or the Supreme Court. The Congress was conceived as the dominant and most powerful of all three branches. It is the subject of the first and longest article of the Constitution—longer than all the other original articles combined. It was given control of the laws of the nation, the finances of the nation, the strength of the armed services, by implication unlimited investigatory powers, the right to impeach and try the President of the United States without recourse to the people and so to impeach and try also all other civil officers, complete supervisory powers over administrative agencies and the right to elect the President if no candidate receives an electoral majority—a power exercised four times, or once in every ten Presidential elections. Because of its supervisory and appropriations powers, the Congress has stronger ultimate administrative powers than the Presidency; and because of its impeachment powers (which can, of course, also be applied to the Justices themselves), it is a higher court of justice than any, including the Supreme Court, in the land. Its powers are tremendous and explicit. Unlike those of the Presidency, they have not, with one or two exceptions, had to be "implied" or construed as "inherent." They are all clearly and almost incontrovertibly Constitutional, detailed carefully to cover eighteen areas of the national life. Members of the Congress, both Senators and Representatives, are the only officials Constitutionally exempt from any kind of arrest while attending sessions (except for treason, felony or breach of the peace) and from the libel law—not even the President and Justices enjoying similar Constitutional safeguards.

In spite of these overwhelming powers, the Congress of the United States has, from the beginning, suffered declining prestige, weakened influence and a more or less chronic inability to get its work done, as the Presidency has in general grown and as the Supreme Court has on the whole held its own. Before inquiring into its present status—and throughout it should be remembered that the Congress is not as dead nor is its usefulness as slight or our basic need for it as reduced as some of its critics would have us believe—it is necessary to understand why it has never been able to employ its vast powers as richly for the nation's good as the makers of the Constitution had hoped.

Primary among the reasons is the fact that the Congress is not, in any very real sense, a national representative body at all. It is a sum of regional, *i.e.,* state, delegations. Its historic development, unlike the Presidency, has been along generally regional lines; its major preoccupation has been the resolution, usually by compromise, of conflicting regional interests; its ordinary approach to national legislation has been through the avenue of the effect of such legislation, not on the welfare or the opinion of the nation as a whole, but on the interests and the reaction of the area from which the Senators and Representatives come and to which they must return. This is a constitutional weakness in the Congress, for it not only accounts for a predominance of provincial minds but, in the Senate at least, prevents the body from being truly representative of all the people. In the upper body of the Congress, indeed, we come upon the somewhat startling situation, as of the 1940 census, of the 13,479,142 people living in the State of New York, having two voices and votes on national affairs of the utmost urgency, while the 13,404,224 people living in the states of Arizona, Colorado, Connecticut, Delaware, Idaho, Maine, Nebraska, Nevada, New Hampshire, New Mexico, North Dakota, Oregon, Rhode Island, South Dakota, Utah, Vermont, Wyoming and Washington had thirty-six voices and votes on exactly the same matters. If Senators were eligible for one term only or if they were elected for life, they might very well cast off their regional cloaks on arriving in Washington, but this they will not do so long as they must return home periodically for re-election.

It was unlikely, therefore, that a Senator from a small dairy state, with some three million people, was going to vote against a discriminatory tax on margarine in the interests of the nation's remaining hundred and thirty-seven million. The particular question was undoubtedly a national one, for it was a Federal tax paid by the people of the entire nation, but the dairy state's Senator viewed the legislation entirely as it affected one forty-sixth of them. The obvious recourse of the people of the nation in such cases is to vote for a strong President, and their vote lends weight to the Jacksonian theory that the only elected official representing all the people is the President.

In the absence of a strong President and if the issue at stake is important, the Congress has not in the past shown itself a capable instrument for coping with it. Two examples come to mind. The first is the period of Congressional dominance that marked the twelve-year interval between Polk and Lincoln in the White House. The long, jagged shadow of civil war lay across the nation in all those years, but the Congress—approaching it as always from a regional view—failed signally to handle the slavery question adequately. Again in 1931 and 1932, although the Congressional elections of 1930 constituted a demand for action to combat the Depression, the Congress was able to do little until national leadership was restored to the White House in 1933. In both these cases, it is relevant to note that Congressional inaction was followed by very emphatic Presidential action.

When it has not actually endangered the interests of the nation as a whole, the regional attitude of the Congress has kept it well behind the temper of the national population, and has resulted in some rather ludicrous anachronisms. Any national body as firmly rooted in regional interests as the Congress is apt to be an unwieldy weapon in the hands of relatively undistinguished men; but the very exceptional powers of the Congress make the whole situation even more disturbing, because during its worst periods it can make a small group of mediocrities the controlling faction in the life of the nation and sometimes, because of the international influence of the United States, in the world. It can also, because of its own peculiar standards, elevate to fame men from its own members who seem in retrospect to have had little, when weighed against any broader criteria, to commend them to anything except a passing notoriety.

In January 1945, for example, very few mature observers were impressed by the conversion of Arthur Vandenberg, the senior Senator from Michigan, who had been a leading isolationist and who was sufficiently moved by the dramatic horror of the Second World War (of which five years earlier, he had said, "This so-called war is nothing but about twenty-five people and propaganda") to concede that the world's most powerful nation must meet the responsibility of assuming a leading role in world affairs. Immediately, his Congressional peers acknowledged his leadership in foreign affairs, as though the sudden change in his considerably retarded thinking under the horribly obvious threat of modern warfare were evidence of one of the most opulent minds of our times. And soon Mr. Vandenberg was spoken of as a challenging white hope for the Presidency, largely because, after seventeen years in the United States Senate, he came around under duress to the view that no nation was an island unto itself—a proposition which had been the opening premise of most newspaper, university and school forums since the beginning of World War I.

The particular case, because it involves the skyrocketing of a man to Congressional leadership in a field in which he had amassed one of the most parochial and backward records imagi-

nable, is an extreme, but it is not without approximations. Of
the ten Senators who became President before Mr. Truman—
his record is not yet completed—only one, Andrew Jackson,
achieved real distinction, and three, Pierce, Buchanan and Harding, were great failures. The parochialism of the Congressional
mind in the twentieth century has, until the threat of atomic
warfare, seriously qualified and compromised the leadership of
the nation in world affairs; perhaps it alone set the influence of
democracy throughout the world back a generation. Jolted out
of its provincialism in 1945, it soon became reluctantly associated
with the temper of its time. But it was still possible in 1949 for
a man who had sat in the United States Senate for thirty-two
years, Kenneth McKellar, to demand the unseating of the Administrator of the Marshall Plan from his effective supervision
of a program that was not only of unique constructive intent in
world statecraft but which alone gave real expression to the
nation's postwar foreign policy. Mr. McKellar was not answerable to the hundred and forty million people of the nation—only
to the half million voters of Tennessee, and politically he could
afford the indulgence of a grudging and narrow view that
would probably have retired a national official at the next election.

II

Since members of both houses of the Congress are in the main
not men of broad vision and assertedly not men who bring a
national rather than a local view to the affairs of the nation, the
Congress has lent itself to the encouragement of shortsighted
actions and has never succeeded in formulating and enacting
long-range and lasting policies—unless they were thrust upon
the Congress by a strong President. Thus, in periods of Con-

gressional dominance of the government, the rule has been an accommodation by the Congress to some single and relatively narrow factor—such as to sectionalism before the Civil War or to the spoilsmen after it. If the law is regarded—as properly it should be—as a codification of the moral judgment of the community as a whole, which in this case is the nation, then the Congress has been strangely and unbelievably obtuse in determining that judgment. It is for this reason—that it lags behind the people rather than that it lags behind the President— that the Congress became in the past the butt of jokes among all the people, the subject of despair among the enlightened and the instrument of hope among the ruthless. For the simple truth is that the Congress of the United States, lacking a membership that must stand on its record before the nation rather than before a state or a tiny fragment of a state, has not evolved into the great and powerful forum the Constitution anticipated. As long as its basic dilemma continues—its Constitutional charge to run a nation versus its inherent nature as a conglomeration of local views and attitudes—it will necessarily be in no full sense a national organ.

Only a Constitutional amendment could effect any solution of this dilemma. Although both the seventeenth and twentieth amendments, respectively providing for the direct election of Senators instead of election by state legislatures and abolishing the right of an old Congress to sit in "Lame Duck" session for four months after the elections of a new, afford precedent for the passage of amendments involving the Congress, there is very little reason to expect either that three fourths of the state legislatures would endorse, as Constitutionally required for all amendments, any proposal to reduce the state as a political unit or that there would be any way of reconciling such a proposal with the Constitutional provision of Article V: "That no state, without its consent, shall be deprived of its equal suffrage in the Senate." This proviso would manifestly require *all* states, rather than the three fourths required for other amendments, to approve any amendment to elect Senators at large nationally. And governors are too fond of climaxing their careers by becoming Senators for us to expect them to influence the bringing about of such unanimity.

There are other now ancient factors which limit the effectiveness of the Congress that do not stem from the Constitution but from its own doing, *i.e.,* its organization and rules.

In February 1945, by concurrent resolution, both the Senate and the House of Representatives of the United States looked inward briefly and concluded to examine its entire organization "with a view toward strengthening the Congress, simplifying its operations, improving its relationships with other branches of the United States Government and enabling it better to meet its responsibilities under the Constitution."

In February 1949, except for the reduction of the number of standing committees and an improved system of aids and services, it was organized and functioning exactly as it had before in all major particulars. Indeed nowhere is there less hospitality to change than in the Congress and nowhere is there more concern for the survival of the interests of individual members. The epitome of both hostility to progress and rigid adherence to self-concern is found in the seniority rule. By this device, the men oldest in point of continuous service on Senate and House committees are automatically entitled to the chairmanship of the committees. Since our legislative business is not conducted by the whole Congress but by thirty-four of these little congresses called committees, the committee chairmen are the real legislative influences of the nation. They are answerable, however, only to the electorate of their district or state. They are, for all practical purposes, unremovable even by their Congressional associates. They are there, whether good or bad, until their departure from the Congress or the defeat of their party's majority representation overtakes them. And they hold their influential posts only because they have been around longer than anyone else. They are usually not only older than the average member but even more parochial because their very seniority bespeaks a political origin in areas not noted for the vitality of close political contests. In the Democratic Party, for example, they are very apt to be entrenched Southerners who win automatically, and are, in the absence of a healthy contest, returned over and over again. The members most assured of heading committees, therefore, are those who come from backgrounds least productive of alert and keen political awareness.

But even if the old retainers are forgotten (and it is not easy to forget the national legislature's being subject to the powerful guidance of men like Senator McKellar, chairman of the Committee on Appropriations, and Representative Rankin, chairman of the Committee on Veteran Affairs), the seniority system still has sinister features. Senator Glen Taylor, a guitar-strumming songster, was elected to the Senate in 1944, when the electorate of Idaho were persuaded for some reason that he had abilities commensurate with the demands made on the Senate. The same year, J. William Fulbright, an able and experienced public servant and an erudite man of far better than average attainments, was elected to the Senate by the voters of Arkansas. Both men have been assigned to the Senate Committee on Banking and Currency, but the eminently unqualified Mr. Taylor was assigned before Mr. Fulbright, and would inherit the chairmanship automatically. Obviously, most members of the Senate would not welcome such an eventuality, nor would the nation, nor would the Committee itself. Yet it could not be stopped. For no one can change the rules of the Congress, according to the Constitution, except the Congress itself and no one is less likely to do so.

One of the most constant complaints of the United States Senate throughout the administrations of Jackson, Lincoln, Grover Cleveland, Theodore Roosevelt, Woodrow Wilson and Franklin Roosevelt, and a loud cry through the administrations of such independent but by no means eminently strong executives as Hayes and Arthur, was that the Presidency was a threat to democratic processes in this country and that the Congress was their major safeguard. Yet the Senate has repeatedly seen itself completely incapacitated to pass on important legislation because one of their number, usually among the least respected, had such a passionate attitude against it that he refused to allow it to come to a vote. In 1935, when major relief legislation of the first urgency came to the Senate floor, that body sat by in total impotence in tribute to a rule of its own perpetration that permitted Huey Long to stop the legislative processes of a great nation while he blurted his way through an endless harangue on everything from the Bible to Louisiana "potlikker." The defenders of democracy against Presidential encroachment saw no inconsistency between allowing themselves to be utterly thwarted by a notorious mountebank and protesting that they are the traditional guards of government by the people. The folly of the rule of unlimited debate has indeed been a direct cause of swift Presidential action that has left the prestige of the Senate seriously reduced before the people. When the Armed Ship Bill of 1917 was before the Congress, following Germany's announcement of unrestricted submarine warfare, the House passed it by the staggering majority of 403 to 14. A statement was signed by seventy-five Senators to the flat effect that they would vote for it when it came to the Senate. But seven Senators conspired to filibuster to prevent its coming to a vote, and the world was treated to the spectacle of the United States' being unable to pass enabling legislation to arm its merchant vessels, although the House of Representatives was for it forty to one and the Senate ten to one. President Wilson armed them anyhow by executive order, and his action is still cited by opponents of a strong Presidency as evidence of dangerous Presidential encroachment upon powers residing solely in the Congress. The question suggests itself whether a duly elected official of all the American people is more dangerous to democratic practices, when he acts to carry out an expressed conviction of an overwhelming majority of the national legislature, than the greatest legislative body of the world, when it allows itself by compact to invalidate that majority by technical concessions to a "little group of willful men."

At Mr. Wilson's insistence, the Senate adopted a cloture rule, providing a one-hour limit on speeches, after this fiasco in 1917, but it could only be invoked by a two-thirds vote and only after the question was put on the signed petition of sixteen Senators. In the past quarter century it has been invoked only three times, rejected fourteen times and either withdrawn or not acted on seven times. The Senators apparently considered this mild qualification of the unlimited debate rule a necessary evil not to be used too freely, because, while it might elevate the prestige of the Senate, it would lower the power of the individual Senator.

Moreover, the Congress, which seems to have no limit to its political masochism, has fettered itself with a mass of other rules and practices, ranging from "Senatorial courtesy" to dilatory devices. It has noted and pondered and publicly bewailed the decline of its influence, and yet it would prefer sticking by its old and outmoded ways to strengthening itself by a real and thorough reform from within. This curious reluctance to throw off its own chains when it alone has the means to do so has been perhaps the greatest single political boon to the growth of the Presidency.

III

What the Constitution-makers planned for the United States
was a representative democracy, with the Congress in a position
of leadership. What has actually evolved, within the specifica-
tions of the Constitution, is a direct democracy, with the Presidency in a position of leadership. This is partly due to those
flaws of inherence and of practice in the Congress that have
been noted above. But it is also due to even broader influences
unforeseen by the members of the Constitutional Convention in
1787 and unappreciated by Congress today. These influences
have been both national and world-wide in their origin, and
they have been not only political but economic, social and even
technological in their nature.

Politically, the main current of American history has been
away from sectionalism and toward unity. A great confirmation
of this unity was the meaning of the Civil War, in which all the
energies of the republic were concentrated, not on freeing the
slaves or on punishing the South, but on asserting for all time
to come the indivisibility of the Union. The Presidency, from
the days of Jackson, had seen this assertion as the essential mission of the Federal Government, and the people under Lincoln's
leadership rallied to the cause. But not the Congress. When the
war was over, the radical Republicans snapped right back to
sectionalism of a more vicious order than ever before had occupied the Congress, trying in impeachment proceedings the
President of the United States, who refused in a score of particulars to lead the nation back to sectionalism, too. In the
years following, the sectionalism of the country was well preserved in the halls of the Congress, and exists there still while
it has long since vanished almost totally from both the other
branches of the government. This unmistakable odyssey of the
nation towards unity, accompanied by a steady affection of

the Congress for sectionalism, has left Congress weakened and somewhat adrift from the main current of our political history.

So now no one is mistaken into judging what the course of the people's thought is by following the thought of the Congress. And it is much easier and more accurate to fix the main historical direction of the nation through reviewing the history of the Presidency than that of the Congress. The Congress had stood apart, adhering to old and repudiated political values long after they were swept aside by the rest of the nation for new ones.

Allied with this divergence of the political values of Congress and those of the nation has been the growing unification of the nation's economic and social interests. The great sectional economic issues are disappearing fast, and the interests of the New England millworker, the Pennsylvania miner, the Decatur letter carrier and the West Coast orchard worker are not contradictory. Indeed, the last four Presidential elections indicate that, aside from the blind emotional attitude of the South, national politics in this country now have very few sectional aspects, and it is not easy to split the country geographically on economic issues. Even socially the Midwest farmer, the Far West rancher and the Eastern plant manager are becoming unified in their tastes and values; their children no longer go solely to their own sectional colleges and universities; their travels and vacations are no longer within sectional limits. In fact, the United States has, since achieving political indivisibility with the Civil War, gravitated economically and socially more and more toward becoming a nation and away from an association of regions. But the senior Senator from Tennessee is no more concerned with or closer to the residents of Oregon than he was two or three generations ago. In the halls of Congress, sectional values, sectional attitudes and sectional roots remain.

In part responsible for this national movement toward unity

have been the great technological advances in communications which have made the people more politically sophisticated than they have been in the past and also more politically critical. Before the motion picture only a tiny fraction of voters ever saw the President, and before the radio a tinier fraction ever heard him. Now, with television giving communications a living quality unequaled by either, his presence is felt in living rooms across the nation even more familiarly than was the best known voice in all history—that of Franklin Roosevelt. The people no longer have to take the word of campaign spokesmen, who were usually returning Congressmen. They have seen and heard the Presidential candidates themselves, over and over again, and tend to place more and more direct reliance on the one of their choice—a tendency which has led the country increasingly toward a direct democracy and away from a representative one. Moreover, the general national news magazines, reaching circulations undreamed of a generation ago, and the syndicated Washington columnists who did not exist in other days, have brought a set of national standards to apply to the actions of the Congress; and even though such influential publications have not been overfriendly to the Presidency, they have been no less critical and sometimes outrightly condemnatory of the Congress. The result is that the people across the land are unwilling to place great faith in a legislature which, while still protecting what local interests remain, nevertheless frequently by procrastination, indecision or opportunistic compromise endangers the national interests.

In short, against the new national standards which technical developments in communications have fostered among all the people, the Congress does not stack up favorably; and the people, knowing it, have come to depend on the Presidency for action. They are themselves the creators of the direct democracy, and the very fact that it has been a long and peaceful revolution indicates that, in the light of the broad changes that have come over the land in the last half century, it is also a logical one.

Meanwhile the Congress suffers. But not enough in its own eyes to attempt to catch up with the age and to demonstrate that representative government and modern life are not irreconcilable.

IV

It is wrong to assume, in spite of its anachronistic practices and values, that the Congress today has become a fifth wheel in the Federal Government. Actually, it is still conducting the increasingly intricate business of the nation with a zeal and application that are worth more than the disdain that seems to be its persistent lot. It continues to make our laws, to appropriate moneys, to supervise through investigations and hearings the administration of the government, to represent the people back home on an almost errand-boy level, and it stands ready, presumably, to exercise its powers of impeachment if necessity requires.

The lawmaking function of the Congress has been said, by various students of Constitutional processes in the last few years, to have been in dangerous degree either usurped by the President or delegated to him by the Congress. An inquiry into our legislative history suggests, however, that these critics have both their chronology and their chief participants wrong. The only outright *assumption* of a regular legislative role in American history was by the Supreme Court when, under Chief Justice John Marshall, it established the practice of judicial review and the power of the Court to declare null and void those acts of the Congress which a majority of the Court could not reconcile with the Constitution. This, in technical effect, put the Court in the position of a third and uppermost house of the legislature, where the opinion of a bare majority of five Justices could defeat the will of the Congress. But, though it has sometimes pondered the prudence of legislation which would require decisions involving the Constitutionality of an act of Congress to be unanimous or subject, like a Presidential veto, to overrule by a two-thirds vote in both houses (which legislation itself the Court would probably promptly judge unconstitutional), the Congress has accepted judicial review in spite of the fact that the Constitution gives the Court no such power and that the Court simply assumed it. By now it is firmly established, and most men of reason would not be anxious to see the Court lose the power.

The American Presidency, however, has assumed no comparable legislative power and has, in fact, been delegated none comparable by the Congress. The Constitutional role of the President in legislative matters is to recommend appropriate legislation and to veto that regarded by him as inappropriate. Essentially his legislative role remains no more than that. However, during the last sixty years, Congress itself has legislated in an increasing number of areas of the nation's economic life and has been technically incompetent to draft regulations necessary to put such legislation into effective practice. Consequently, as has already been indicated in the preceding chapter, in order to make it possible for the President to meet his Constitutional responsibility to "take care that the laws be faithfully executed," the Congress has authorized him or the executive agency acting for him "to issue such regulations and orders as it may deem necessary or proper in order to carry out the purposes and provisions of this act." Frequently the Congress has not relied on the Presidency, through regular executive channels, to carry out such acts but has created an independent commission, fixing by law its general nature and detailing its functions, and has given such commissions the power independently to issue orders and regulations. Because they are law-executing agencies, these have been frequently associated in the public mind with an extension of the powers of the Presidency when actually they are the creations of the Congress, deriving their regulatory powers and both their quasi-legislative and quasi-judicial natures from the Congress. Moreover, they are answerable to the Congress, which controls their appropriations and can rescind the powers it delegates to them, and not directly to the President.

It is confusing the issue completely to imply that in the case of such commissions, which do indeed have wide and great powers within their areas, Congress has delegated or abrogated its own essential lawmaking powers. The difference between the quasi-legislative function of a commission and the true legislative functions of the Congress is that the latter is expressive of a national policy and the former exists merely to frame reasonable rules to carry out that policy.

For example, in the 1880's the railroads of this nation were engaged in practices that aroused vigorous protests from the public, from other businesses and from the more farsighted of the railroads themselves, when cutthroat competition, rebates to favored shippers, pools and rate-fixing schemes had rendered the whole national economy subject to the whims and evils of some of the railroads. In 1887 the Congress passed the Interstate Commerce Act to regulate the railroads, and a five-man commission was established to carry out the meaning and purpose of the act. Now the Forty-ninth Congress would obviously still be in session if it had sought to hold hearings, weigh evidence, amass technical reports and secure economic evidence to incorporate in the act all the regulations necessary to its effective realization. Consequently, the Interstate Commerce Commission was authorized to issue such orders and regulations—not as a quasi-executive agency on behalf of the President but as a quasi-legislative one. After a series of adverse decisions in the courts had severely weakened the Commission and reduced its powers, the changes that came over the judicial mind with the turn of the century gradually permitted it to function—subject, as it properly should be, to judicial review—fully within the intent of the law.

As originally established, the Commission was empowered to act only with regard to railroads. In 1906, 1935 and 1940, Congress was faced with the demand and need for regulating interstate pipe lines, motor carriers and water carriers, respectively. To preserve its Constitutional monopoly on lawmaking, it would in each case have to go into perpetual session to equip itself with the technical and economic information necessary to conduct daily hearings and to frame detailed regulations in each of these three new fields. Instead, however, it passed broad legislation to put into the law the policy of the people of the United States to the effect that such areas were to be regulated in the national interest, and then, since the Interstate Commerce Commission was already in existence and these new concerns fitted logically into its sphere of competence, empowered it to issue the orders and regulations necessary to carry out the legislation. In no case did the Commission itself, the President or the courts assign these new areas to the supervision of the Commission. The Congress alone did it. There is consequently no question whatsoever of the usurpation of legislative powers involved.

Nor is there any real support to the familiar charge that the giving of such powers to Federal commissions constitutes an abrogation or delegation of its essential lawmaking function by the Congress. For the Congress alone passed into the body of the law the policy of regulating all these phases of interstate commerce, and the Commission was empowered only to issue such orders and regulations as were required from time to time to carry out that policy.

Throughout the years, in eight other cases, the Congress

passed similarly broad legislation and created independent commissions (not directly under the President) with quasi-legislative powers in the indicated field to carry out the intent and meaning of its acts: in 1913, the Federal Reserve Board; in 1914, the Federal Trade Commission; in 1916, the U. S. Shipping Board, later called the Maritime Commission; in 1920, the Federal Power Commission; in 1934, the Securities and Exchange Commission and the Federal Communications Commission; in 1935, the National Labor Relations Board; and in 1938, the Civil Aeronautics Board. The two striking aspects of the list are, first, that in each case intelligent detailed legislation presupposes a specialized knowledge beyond the general competence of any Congress and that Congress for this reason alone had to entrust it to the relevant commission; and, second, that, with one or two exceptions, the creation of the new commissions parallels the introduction of new economic or technical complications in the national life.

It is, of course, always fashionable to regret the increased activity of the government, but to give his complaint validity one would have simultaneously to regret modern life itself. It is patently ridiculous to observe ruefully that there was no Federal Communications Commission in President Hayes's day when there was no telephone, radio or television or that there was no National Labor Relations Board in President Adams' day when organized labor was virtually nonexistent and the country was largely agrarian anyhow. It is even more fatuous, however, to suggest that the nation's legislative power is slipping away from the Congress because it prudently leaves the hundreds of detailed orders and regulations, necessarily incidental to an act incorporating a broad purpose, to appropriate commissions. Justice (later Chief Justice) Edward D. White, writing a majority opinion in 1904, declared that inability of the Congress to do so would be tantamount to saying it had no power to legislate in such fields at all. Nor do such commissions necessarily pass, once they are created, under the direct control of the President. He must appoint their members, with Senate confirmation; but, according to a Supreme Court decision in 1935, he cannot remove them without cause from six of the nine commissions, and the Hoover Commission has recommended statutory amendments to protect similarly the tenures of the other three.

If Congress is frequently and erroneously accused by critics of voluntarily delegating its legislative functions to such agencies, it is even more often charged with selling out to the President. The best refutation of any such charge as this is that as often as not the Congress, even when of the President's own party, goes its own way and either legislates diametrically opposite to what the President has recommended or else refuses to act on a Presidentially inspired measure at all. What confuses the issue, however, is that in an increasing volume of legislation, almost entirely within the economic field, the Congress has given the President great interpretive powers, so that he has more latitude on the extent and incident of the application of the law, and great discretionary powers, so that in matters not entrusted to the nine independent commissions he is able, through directly controlled administrative agencies, to issue orders and regulations to give a specific law expression. But the important point is that this is not lawmaking in any real sense. The Congress still makes the laws, and the delegation of so-called "lawmaking" power to the President has been in fact merely the delegation of regulatory powers to executive rather than to independent commissions—with the additional safeguards that if the people do not like the way the President uses such powers they can turn him out of office at his term's end and that if the Congress suspects that he misuses them it can impeach him or repeal the act granting the powers.

V

Although the powers of the Congress are defined in eighteen distinct clauses of the Constitution, nearly all these functions come under the broad head of its lawmaking function. "To lay and collect taxes" and "to raise and support armies" are, for example, invariably the subject of Congressional acts.

Even such collateral functions as the reflecting and the informing of public opinion on major issues and of keeping a supervisory and reviewing eye on the administration of the government are related to the business of lawmaking, for theoretically the Congress could not legislate very wisely without knowing whether or not the people of the nation were for their action and without knowing whether or not the government was likely to administer it wisely. Outside the general field of lawmaking, however, the Congress is equipped by certain usages and practices, some of them entirely extra-Constitutional and of their own devising and some of them very literally Constitutional, to control the executive; it can grant or withhold appropriations; it can bury a bill in Committee so that, before their constituents, members cannot be accused of being for or against it; it can attach irrelevant riders to bills so pressing that the President, violently opposed as he may be to the provision of the rider, cannot veto the entire bill; it can launch investigations and conduct public or executive hearings; and the Senate can grant or withhold confirmations.

Cynical uses of all of these are not rarities in the history of the Congress, but sentiment against such use within the Congress—while not sufficient to defeat them definitely in rule changes—has increased in recent years, perhaps largely because of increased public resentment and journalistic vigilance. But one of them—the Congressional investigation—is growing, and Congressional sentiment favoring it seems also to be growing.

The increased use of the investigatory power is not entirely a political phenomenon. As Congress has been required to extend the area of government concerns, it has been compelled also, as we have seen, to delegate regulatory powers, to authorize wide increases in the number of administrative bureaus and to support by appropriation and sustain by law a great and complex government machine involving the expenditure of over $42,000,000,000 annually and the activities of over two million government employees. The dimensions of the problem can be conceived by relating it to the general structure of the nation: an amount equal to two thirds of the dollar value of all the manufactured goods produced in a year in the country is spent annually by the Federal Government; and one out of every fifty adults in the nation is employed by the Federal Government in civil posts. This is all very staggering to the conscientious Congressman, and he is apt to be anxious to ask the administrative officials what is going on before he will make up his mind about additional or renewed appropriations. Moreover, it has already been noted that the Congress is required in modern life to legislate on highly specialized matters and must conduct investigations or hearings to adduce the information prerequisite to legislation, from private citizens in a position to know.

The somewhat fearful implications of the Congressional investigatory powers and, to an infinitely greater extent, its extravagant abuse by the unintelligent accidents who sometimes inspire and preside over them have led many Americans of sober judgment to conclude that they are un-American to begin with and should be outlawed. Actually, although there is no Constitutional provision for investigations, they are deeply rooted in American legislative processes. Both the English Parliament and the colonial assemblies of America were authorized to conduct specific investigations, and the constitutions of some of the original thirteen states contained general authorizations. Since the establishment of the United States, investigations by committees of the Congress are as old as the Congress itself. Alexander Hamilton and the Treasury Department were investigated by the Second Congress, and both the Presidential and cabinet offices have been frequently investigated ever since. Corruption and bribery have often been revealed only through Congressional investigations. The inadequacy of old laws and the necessity for new ones have been determined only by investigations. The abuse of offices, inefficiency, misapplication of powers have all been curtailed not only by investigation but by the constant possibility of an investigation.

On the other hand, there has also been directed to the investigatory power of the Congress severe and sometimes quite general criticism, although this has in most recent cases been addressed largely to the bad manners, limited intelligences and obvious exhibitionism of such performers as J. Parnell Feeney of New Jersey, who had changed his name, some time before a rather obscure career of selling insurance, to Thomas. At the occasional mercy of such vociferous mountebanks, the Congressional investigation has not only seemed a great evil but has also had the appearance of a somewhat sinister innovation with no apparent usefulness and no institutional standing. Actually, legislative investigations are a fairly effective tool of democracy but, like all the tools of democracy, are subject to all the variations in degree of merit that the men who use them are. Nevertheless, with the impeachment power of the Congress all but nullified in its application to the Presidency by the fiasco of 1868 and with the Presidency as a result of entirely natural forces, democratic processes and judicial approval continuing to grow in power, the investigatory function of the Congress must also grow in both the incidence and efficacy of its use. Indeed, it has already grown—commensurate, like the Presidency and the general extension of government activity, with the growth of the nation. From 1789 through 1925 there was a total of 285 investigations on the part of both the Senate and House by standing and select committees of the first sixty-eight Congresses in 136 sessions, an average of 2.1 investigations per session. In 1945, on the other hand, the Seventy-ninth Congress alone launched a total of fifty investigations in one session.

Not all of such investigations are aimed primarily, or sometimes at all, at the administrative branch of the government. Indeed, some of them have been directed inward, and have been concerned exclusively with the conduct of Congressmen. In 1857 the Thirty-fourth Congress investigated itself and expelled four of its own members for bribery and, in view of difficulties in the proceedings, passed an act requiring appearance on demand before a Congressional committee on penalty of indictment for misdemeanor. Similarly, in 1872, both the Senate and the House launched investigations into the financing of construction of the Southern Pacific railroads and censured some members of both houses, recommending some for expulsion. In general, however, the Congress has been increasingly sparing in its investigations of itself. (Probably largely due to a wide elevation in national ethics, Congress has, as a matter of fact, been much less given to corruption in this century than in the last.) But, as shown by the case of Representative Andrew J. May, chairman of the House Military Affairs Committee, in 1946, it is not inclined to extend any special consideration or protection to its own members.

In recent years a far more active purpose of investigating committees has been legislative, and in this area the Congressional investigation has been of first creative use in our democracy.

It is natural and perhaps inevitable that during the periods in which Congress has had to legislate in an increasing number of new fields, it has had also to exercise its investigative power more. Consequently, the last and greatest period of legislative investigation was in the 1930's, when the broad economic problems of the time and the accelerated economic expansion of the preceding decade led to national concern about the inadequacy of existent legislation. It is, indeed, one of the ironies of history that the economic reforms of the era have been viewed, by those observers more emotionally attached to the past than clear-thinking about the present, as evidence of an unhealthy growth in the Presidency, when as a matter of fact they were the product of uniquely stimulated legislative processes.

Thus, the Banking Acts of 1933 and 1935, incorporating into the law such obvious safeguards as separating commercial banks from investment affiliates, insuring deposits and controlling credit, discount and open-market operations, were directly indebted to the most extraordinary Congressional investigations in history—those conducted by the Senate in 1933 and 1934. Not only was the total absence of any morality in the most respected quarters of American business revealed, but the nation was stunned by an incredible revelation of the complete lack of personal ethics on the part of one name after another that had previously won itself a high place in the affairs of the community, the churches and countless philanthropies. Names, not of known criminals, but of esteemed men who had had the richest advantages of education and background were splashed across the pages of the press and committed to history as those of practitioners of acts which while within the law were morally repugnant to a great segment of the public and seemed completely careless of the real health of a free capitalist system. Twenty Morgan partners had paid virtually no income taxes for the three years preceding the investigations; Charles Mitchell, Chairman of the National City Bank, Otto Kahn of Kuhn, Loeb Co., Thomas Lamont of Morgan, Albert Wiggin of the Chase National Bank—all these and many more blandly admitted to such practices outrightly designed to take advantage of loopholes in the laws as selling million-dollar blocks of stock to their wives at a loss to avoid income taxes and then buying them back shortly after. In banking practice, Federal Reserve credit was revealed to have been diverted to the stock market, investment affiliates were formed to snap up the use of the money of depositors, huge holding companies were created to concentrate profits and then the profits were concealed in tax returns.

Meanwhile, with a blissful indifference to the health of the capitalist system which they had bled white, some offenders acted as though the Congress of the United States was guilty of a conspiracy because it sought legislation designed to restore vitality to that system and prevent in the future abuses that had all but brought it to extinction. But the Congress persisted and, after turning up the most depressing collection of irresponsible and amoral practices imaginable, proceeded to enact the Banking Act of 1933, the Securities Act of 1933, the Securities Exchange Act of 1934, and the 1934 Amendment to the Revenue Act, as it digested the 12,000 pages of evidence adduced at its investigations. All these were acts of the Seventy-third Congress; and though they were in response to Franklin Roosevelt's first legislative recommendations, they were outstandingly acts by the Congress itself, rooted not in the minds of isolated bill drafters but deep in the institutional legislative processes of the republic. And, significantly, they emphasize even more than the threats of wartime that democracy is equal to any dangers that arise, that Congress can rise to greatness and that a free capitalism cannot be murdered if those who abuse it are ferreted out. Indeed, within eight years, the nation—still a democracy and still with a capitalist economy—was able to fight and win a war on two hemispheric fronts simultaneously. The death knell sounded by President Hoover as he trudged, a pathetic victim of his own philosophy of the helplessness of a democratic government, out of office on March 4, 1933, was fortunately premature: "We are at the end of our string," he had said. "There is nothing more we can do"—while one state after another closed its banks.

In 1880, Mr. Justice Samuel Freeman Miller had held that in the majority opinion of the Supreme Court there was no Congressional right to inquire into the nine claims of the government against the insolvent bank of Jay Cook. Privately he also observed—as though he had witnessed some of the emotional, headline-seeking exercises of the investigatory power in later days—"The public has been much abused, the time of legislative bodies uselessly consumed and rights of the citizen ruthlessly invaded under the now familiar pretext of legislative investigation . . . Courts and grand juries are the only inquisitions into crime in this country. I do not recognize that Congress is *the grand inquest* of the nation."

Although perhaps one of the ablest judicial minds of his day, the Associate Justice missed a very basic point with regard to the legislative function of the Congressional investigatory power. The purpose of grand juries is to inquire into the breaking of existing laws and to indict those suggested where first cause is found; the purpose of the courts is to try those indicted to see whether they have in fact broken the existing laws. The legislative function of the Congress, on the other hand, is to inquire into conduct, practices and deeds which, while not necessarily breaking any law, are nevertheless detrimental to the national interest and might therefore, where just cause is found, be a fit subject for new legislation. It is then up to the Congress to ponder the case and to frame and pass such legislation if it is found necessary or desirable. The grand jury and the courts are both concerned with infractions of the law after it is written; and they may be curative if they work well. The Congressional investigation is properly more concerned with infractions of principle or with actions that should in the future be barred by law; and it is preventive, if it works well.

Thus, there was no law against Mr. Charles Mitchell's avoidance of paying income tax at all one year because he sold stock to his wife at nearly a three-million-dollar loss and bought it back later. (He was, in fact, tried and acquitted.) But the Seventy-fourth Congress responded to the opinion of the great body of indignant citizens, whose views were reflected by scores of editorial commentators who said that Mr. Mitchell's action was not only dishonorable but also, in fact, if not in law, a crime against the people. Congress put the evidence unearthed by its investigation to practical use in passing the Revenue Act Amendments of 1934, making such conduct impossible with impunity in the future.

On a broader scale, Ferdinand Pecora's skilled and relentless handling of the Senate's Banking and Currency Committee's investigation on the sale of stocks led to the revelation of practices, entirely legal, that very obviously could permanently wreck the lives and properties of millions of citizens. Those who ruthlessly adopted such practices were entirely immune to the courts and grand juries mentioned by Mr. Justice Miller, and a man desirous of making two million dollars by conspiring to wipe out the honest investment of a man with ten or twenty thousand was not answerable to any court in the land. But, according to a rejection of Miller's opinion by Chief Justice Taft some fifty years later, such acts were appropriate fields for Congressional investigations, and the Congress could, under threat of contempt, compel the appearance of witnesses and giving of testimony relevant to the inquiry. Without such appearances and testimony, neither the need nor the suitable extent of new legislation could be soundly established.

Mr. Taft, in his decision, however, emphasized pertinence "to the question under inquiry," and nearly every case of contempt of Congress in the exercise of its investigatory function has involved a conflict between Congressmen and witnesses over such pertinence. In the Un-American Activities Committee's investigations of 1948, this problem hit a new high, in no small part due to the peculiar genius of its chairman, Mr. Thomas, to disgust even objective observers with his blundering and loudmouthed conduct of the sessions, and partly due also to the pitiable basic confusion of the "unfriendly" witnesses. The question here, stripped of the emotional ravings of Mr. Thomas and the hysteric hostility of his guests, was whether, "pertinent to the question under inquiry" or not, the Congress could force a man to testify about his personal political beliefs. This, despite the seeming novelty of their situation to the witnesses, is a question which was at least a hundred and sixteen years old by the time it involved them. For ex-President John Quincy Adams raised it in the House in 1832, when the political affiliations of the directors of the Bank of the United States, a private depository for Federal funds, were the subject of much Congressional interest. Moreover, whenever any appointment has been made to any one of the nine independent commissions of the Federal Government, with the exception of the National Labor Relations Board and the Federal Reserve Board, the nominee's political affiliation is automatically subject to Congressional inquiry, for it is illegal for any more than a bare majority of those commissioners to be of the same political party. Obviously, then, a Congressional inquiry into a nominee's desirability could appropriately ask him his political affiliations. Since the apparent purpose of the Un-American Activities Committee was to determine the need for protective legislation against subversive activities, and since Communism theoretically qualifies as subversive to our political institutions, it would seem not only logical but necessary for the investigating committee to determine whether its witnesses were Communists—quite as pertinent, in fact, as asking Mr. Mitchell at the banking investigation whether he was a banker.

Probably the greatest immediate result of the stand of the witnesses at the subversive-activities investigation will be the opportunity to have the courts settle the question of the inviolable privacy of one's political affiliation—a matter which, despite the persistent protests of the witnesses, who appear not to have read the document, is nowhere mentioned in the Bill of Rights amendments to the Constitution.

VI

When the Congressional investigation has as its immediate purpose the adduction of information for use to determine the need and best nature of new legislation, its role is an essentially creative one. When its purpose is to check on the administrative branches of the government, on the other hand, its role is essentially a critical one. In the latter case, although remedial legislation may result from its proceedings, the investigation is not concerned primarily with ascertaining the need for new laws but with fixing the effectiveness and prudence with which the existing laws are being executed. Possibly because it approaches more closely the functions of the courts and especially the grand jury and more certainly because of the traditional doctrine of the separation of powers, the administrative investigation has received far less judicial encouragement than the legislative investigation.

Indeed, as a general rule, the Supreme Court has been careful to sustain the assertion of the Presidency that it is equal and not subservient to the Congress. As a result, the Congress has tended to associate such inquiries as it launches into the executive conduct with specific Congressional functions, such as the appropriation of moneys or the confirmation of appointments. Even in such cases, however, the Congress has been unable to secure judicial support for pressing its inquiries into the privileged relationships of the President and his administrative aides, including, of course, Cabinet members. In fact, the Supreme Court held in 1803 that officials of the Executive Department were not required even to divulge confidential matters before that august body, let alone a Congressional committee. Moreover, the President has as recently as 1948 issued a direct order forbidding officials of the Executive Department from furnishing to the Congress or any of its committees reports in the possession of the Department concerning the loyalty of its employees. Similarly, in 1941 and again in 1944, Attorneys General Jackson and Biddle both refused to accede to Congressional requests for information in the possession of the Department of Justice, for communications from the President and for the appearance before a Congressional committee of the Director of the Federal Bureau of Investigation. And in March 1948 the Secretary of Commerce, W. Averill Harriman, ignored a Congressional subpoena to produce a departmental file. Two months later the frustrated House passed a bill to force, under penalty of imprisonment, officers of the Executive Department to produce information on Congressional demand; but if the bill had not bogged down in the Senate it probably would have in the Supreme Court, for it is not likely that the Court would have acknowledged an essentially judicial power to the Congress that it had, in the *Marbury* v. *Madison* decision, denied itself.

Contributing further to the reluctance of the Court to return a broad interpretation of the Congressional investigatory power, as Mr. Justice Miller, who as a jurist was considerably inclined to pragmatic values, indicated as far back as seventy years ago, is the history of such committees as the House Committee investigating the government withdrawals from the Bank of the United States in 1832, the Joint Committee on the Conduct of the (Civil) War, whose sole purpose was an attempt to assert Congressional supremacy over Lincoln, the Senate Lobby Investigating Committee of the 1930's, the House Un-American

Activities Committee, the Brewster Committee investigation of Howard Hughes and the Hickenlooper investigation of the Atomic Energy Commission, all of the 1940's. No court decision and no executive protest has brought the investigatory power of the Congress more damagingly before the bar of public opinion than these proceedings. Indeed, nothing so startled informed citizens in 1949 as the threat of certain members of the House Un-American Activities Committee to investigate the fairness with which a Federal judge had presided over a perjury trial in New York; it was alarming enough to think of any trial which did not end according to a Congressman's prejudged private verdict being subject to an investigation but even more so because the threat came from members of a Committee that was notorious and arrogant in its own unfairness. It was a jet-black pot calling a pale-gray kettle black. Even the thoroughly estimable achievements and methods of such bodies as the Truman Committee of World War II cannot balance, in the public mind, such shenanigans as this.

The obvious answer to the disrepute into which Congressional investigations have fallen would appear to be a codification of some standards of justice for the required observation of the investigating committees. The most important of these would be to permit the witness to make a statement unmolested by committee members in addition to answering their questions, too many of which are purposely of the "Have you stopped beating your wife?" variety. The next most important would be to curb the swollen powers of individual committee members, particularly the chairmen, and bring the investigating committee more under democratic methods by requiring subpoena and the extent of questioning to be fixed by a majority of the committee concerned. Thirdly, the witness should perhaps have the right to counsel in such proceedings, although such a right would be largely meaningless if the counsel did not himself have the right to object or to cross-examine. This last reform might well turn into a boomerang, however, for it would strengthen rather than alleviate the false appearance of such investigations as courts and might also stretch the proceedings out intolerably. Indeed, none of the indicated reforms would be an assurance of the correction of the evils of the Congressional investigation or of the promotion of its usefulness, for the difficulties are related to deeper and more general problems that beset the whole Congress and will be fully eradicated only when the latter are solved.

Just as in the case of the Presidency, the Congress is ever broadening the area of its concern, especially in the field of investigation, where the need for reform is most pressing, not only because the abuses have been excessive but because the function is of growing importance. We have seen how the complexity of modern life, the intricacy of national affairs and the inevitable expansion of government have made the resort to regulatory commissions increasingly necessary. Such quasi-judicial and quasi-legislative organs, to remain a great good and avoid becoming a great evil, must be subject to a constant, calm, mature and informed surveillance by the Congress. So also if the great good of leadership is not to become the great evil of one-man government, must the strengthened Presidency be subject to the enlightened oversight of the Congress. And unless the Congress can improve its investigatory methods and rally to its support the best minds of the country, it—and not the Executive Department—will ultimately have to answer for any decline of the Congress to complete impotence.

VII

One of the major political preoccupations of the American people and also of the Congress itself has been periodic efforts to "reorganize" the Congress—a field for which there is wide Constitutional latitude inherent in the second clause of Section 5 of Article I: "Each house may determine the rules of its proceedings..." Actually such reorganization has been continuous in the case of the Senate, because there has in fact been only one Senate from the beginning, since only a third of its members are up for re-election at one time and there has never been a Congressional session when a majority of the Senate was not held over from the previous session. But while the Senate is a continuing body, the House is theoretically a brand-new one every two years. Consequently, the House has been quicker to welcome reorganization than the Senate and more congenial to throwing out old customs. However, the structural and working organizations of both houses have had general similarities, not the least of which is the committee system.

Although the Constitution manifestly intended the houses of Congress to be great deliberative bodies, they have exhibited a conspicuous reluctance from the start so to act. We have seen how President Washington appeared before the Senate to "advise" with it on an Indian treaty and how the Senate promptly referred the whole thing to a committee, thereby infuriating the President, who never repeated the experiment. For many years the Senate continued to refer every individual piece of business to a special committee appointed for that single purpose and which went out of existence as soon as the specific matter was settled. By the end of the first quarter century, the volume of business so rose that in a single session a hundred or more such special committees might be appointed. It then occurred to the Senate that it might name standing committees devoted to some general spheres such as foreign relations, and, instead of assigning for consideration one measure involving foreign affairs to one committee and naming a new one to consider the next measure, the standing committee would handle all such business. Four standing committees were in existence by 1816, when eleven more were added. This number had grown to forty-two by 1889, when the Senate was a hundred years old, and to seventy-four by 1913. At this point the number of standing committees, many of which were overlapping, was as unwieldy as the volume of old special committees, and the Senate, by combining some and eliminating others, reduced the number to less than half, thirty-four, in 1921. In its second major re-organization, the Senate reduced the number further, again by more than half, to fifteen, in the Legislative Reorganization Act of 1946.

The House followed a similar pattern: seventeen standing committees in 1816; twenty-nine in 1889; thirty-three by 1909; forty-eight by 1946, when the number was slashed over a half to nineteen. Moreover, the powers of the committees are more clearly defined, and Senators are limited to two and Representatives to one assignment each.

These measures, and others incorporated in the Legislative Reorganization Act of 1946, unquestionably will improve the workshops of the Congress, which the committees are, for no member will have to scatter his efforts over half a dozen committees; minor committees—being obliterated—will no longer labor to make mountains out of molehills (although this is a pastime that we may be sure the Congressional temperament will not allow to become completely extinct); all committees, since appropriations for the committees will not have to be split so many ways, will be able to afford paid staffs of experts.

Despite these reforms, a major flaw in the committee system—perhaps its most serious one—still exists: the seniority rule for committee chairmanships. This rule is not so ancient as the stoutness of its defense would suggest. Actually the Senate once balloted for committee chairmen; nor has the House from the beginning practiced the seniority rule. Yet the Congress is unwilling to change the custom, although it may be distressed by such sights as the Mississippi mountebank John Rankin heading the House Committee on Veteran Affairs. But both houses are rendered powerless by their own rules, which only they can change. Moreover, the Senate has not solved the problem of the filibuster, which is a far more final obstacle to democratic procedure than any other evil in the entire Federal Government. The House has not corrected the usurpation of the powerful Rules Committee, which virtually controls the introduction of new legislation in the United States and frequently whether or not it will have a hearing at all. Indeed, when the Legislative Reorganization Act of 1946 itself was transmitted from the Senate to the House, the leadership of the latter insisted on amputating it in some important particulars, refusing it a presentation for a vote at all unless their personal desires were respected above the findings of the United States Senate and the report of the joint Congressional committee. That action itself is perhaps the measure of the problem of the Congress.

Political scientists, the press and informed laymen have been urging far broader Constitutional reforms in the Congress than have ever been entertained by any Congressional committees. The most common of these usually suggest some form of legislative council or cabinet, ranging from the proposal that the Vice-President, the Speaker, the majority leaders in both houses and the chairmen of standing committees constitute a kind of legislative liaison body with the President and a joint steering committee to get the legislation through the Congress, to an adoption of a system allowing Cabinet members a seat but not necessarily a vote in the Congress. Other suggestions have been more radical, denoting such very fundamental changes as a shift to the Parliamentary system of England.

It is difficult to see either the need or the advantages of such very broad changes. Access to the President is not currently barred to such dignitaries as the leaders in Congress, and whether Cabinet members could profitably employ their time sitting in Congress is highly questionable. There would seem sufficient opportunity for Congress to do an intelligent job without altering its fundamental nature at all but simply by improving the quality of men sent there. There is no example in our history where the Congress was prevented from doing its job because of restrictions on it or because of inaccessibility to the President. It has been inhibited only by the severe limitations of some of its own members, many of whom would sacrifice national interests to sectional interests, or public interests to personal interests, and who are often too small as men to comprehend the implications of their own actions.

Nor is this condition in any way strange. A man in the State of Nevada can be a United States Senator and possibly, through a committee chairmanship, be powerful enough to defeat the will of the President if he can prevail on 30,000 voters of his state to support him. Obviously, if a legislative talent who has to secure only 30,000 votes is to be charged with a great measure of weight in directing the destiny of 140,000,000 people, those people are running a considerable chance. The obvious answer would be to elect the entire Senate at large from the whole country, possibly cutting its size in half in the process. But if the regional anachronism must persist, then the Senate could preserve its present numerical strength, with one Senator to each state allowed and the remaining forty-eight elected at large, with chairmanships restricted to Senators-at-large.

The House represents a more serious problem. There are now 542 Representatives (six times as many as there are mayors of cities of over 100,000 population), obviously too large a number to avoid attracting big toads in very small puddles who cannot reconcile themselves, on getting to Washington, to becoming small toads in a very big puddle, and also much too large a number to permit very efficient legislative processes. As a result the people do not value the office of Representative and have frequently shown their casual view of it by electing the widows of deceased Representatives to replace them. The Representative, on the other hand, conscious that he is not much of a political rarity, is apt to make up for it in various forms of political infantilism or exhibitionism. The basic solution is probably to reduce the number of representatives by something like 70 per cent and to elect half of them from the states at large and the other half from the nation at large.

The bane of the Congress from the beginning has been the small mind grappling with the large problem, the local wonder who can capture a localized electorate pitting himself against national issues, the spokesmen of a few thousand people holding out to defeat the will of the millions. And no institutional change in the Congress can effect much improvement until the outmoded regionalism that is the root of the trouble is exorcised. Meanwhile, however, the law of averages is—as it always is—on the side of democracy, and the Congress grinds its way along under the general compulsion of the handful of wise and competent men that you have a reasonable chance of drawing in any collection of 640 men who have commended themselves favorably for one reason or another to their neighbors.

Chapter Four

The Supreme Court

HOW THE COURT, UNDER THE INFLUENCE OF A GREAT REALIST
NAMED JOHN MARSHALL, CAME TO PARTAKE OF THE POLITI-
CAL SUBSTANCE OF AMERICA AND WHY, THOUGH IT HAS BE-
COME INVOLVED IN POLITICAL STRUGGLES, WE NEVERTHELESS
PRIZE IT AS A MODERATING INFLUENCE IN THE
NATIONAL LIFE

I

MORE remote from the citizen than the Congress or
the President and certainly far less vulnerable to his
criticism is the Supreme Court of the United States,
which wields its mighty power over both the Presidency and
the Congress but is substantially immune from the effects of
the powers of either of them. At best, it is the conscience of the
government, the Kantian inner check, the stabilizing influence,
the second and more mature thought. At worst it has been many
things: a delaying factor, a throwback, an agency of negativism,
an undoer of legislative progress, and even—particularly, at the
present time—that masterpiece made by confusion of which
Shakespeare wrote, a maelstrom of divisions, contradictions and
intrajuridical differences. Yet it is the most venerated if the
least understood of all our political institutions, the only one
with a mystical halo conferred on it by the people and one
which the lowliest citizen, knowing next to nothing about it,
will rise in wrath to protect if anyone threatens to do anything
about it. The Congress can recommend reorganizing the Executive, and the Executive can urge reorganizing the Congress,

and each can start reorganizing itself—and nothing much happens. But let anyone—including such popular idols as both the Roosevelts or a Jackson or a Jefferson—suggest reorganizing the Supreme Court and a chorus of protests arises in such volume that the effort is promptly abandoned. By consent of the people the Supreme Court is to be left alone, its majestic power unimpaired, its aloof dignity uncompromised.

Perhaps this is due to an intuitive awareness by the people of the peculiar position of the Supreme Court and a conviction that they can afford the occasional luxury of an incompetent President or an unprincipled Congress so long as it is there. Since 1803 this nation—preoccupied as it has been with the elections of Presidents and with the acts of Congress—has actually been living under a system of judicial supremacy. "We are under a Constitution, but the Constitution is what the judges say it is," said Charles Evans Hughes. Five of those judges, not answerable to the people at all, can nullify an act of the Congress and stay the hand of the President. Moreover, they can also nullify the acts of the several state legislatures and stay the hands of the several governors. There is no appeal from their decision, and they can't be removed from office if their decisions are not liked. Functioning in a democracy, they are neither part of any democratic processes nor necessarily sensitive to any democratic pressures. Nor are the Supreme Court's powers subject to any interpretation but its own, whereas the powers of both the President and the Congress are subject to the interpretation of the Court. Harlan Stone, late Chief Justice, put it clearly enough: "While unconstitutional exercise of power by the executive or legislative branches of the Government is subject to judicial restraint, the only check upon our own exercise of power is our own sense of restraint."

Despite all this, the Court is totally without any force behind its decisions except its institutional standing. As Hamilton noted, the President "holds the sword of the community" by his Constitutional command of the armed forces, and the Congress "commands the purse" by its authority to raise taxes and make appropriations. The Supreme Court has nothing but its library and yet, paradoxically, has supremacy over both President and Congress and is paid more popular respect than either. The most autocratic of our political institutions, it oddly enjoys a certain exemption from the kind of popular resentment which is apt to appear chronically in a democracy against its officials and which no President and no Congress has ever entirely escaped.

II

One would assume, from the success with which the Court has historically asserted its position and from the public's adoption of the hands-off dictum so far as the Court is concerned, that it had somewhat more solid and precise Constitutional origins than either the Presidency or the Congress. Actually, the Constitution is both shaky and vague on the Court, and Article III, establishing the Court, is the briefest and least specific of the three articles providing for the separate branches of the Federal Government. It simply catalogues the types of cases that may be brought before the Court, defines its jurisdiction, and lets it go at that. It does not anywhere state that the Court has the power or the duty to review acts of the Congress and decide whether or not they are unconstitutional. It does not anywhere say how many Justices there will be. It does not anywhere say whether those Justices shall have judicial experience, legal experience or even legal training. It does not anywhere say how old a man must be to be named to the Court, although the Constitution specifically requires the President to be at least thirty-five, a Senator to be thirty and a Representative twenty-five. It does not anywhere say that a Justice shall be a citizen or even a resident of the United States, though it specifies that the President must be a native-born citizen and a resident of at least fourteen years, a Senator a citizen for at least nine years and a Representative a citizen for at least seven.

But despite this complete absence of any precise provision for the composition of the Court and the relative vagueness of any definition of the real power of the Court, there is little doubt that the framers of the Constitution meant the Court to be as powerful as it has become. In fact, some of them said so. The foundation of the Court's power rests on its authority to nullify Congressional or state legislation which it holds unconstitutional. Hamilton wrote in *The Federalist* that it was the duty of the Court "to declare all acts contrary to the manifest tenor of the Constitution void." At the Constitutional Convention, Oliver Ellsworth (later, the second Chief Justice) suggested that the Court should share with the President in the exercise of the veto power—a device which might, incidentally, have had the virtue of assuring an act's Constitutionality before it was put into effect rather than afterward. Moreover, although occasionally a delegate denounced the implied supremacy of the Court, as Richard Spaight did, the proceedings of the Convention reveal that most of the delegates assumed that the power of judicial review resided in the Court, and they shared largely in Hamilton's view.

Because the Constitution was nevertheless silent on the power of the Court to rule on the Constitutionality of the acts of the Congress, the Court has never established a procedure for the automatic review of such acts. Nor has it ever exercised any advisory function warning either the President or the Congress in advance of its negative view of the Constitutionality of a proposed act. As a matter of fact, if the Congress of the United States passed and the President approved a bill prohibiting anyone but bald Episcopalians with at least a million dollars in the bank from voting for Federal officials, the Supreme Court would do nothing about it unless some state or private party instituted litigation to stop the enforcement of the law. Even at that, if it were satisfied with the judgment and procedure of the lower court, the Supreme Court would not review the case. For despite its attachment to the power of judicial review, the Court has invariably rejected any method but the litigatory one, and it has not been without wisdom in so doing, for among other things it makes self-reversals more graceful. Furthermore, its method is eclectic, and the number of cases it refuses to review is greater than the number it admits to its docket.

In practical effect the Supreme Court, among other things, reviews the laws enacted by the Congress. Technically it does no such thing: it merely listens to the arguments of two parties (one of them often being the government) whose interests conflict and involve the Federal law, and decides which of the two is right. At one time each Justice wrote an opinion, which made for individual responsibility, but it later became customary for the Chief Justice to assign a case to a particular Justice, who would write the opinion of the Court—the majority opinion which is, in effect, the final word. The dissenting (minority) opinion—pointing out why the dissenting Justices disagree—is written by one of the minority and has no legal force at all, but—in the case of such dissents as those of Oliver Wendell Holmes or of Robert Jackson—they have as much weight in the future shaping of the law as a majority opinion (and often more). Both the Justices concurring in the majority and those in the dissent may write their own separate opinions, particularly if they arrive at their conclusions through different reasoning—a popular practice in the present Court. However, each opinion is applicable only to the actual case before the Court. The Court speaks *ad hoc,* and it does not send a marshal around to the Congress to make it rescind formally an act held unconstitutional. What it does do is find against the party (usually the government, which has to enforce the act) who appears supported by and in support of such acts. Obviously, however, this invalidates the act, because otherwise every party against whom the government enforced the act would rush to the Court to get vindication of his resistance to it. Consequently, a Court opinion finding an act unconstitutional marks the end of the government's execution of such an act and, since the act is thenceforth inoperative, an end to the act itself.

Although the application of the law is through litigation, and, therefore, technically the opinion of the Court is addressed to a particular case, the opinion immediately assumes a stature more lofty than a Congressional act or a Presidential veto. It becomes, indeed, part of that great body of legal principles that both shapes and recalls, both guides and documents, our civil history. It is subject to reversal only by the Court itself or by its successors in future cases. Unlike acts of the Congress, it is immune to Presidential vetoes; and unlike Presidential vetoes, it is immune to overriding by Congress. Moreover, as the nature of the case and the wisdom of the Court allow, an opinion is not necessarily limited to the Constitutionality of the law involved but may involve also broad ethical, political, social, economic or even religious principles. Indeed, if the laws of a nation are the measure of that nation's civilization, then the opinions of our Justices taken as a whole are the standard of our maturity and our wisdom.

III

In general, the largest function of the Supreme Court is that of judicial review rather than the dispensation of justice, even though the Court technically deals only with specific cases. The

major purpose of judicial review as exercised by the Supreme
Court is to decide if the law—whether it be of Federal or of
state origin—is unconstitutional (which does not apply to what
is not in the Constitutiton, incidentally, but rather to what conflicts with what *is* in it) or Constitutional (which, similarly,
doesn't mean what is in the Constitution but rather what is in
essential harmony with it). One example will suffice.

In 1936 a case involving the Agricultural Adjustment Act of
1933 was decided by the Court. The purpose of this early New
Deal measure was to relieve farmers, whose income had dropped
70 per cent in three years, to arrest the wholesale foreclosures
of farm mortgages and to reduce crippling farm surpluses. The
act provided for specific aid by extending farm credit and relief
for mortgages, and it also authorized the Secretary of Agriculture to reduce production and set up a system of market quotas.
The government was further to make compensatory payments
to participating farmers, which were to be paid for by a tax on
the processing of farm commodities. In May 1933 the act became operative. The Court, however jaundiced a view it may
have taken of this legislation, said nothing about it, and for
close to three years it was in actual effect. Then the Court
listened to a case involving a cotton mill which protested paying
the processing tax. The Court in a six-to-three decision found
for the mill. The majority opinion held that the tax was unconstitutional and invalid, because the benefits payments were
unconstitutional and invalid, because only the several states and
not the Congress had power to regulate agricultural production,
and Congress had no power to tax in order to compensate farmers for production cutbacks.

As Charles P. Curtis observed, after some years of practice,
the Court "backs into questions it ought to face." Mr. Justice
Roberts, of the majority, thought he was facing it: the Court's
job, he said, was "to lay the article of the Constitution which

is invoked beside the statute which is challenged and to decide whether the latter squares with the former." That was all. "The Court neither approves nor condemns any legislative policy." But Brandeis, Cardozo and Stone dissented in a very great dissent written by Stone. They found that the Agricultural Adjustment Act squared with the Constitution all right; that thus to relieve farmers was merely, in the language of the Constitution, taxing to "provide for . . . the general welfare"; that (Mr. Justice Stone threw the argument back at Mr. Justice Roberts) "courts are concerned only with the power to enact statutes, not with their wisdom. . . . For the removal of unwise laws from the statute books appeal not to the courts but to the ballot and to the processes of democratic government."

The majority won the battle but lost the war. In 1938, two years later, Mr. Justice Roberts wrote another majority opinion, this time holding that the Agricultural Adjustment Act of 1938 (which also had the government regulating agriculture) *was* Constitutional, and Mr. Justice Butler, dissenting, used Mr. Justice Roberts' 1936 opinion to prove that it was *un*constitutional. Finley Peter Dunne had observed that Supreme Court Justices also read election returns, but cantankerous old Senator William B. Giles put it more gracefully back in 1808: "I have learned that judicial opinions . . . are like changeable silks, which vary their colors as they are held up in political sunshine."

IV

Concentrated in that case are all the juridical elements that make up the unbecoming conflict over the Supreme Court since it first got really supreme in the days of the famous and able John Marshall, third and greatest Chief Justice and, next to Lincoln and Washington, the greatest name in American history. It was he who, in 1803, first held an act of the Congress unconstitutional, and, though his opinion asserted for all time to come the right of the Court so to review Congressional acts, it was also, oddly, a nice example of judicial restraint. For the act involved was the Judiciary Act of 1789, among other things empowering the Court to issue writs of mandamus (that is, court orders to an inferior tribunal or to a person or a group of persons directing the performance of a public duty) in the exercise of its original jurisdiction, and Marshall's opinion held that this would enlarge the original jurisdiction of the Court, that the Congress had no power so to enlarge it and that the act was therefore unconstitutional.

For the next fifty-four years no act of Congress was held unconstitutional until the Dred Scott Decision of 1857 held the Missouri Compromise of 1820, excluding slavery from some territories of the United States, unconstitutional. Ten post-Civil War acts, however, the work of notoriously bad Congresses, were held unconstitutional in eight years from 1865 to 1873. Then as the area of Federal legislation necessarily expanded with the growth of the nation, the scope of judicial review automatically broadened, until in the early 1930's not only Congressional acts but regulations of independent government agencies were popping up regularly before the Court, and in one period of a few months seven out of nine Federal statutes reviewed were invalidated by the opinions of the famous Court of "Nine Old Men." A different record was made in the late 1930's and early 1940's, when a new Court distinguished itself by accumulating a score of thirty-two reversals of earlier opinions of the Court dating back over the century.

Except for one very large fact, this record would constitute an extraordinary dilemma in American history and would probably have long since precipitated a complete collapse of the Court. This one large fact is that the Supreme Court is in reality a quasi-political body, subject to political compulsions and operating not in a judicial vacuum at all but in a whirling political climate. Indeed, the doctrine of judicial review fairly confers on the Court a political nature, for how are nine mature men to sit in prolonged puzzlement over whether or not a statute is literally Constitutional? That is an exercise in pedantry for the semasiologist. What the Court does, in fact, is to decide on the prudence of the statute as related to the spirit and guarantees of the Constitution. Indeed, to suggest that any act comparable to the Fair Labor Standards Act is literally unconstitutional is a useless elucidation of the obvious, not unlike noting that the use of the atom bomb is literally inconsistent with the rules of chivalry. Consequently, the Court's major function has been to examine new legislation, as it has come before the Court in practical application, against not only the background of the Constitution but of the economic, social and political conditions of the day, the needs of the times and the experiences of the past. This has made the Court in practical effect a continuous legislative body, for laws are made not only through enactment (which merely launches them) but through the juridical process, which gives them meaning.

"Thus, the Supreme Court is not only a court of justice," said James M. Beck, a very conservative Solicitor General, "but in a qualified sense a continuous Constitutional convention. It continues the work of the Convention of 1787 by adapting through interpretation the great charter of government; and thus its duties become political, in the highest sense of that word, as well as judicial."

Mr. Justice Holmes found the best of men more political than judicial in temperament anyhow: "The felt necessities of the times, the prevalent moral and political theories, intuitions of public policy, avowed or unconscious, even the prejudices which Judges share with their fellow-men, have had a good deal more to do than the syllogism in determining the rules by which men should be governed." He had also been inclined to take a restrained measure of judicial review: "I do not think the United States would come to an end if we lost our power to declare an Act of Congress void."

But the Court has the power of review, and you can't have a political nature without a political complexion. Mr. Justice Roberts' parlor game of putting a clause of the Constitution next to a clause from a contested statute "to see how they square" just doesn't work. "The life of the law has not been logic; it has been experience," said Holmes. And if the exercise of Justice Roberts had value, a law would be equally unconstitutional in 1936 and 1938, in 1842 and 1947. But it is not, because there is nothing so simple as all that—not in either legislative or judicial processes. And judicial review itself means more.

In one of the immortal opinions of our history, Chief Justice Marshall told his contemporaries and his successors what judicial review was all about: "Let the end be legitimate, let it be within the scope of the Constitution, and all means which are appropriate, which are plainly adapted to that end, which are not prohibited but consist with the letter and spirit of the Constitution, are constitutional." Now this would necessarily involve the Court in appraising changing national conditions in interpreting the Constitution—and that is a political and not a legalistic activity.

It involves the Justices also, whether they choose or not, in appraising economic and social conditions. Mr. Justice Brandeis mentioned a specific case: "The change in the law by which strikes once illegal and even criminal are now recognized as lawful was effected in America largely without the intervention of legislation. This reversal of a common-law rule was not due to the rejection by the courts of one principle and the adoption in its stead of another but to a better realization of the facts of industrial life." Justice Jackson has similarly said, "Supreme

Court decrees prick out roughly the drifts of national policy."
And since they do, those who write them are in the political
waters up to their ears. For from as early as Marshall's 1819
decision, the considerations of what is politic and what is reasonable have tempered the consideration of what is Constitutional. And no tribunal can weigh those considerations without
disturbing its judicial antisepsis. Moreover, the Court has, like
the Presidency, undergone a process of evolution that has both
expanded its powers and extended the framework of its standards of reference. It has, in a sense, become more outrightly
political.

v

The substance of the changing political philosophy of the
Supreme Court is its opinions regarding the Constitutionality of
Congressional acts, or, in other words, the area of Congressional
competence. The character of it is in its reversals of itself. The
core of it is the simple question, What does the Constitution
mean?—for not only has the Supreme Court in one session said
it meant one thing while another Court in another session has
said it meant another, but Justices of the same Court have held
in the same session divergent and sometimes opposite views of
what it meant in application to the same case. These reversals
and split decisions have shattered the illusion of extrapolitical
opinions, and not many people today would claim or wish that
the Court looked at legislation stripped of its political context.
Consequently, where the reversal might be evidence of a singular lack of consistency if opinions were solely judicial, it is
evidence of a healthy flexibility when it is remembered that they
represent a large and often determining political content. There
is, therefore, not so much stigma attached to a five-to-four decision of the Court as would superficially appear, for as there is

politically nothing to dread more in a democracy than a unanimous legislature or a unanimous electorate (which means one
party), there is something repugnant also about an opinion,
even though it comes from the Court, if it has any controversial
political element, that is unanimous. Indeed, the great strides
made by the Court in the application of the Constitution to the
ever growing and the ever more complex affairs of the nation
have been when the Court has been divided. Great opinions
have provoked great dissents, and fallacious opinions have provoked resounding dissents that the nation has justly prized. Our
political history would be far more barren without them, and
our institutions no more secure.

Much of what has come to form the body of ethical principles
by which the nation lives has its prologues in dissents of the
Court. One thinks immediately of perhaps the most famous
dissent in our judicial history, that of Justice Oliver Wendell
Holmes, Jr., in the case of *Hammer* v. *Dagenhart* in 1918. Two
years earlier the Sixty-fourth Congress passed an act, effective
in 1917, prohibiting commerce between the states in goods produced in factories, quarries or mines employing children under
fourteen or children between fourteen and sixteen for more than
an eight-hour day or six-day week, or at night. The Western
District Court of North Carolina declared the law unconstitutional. In June 1918 the Supreme Court upheld the district court
by a five-to-four decision, with Mr. Justice William R. Day
writing the opinion that the act regulated manufacturing rather
than commerce and was therefore beyond the competence of
Congress. What this decision meant in effect, of course, was
that only transportation industries were subject to Congressional
legislation. In his brief, tightly reasoned and closely documented
dissent, Holmes pointed out that the Congressional power to
regulate interstate commerce meant nothing without the power
to prohibit, that among such prohibitions were those already in

effect in the White Slave Act (which invoked the interstate-commerce power in order to enable Congress to legislate against prostitution) and the Pure Food and Drug Act (which invoked the interstate-commerce power to enable Congress to legislate against harmful foods and drugs). Consequently, he held that the Court was putting an arbitrary limitation on the use by the Congress of a power long since acknowledged and exercised. And he saw no reason why the prohibition element of the regulatory power was "permissible as against strong drink but not as against the product of ruined lives."

In 1919 the Sixty-fifth Congress tried another tack: forgetting the interstate-commerce power, it sought to destroy child labor by using its tax power and clapped a 10-per-cent profits tax on all companies using child labor. In 1922, the Supreme Court, speaking through Mr. Chief Justice Taft, invalidated the effort on the ground that it was utilizing the tax law for something other than to raise money. In his decision the Chief Justice had the astonishing naïveté to refer favorably to the tax differential on yellow versus white oleomargarine. Certainly he knew that yellow oleomargarine was not taxed ten cents a pound because it was a handy way to raise money. His refreshing view was that if "another motive than taxation" was "not shown on the face of the [tax] act" but was hidden, then the tax power could be used for such other motive. But if that motive was manifest rather than hidden, then the tax power could not be so used. By 1922, then, it was established that by use neither of the tax nor of the interstate-commerce power could Congress control the labor of children. But Mr. Justice Day's opinion of 1918 and Mr. Chief Justice Taft's of 1922 are both forgotten, and appropriately so, while Mr. Justice Holmes's eight-paragraph dissent lives both as a legal foundation and a literary masterpiece.

There is no more striking illustration of the political character of the Court than its list of reversals, and there is probably also nothing which has so consolidated the position of the Court. Democratic processes are not congenial to rigid and inflexible institutions, and the Court—made up, for the overwhelmingly largest part through the years, of men of wisdom and political prudence—has been profoundly aware of this. Mixed by the wise jurist with the strain of Constitutionalism is the strain of what is prudent and good. "The very considerations which judges most rarely mention," said Holmes, "and always with an apology, are the secret roots from which the law draws all the juices of life. I mean, of course, considerations of what is expedient for the community concerned. Every important principle which is developed by litigation is in fact and at bottom the result of more or less definitely understood views of public policy . . . the unconscious result of instinctive preferences and inarticulate convictions."

Not even the strictest Constitutional constructionist would claim that such preferences and convictions are unchanged from one century to another or from one decade to another. What then would be the value of a Court of legal pedants, unable or unwilling to adapt the broad principles of the Constitution to the shifting requirements and demands of the generations? And, so hemmed in and fettered by frozen legalisms, what chance would the Constitution itself have had to survive? "But in cases involving the Federal Constitution," said Brandeis, "where correction through legislative action is practically impossible, this Court has overruled its earlier decisions. The Court bows to the lessons of experience and the force of better reasoning, recognizing that the process of trial and error, so fruitful in the physical sciences, is appropriate also to the judicial function. . . . Moreover, the judgment of the Court in the earlier decision may have been influenced by prevailing views as to economic or social policy which have since been abandoned."

The Court indeed bows to experience, and the dissents of

yesterday are used to bolster the majority opinions of today—
the ultimate reversal. Mr. Coolidge's appointee, Harlan Stone,
shattered the majority opinion of Mr. Justice Day invalidating
that Child Labor Act of 1916, by using Mr. Justice Holmes's
classic dissent to support the unanimous upholding of the Fair
Labor Standards Act of 1938. Here was the Court unanimously
declaring the decision of an earlier Court all error and no
trial. But the enabling clause of the Constitution had not been
changed. So which Court was court and which legislature?

Not all Justices would care to be as direct as Brandeis; but
the legislative role is there all the same, and the legislative role
is a political role, one increasingly played by the Court. Before
1865 the Court in all its history held two Congressional acts to
be unconstitutional. Since the Civil War up to the Roosevelt
barrage at the Court in 1937, there were almost seventy invali-
dations of Federal statutes. The average increased from one in
thirty-five years to slightly less than one in every year. Every
such opinion of the Court, of course, reverses the elected Congress of the United States and, because much legislation has its
springboard in the recommendation of the Executive, also reverses the President. Inevitably, political repercussions follow.
Nor is that all. Frequently a political conflict has resulted from
the Court upholding the Constitutionality of an act, the most
noteworthy examples being the sustaining of the first Bank of
the United States charter and the Fugitive Slave Act of 1850.
Moreover, in every such case, the Court has come in conflict with
the President or the Congress, and usually with both. Political
institutions face political risks, and the Court has shown itself
capable of taking care of itself. The Supreme Court has never
been characterized by a majority of politically naïve minds; and
many have been deeper rooted in political than in judicial experience, while all, of course, have been politically appointed,
with only four out of thirty-two Presidents appointing men not
of their own political party.

Consider only the Chief Justices.

Sixteen men in a hundred and sixty years have been named to the office. One of them, John Rutledge, named by George Washington in 1795, was rejected by the Senate after taking his seat, because of his political opposition to the Jay Treaty the previous summer. William Cushing, named in place of Rutledge by Washington, was confirmed but declined the office, pleading ill health though he sat as an Associate Justice for sixteen years afterward. Two others of those named as Chief Justice, both by Republican President Ulysses S. Grant, had their names withdrawn. The first, George Henry Williams, was refused approval by the Senate Judiciary Committee in January 1874. That same month Grant nominated Caleb Cushing, the best-equipped man of his time, for the post, but he was the victim of a strictly partisan opposition and Grant had again to withdraw his nominee. It is significant that each of these men already had judicial experience of a high order. Of the twelve named who actually served in the office with Senate confirmation, only five, Jay, Ellsworth, White, Taft and Vinson, had any judicial experience before coming to the Supreme Court. The other seven, Marshall, Taney, Chase, Waite, Fuller, Hughes and Stone—far greater in reputation on the whole— had no judicial experience whatsoever before joining the Supreme Court, for even Hughes and Stone had been Associate Justices without previous judicial experience. If these men were not named for their juridical reputations, as they manifestly were not since they had none, then they must have been appointed for political reasons.

Now consider briefly that a total of eighty-five men have served as Associate Justices from the beginning, twenty-eight of them having been named in the last fifty years. Of these twenty-eight named since 1900, only ten had had any major judicial experience. The rest had been Cabinet members, Senators, governors, teachers of the law. Of the fourteen named since 1925, four have been elevated from the office of Attorney General and one from that of Solicitor General. All of these men, with the possible exception of the occasional teacher of the law, were men primarily of political backgrounds rather than juridical, used to thinking in political terms and dealing with political values. It may justly be said, therefore, that the composition of the Court for the most part has been strongly political, not only in that the method of a Justice getting there is political in the first place, through the Presidential appointment and the Senatorial confirmation, but also in the major past associations of most of the Justices.

No one was more ready to dwell on this political nature of the Court than William Howard Taft, one of the few Chief Justices who had come to the Supreme Court with a background including juridical experience. Taft knew the Court well. He had served on the Ohio Superior Court for six years in his thirties; in 1890 he was President Harrison's Solicitor General, argued eighteen cases before the Supreme Court and won fifteen of them; for the eight years following, he was a Federal circuit judge, the second highest judicial post in the land; he twice declined appointments to the Supreme Court by Theodore Roosevelt in order to continue his work in the Philippines as President of the Commission; as President of the United States, he named six men to the Supreme Court in four years—more than have been named by any President in one term since Washington; for eight years he taught Constitutional Law at Yale; for nine years he presided over the Supreme Court as Chief Justice, the best administrator of the Court's affairs in its history if but an indifferent jurist. He was also the finest political manipulator of the Court that ever lived, and would probably have shaken his generous bulk with laughter at the thought that the Court was not a political institution. In fact, he was much more at home with the politics of the bench than with those of the White House. He regarded the purely accidental stroke that he had been able to appoint six Justices as the major achievement of his administration. But he was aware also that death substitutes for the ballot box in removing Justices and in upsetting the applecart of judicial politics. And, from his own accounts, the jovial Taft would rather campaign against death than an opposition candidate. As he left the White House to make room for the liberal Democrat, Woodrow Wilson (who was very apt to appoint latitudinarian constructionists to the bench), he reminded his six Justices of their political function: "I have said to them, 'Damn you, if any of you die, I'll disown you.'" The strategy was obvious: stay alive until a Republican is back in the White House to name conservative successors.

Two of Taft's appointees paid little attention to his admonition, and a third one, Hughes, resigned to run against Wilson. But the other three, including Chief Justice Edward D. White, stayed on. Then as the 1920 campaign approached Taft began to get nervous—for it was a campaign that batted every political issue back and forth, except what Taft regarded as the greatest political issue of all—the Supreme Court. He studied his vital statistics again. "Four of the incumbent Justices are beyond the retiring age of seventy," he noted with alarm, "and the next President will probably be called upon to appoint their successors. There is no greater domestic issue in this election than the maintenance of the Supreme Court as the bulwark to enforce the guaranty that no man shall be deprived of his property without due process of law." In other words, without Republican appointees to the Court, confiscation of property would quickly ensue. But the four beyond seventy held out, and Warren Harding was safely in the White House. As became an ex-President of the same party, Taft dropped by to see him. He mentioned the Court.

One of the Justices over seventy was Chief Justice Edward D.

White, whom Taft had elevated to the post in 1910. Now, as Taft told Harding, there was something of a political bargain involved in the promotion. White had been a Democrat, but Taft promoted him anyhow, and White then told Taft that "he was holding the office for me and that he would give it back to a Republican administration." This left Harding a little disturbed, because he had promised the first opening to George Sutherland, who was one of his closest friends from the Senate. Taft then went around to see the aging Chief Justice White, who had promised those ten years earlier to save the office for Taft and give it back to a Republican administration. He had sat out the eight years of Wilson all right, but he made no move, now that a Republican was back in the White House, to retire from his office and "give it back." In the words of Taft's biographer, Henry Pringle, "Taft's anxious appraisal of the jurist's health was a degree ghoulish." Fortunately, however, White had the good grace to die shortly, and the only obstacle to the conclusion of this strange political bargain between a Chief Justice of the United States and a President of the United States was Harding's promise to Sutherland (who was, by now, out of a job, having been defeated for re-election to the Senate). The Attorney General of the United States, Mr. Harry Daugherty, stepped in to handle the matter. He went to Harding and arranged for ex-President Taft to get the Chief Justiceship and for ex-Senator Sutherland to get the next opening as Associate Justice. Taft thus managed to appoint seven members of the Court—the seventh being himself after leaving office.

After donning the judicial robes which represented the only office in the world that he really wanted desperately, Taft continued to take a political view of the Court as an institution. Coolidge was in the White House in a little while, and Chief Justice Taft returned the compliment to Attorney General

Daugherty, who had interceded with Harding on his behalf, and asked him to resign to relieve Coolidge of embarrassment. Coolidge, having had Taft's help in easing Daugherty out of the Attorney General's office, put Harlan Fiske Stone in it, and promoted him to the Supreme Court the next year. A great scholar, a great lawyer and a great jurist, Stone was the best appointee to the Court in a decade. But Taft was not happy with his new associate. "A learned lawyer in many ways," he called the Coolidge nominee, "but his judgments I do not altogether consider safe. He definitely has ranged himself with Brandeis and with Holmes in a good many of our Constitutional differences." Coolidge had let Taft down!

But what terrified Taft even more was the specter of Herbert Hoover, a seeming radical of sufficient violence to nominate almost anyone. He determined to campaign against death again, for the only hope now was for all the old Justices, including himself, to live forever—a repetition of the strategy of the four over seventy who sat out Wilson. Only now there was no Republican to wait for, Hoover was a Republican and presumably also a Bolshevik: "I am older and slower and less acute and more confused," wrote Taft the year Hoover was inaugurated, in a rare appraisal of the highest juridical mind of the land. "However, as long as things continue as they are, and I am able to answer in my place, I must stay on the Court in order to prevent the Bolsheviki from getting control. . . . [T]he only hope . . . is for us to live as long as we can. . . ." In the same vein he wrote to Pierce Butler the same year: "The most that could be hoped for is continued life of enough of the present membership to prevent disastrous reversals of our present attitudes. With Van [Van Devanter] and Mac [McReynolds] and Sutherland and you and Sanford, there will be five to steady the boat. We must not give up at once."

Thus to the end, both from without and within, Taft not only regarded but treated the Court as a political institution, the conservative factor in politics that can outlive an unpredictable Congress and "radical" Presidents like Wilson and Hoover, and he had long life and old age on his side. For the Court is frequently not merely political but a political afterglow in both its composition and its function.

This is largely due, as Mr. Justice Jackson has pointed out, to the fact that "the Court is almost never a really contemporary institution." (The present Court is one of the rare exceptions.) The reason is obvious. The President is elected every four years, a third of the Senate every two and the entire House every two. But a Justice averages some fifteen years on the bench, the actual average tenure, from the beginning and excluding those still in office, amounting to fourteen years and eight months, while the average Presidential tenure has been only a third of that time or five years. Consequently the Justices have a natural tendency to relate the problems of one period and the legislative solution to them to the values and the Constitutional views of a preceding period. Moreover, both the President and the Congress of one period are usually there by virtue of a popular rejection of that earlier President and Congress by whom the Justice was appointed and confirmed. The judicial rejection of the New Deal was the work of a Court largely representing the political philosophy of the twenties which had itself been overwhelmingly rejected by the people.

The salubrious effect of the juridical temperament on longevity is a real factor here. Eight Justices have served over thirty years—three of them for thirty-four years—the equivalent of over eight Presidential terms. By this standard a mind opulent enough to be on the Supreme Court in McKinley's day could be expected to be flexible and enduring enough to review with wisdom the legislative solutions of the intricate problems of the Great Depression that faced Franklin Roosevelt. Sixteen

Justices have served over twenty-five years, representing in Presidential history the span from Harrison through Tyler, Taylor, Fillmore, Pierce, Buchanan, Lincoln to Johnson. Chief Justice Taney, a pitiable but stubbornly active figure at the end, sat through the administrations of ten Presidents—well over half of all the Presidents who had then been in office.

Moreover, men are not usually nominated to the Supreme Court in the first flush of youth, so that their average age on completing their service has been seventy as opposed to fifty-nine for the Presidents. And Justices do not like to resign or retire. Only thirty-three have done so (including those who left to take other offices), while forty-seven have died with their robes on. These are not apt to be—if we willingly except the rarity of a Holmes or a Brandeis—the most progressive minds of the period. And they are bound to be conservative, no matter how liberal in the beginning, for yesterday's liberal is often today's conservative, and the Court usually is of political yesterdays. Even the younger generation today is a little shocked to hear Frankfurter and Jackson spoken of as belonging to "the conservative wing" of the Court.

Of course, what is conservative now, even in the Supreme Court, was fairly radical once, and politically age goes to school to youth. So that while there always has been a conservative and liberal split in the Court, the split has not always been over the same thing. In one period it was the question of supremacy of the Court over the highest state courts; at another the rights of the Congress to enact broad legislation affecting interstate commerce; at another the right to police monopolies; at another the extent of economic and labor legislation; at another the right of the Court to protect traditional property theories against legislative encroachments; and at yet another the right of the Court to sustain the rights of the people against the legislature itself.

Now we are in the latter phase, with an all Roosevelt-Truman Court splitting between conservatism and liberalism. The conservatives, led by Frankfurter, are for a measure of judicial restraint, inclined to the view that the legislature has the prerogative and speaks for the citizen. The liberals, led by Douglas and Black, incline to the view that the Court has the prerogative and speaks in behalf of the rights of the citizen even against the legislature. The shift in intrajudicial politics would spin the Nine Old Men of fifteen years ago in their graves. For it was the liberals Brandeis and Cardozo then who favored legislative prerogative and the ancient and conservative survivals who said the Court should veto legislation to protect the people.

Liberalism and conservatism on the bench then seem to be related to the nation's legislative affairs. There would not appear to be a more certain way for the Court to preserve its political nature.

At the same time, the Court has rarely been politically partisan, which is one of the very great and rewarding facts about it as an institution—one, indeed, that has made it politically unique in this country, for the Congress is outrightly and formally partisan in organization and no one but a fool would claim that the Presidency is a nonpartisan office. Partisanship— an absolute necessity in the two electoral branches of the government—would be an evil in the Court; it would serve no useful purpose and turn the body into a petty and perpetual Senate. For all its political associations, the Court has avoided outright partisanship. Before this single fact the inherent disadvantages already suggested in the appointive and life-tenure character of the Court wither, and it remains the purest of our institutions because its Justices are politically independent once in office.

Every student of the Supreme Court has been stopped in his tracks by Brooks Adams' indictment in *The Theory of Social Revolution*: "In fine, from the outset, the American bench, because it deals with the most fiercely contested of political issues, has been an instrument necessary to political success. Consequently, political parties have striven to control it, and therefore the bench has always had an avowed partisan bias."

Adams' theory is perfectly sound, but theory doesn't go too far in politics, and that of Adams breaks down in his second sentence. In general, the Court has been without a partisan bias, avowed or otherwise, in spite of its dealings with the most fiercely contested of political issues. Witness Harlan Fiske Stone, Coolidge's Republican appointee, whom Franklin Roosevelt promoted to Chief Justice for his closely reasoned dissents on opinions invalidating the New Deal. Witness again the record of Hoover's appointee, Benjamin Cardozo, who differed with his brethren on the unconstitutionality of one New Deal statute after another. Witness, for a little while, the "Roosevelt Court"—those who were supposed to be, according to the opposition, a "rubber stamp" for any directive mystically communicated to them from the White House. By 1943, Roosevelt had named an entire Court except for the remaining Roberts. In 1943 there were one hundred and thirty-seven opinions, eighty (58%) of which were split and sixteen of which were five-to-four decisions. What kind of partisan bias is that? In 1946, by which time the Roosevelt Court was not new and there was plenty of time for the members to get on with their partisan bias, there were one hundred and forty-four opinions, ninety-two (64%) of which were split, with twenty-six of them five-to-four decisions.

Similarly in the Court presided over by Charles Evans Hughes, whom Hoover appointed, Justice Stone (appointed by Coolidge), Justice Brandeis (appointed by Wilson) and Justice Cardozo (appointed by Hoover) aligned themselves regularly against Van Devanter (appointed by Taft), Sutherland (appointed by Harding), Butler (appointed by Harding) and Mc-

Reynolds (appointed by Wilson). Hughes and Owen Roberts (both appointed by Hoover) were the Court's swing men and went first to the one wing and then to the other. Where was the partisan bias? There may have been—unquestionably there were—political attitudes involved and political values. But certainly there was no partisan bias when Wilson, Coolidge and Hoover appointees arranged themselves against a Wilson, a Taft and two Harding appointees—with two more Hoover men running from one wing to the other and back again.

Nor is all this too late for Brooks Adams' observation, for by Hughes's day the Court was historically nonpartisan. Andrew Jackson appointed a complete Supreme Court (the only man but Washington to do so) between 1829 and 1837, and Jackson's policy of seeking that Spanish land claimants prove their claims was repeatedly rejected by the Court. The Fugitive Slave Law, which such antislavery men as Emerson said they would not obey even after the Court asserted its Constitutionality, was upheld by antislavery judges. State-rights Democrat-Republicans joined Marshall in the establishment of judicial nationalism. The carpetbagger Reconstruction laws of the exclusively Republican Congresses after the Civil War were invalidated by an exclusively Republican Court. Thomas Jefferson's first appointee, William Johnson, held Jefferson's directive under his favorite Embargo Laws to be without force or authority. Similarly, throughout its history, members of the Court have clamped legal restraints on the Presidents who appointed them and have invalidated acts of the Congresses whose Senators confirmed them. The Court has been political but not partisan.

VII

The level of politics on which the Supreme Court operates is the highest one: by judicial review it establishes the policy of the nation, for the Court has as frequently used the Constitution for a springboard as it has for a fence rail. Indeed, John Marshall, who was more powerful than any man in the welding of a loose confederation into a real nation, took a very broad view of the powers of the Federal Congress and a very limited view of the Constitutional safeguards for the rights of States; and, with the able collaboration of Joseph Story, he proceeded in a series of great opinions to use the Constitution as a point of departure for the construction of a whole supplementary body of Constitutional law. Much of this was virtually written by such nationalist lawyers as William Wirt and Daniel Webster, whose eloquent arguments before the Court were incorporated by Marshall in his decisions. The tradition established by Marshall in his thirty-four years of judicial leadership has never been broken permanently, and the Court has a large place in American history because it developed from his time on as a policy-determining body rather than a huddled group of pedantic legalists. The Constitution became the guide and not the road block.

But you cannot, whether on the level of legislative expedience, executive conviction or judicial prudence, act in the area of determining public policy without becoming subject to political reaction. Consequently the Court's history is one of recurring conflict with the President or with the Congress and, sometimes, with both. This is most natural, of course, at those times when the Court is relatively old, for then the judicial point of view is usually that of an older generation—and no older generation is ever convinced that the younger one isn't moving too fast for safety. In such cases, the core of the Judicial-Congressional or Judicial-Presidential conflict is usually a political anachronism. Moreover, old age is stubborn and youth is impetuous, and the conflict from time to time blows up into dimensions which are usually somewhat larger than the real circumstances warrant. Holmes had written: "I do not think the United States would come to an end if we lost our power to declare an act of Congress void." Nor has it come to an end because the Court retained the power. The aftermath is frequently worse than the storm or, even more disturbing, the cure worse than the ailment. And Franklin Roosevelt, the most gifted of American politicians, made a political error of the first rank when he blew the balloon of juridical antediluvianism up to such dimensions that it burst in his face. There is such a thing, as we will see further when we get down to somewhat lower aspects of our political nature, as political evolution. Lincoln knew this and never forgot it. Franklin Roosevelt knew it but forgot it at least once. But he wasn't alone in our history.

The earliest conflicts of the Court with crasser political elements were not with national agencies but with individual states—for example, Pennsylvania, Georgia and Ohio—over the Court's review and voiding of state legislation. Marshall, nearly always the voice of the Court, found a succession of state laws repugnant to the Constitution. He also tended to irritate the legislatures of individual states by a succession of very conservative opinions on the law of contracts and by his decision upholding the chartering of the first Bank of the United States and forbidding taxation of the Bank by the states. Similarly, the regional and state view of his broad construction of the interstate-commerce power granted by the Constitution to Congress was passingly dim. But though there were sporadic defiances of the Court by the states, judicial nationalism triumphed and left Marshall with an odd place in history, for more than anything else his latitudinarian attitude toward the Constitutional powers of the Federal Government, which infuriated the most liberal thinking of his day and pleased the most conservative, established a mechanism and a tradition that a century later permitted the intrusion of the Federal Government into the economic life of the nation, which infuriated the most conservative thinking and pleased the most liberal.

For all practical purposes there was little the individual state could do to break down national judicial supremacy, and Marshall and his Court were not unaware of it. But when the Court conflicted with the President or the Congress, it had to maintain itself against lions rather than terriers. Nor has this most fundamental conflict been either rare in incidence or mild in temper, and it has had complete lapses only in such rare periods as the present when the Court catches up chronologically with the elected branches of the government. Such conflicts have usually originated with an opinion of the Court that was in opposition either to the program or dominant policy of the President or to the legislative will of the Congress—sometimes to both. In such cases the customary reaction has been to threaten "reform" of the Court or of judicial procedure.

In general the attacks of the Congress against the Court have been aimed at its institutional status while the quarrels of the Presidents have been personal. Consequently the Congress has, from time to time, sought to limit or condition the power of the Court while displeased Presidents have thought of correction in terms of new Justices. Since it has power to impeach Supreme Court Justices along with all other Federal officials, the Congress has always had completely within its competence a means of calling the Justices to personal account, but after one experiment it has exhibited unexpected restraint in the exercise of the impeachment power over the Court. In 1805 Mr. Justice Samuel Chase was tried in impeachment proceedings, inspired by President Jefferson, for incorporating some political observations of a fairly heated intensity in his charge to a Baltimore jury (Supreme Court Justices, until 1891, had to sit as Federal circuit judges in addition to their Supreme Court duties). The real purpose of the impeachment effort, of course, was to institute a method of recall of judges for being politically incongruous with the Congress. The impeachment, despite Jefferson's influence, fortunately failed, and finished the threat of the use of impeachment for political removal of Justices, as the 1868 impeachment of Johnson did the same with regard to the Presidency. But Congress was still periodically inflamed with the actions of the Court and was visited with some strange and alarming inspirations toward curbing its powers.

The first of these came as soon as Chase was acquitted when it was proposed in the House that "the Judges of the Supreme Court and all other Courts of the United States shall be removed from office by the President upon joint address of both Houses of Congress requesting the same." The astonishing proposal, virtually assuring a new bench with every party shift in Congress, was opposed even by the current Court's enemies and twice failed of adoption. But the proposal died hard: four times it was introduced again between 1808 and 1816, and each time defeated.

In the following decade, during the 1820's, the Court was again the object of worried concern—largely because of a fear not of the Court's ascendancy but of that of the whole Federal Government. Many people, among them Jefferson, took a dismal view of the Court's increased custom of caucusing the opinions of the Justices in conference and issuing only one majority opinion. They felt that the Justices were more accountable if each had to write a separate opinion. The theory, of course, was to line up the unacceptable Justices and make them politically rather than judicially answerable for their opinions. This led to rather awkward ramifications, and some weird suggestions were made by some of the great men of the day: let the Senate review the opinions and fire the Justices whose opinions the Senate found "unconstitutional," for example, or limit the terms of the Justices to six years. In 1821 the Senate pondered a bill to make itself the appellate court in cases involving conflict of state laws with the Constitution—on the grounds that the Supreme Court was too liberal in construing the powers of the Federal Government. There followed, somewhat naïvely, resolutions in Congress to nullify specific decisions of the Court. In 1823, a Senate bill was proposed requiring the concurrence of seven Justices (at that time a unanimous concurrence) in order to invalidate any state statute or act of Congress, and another was introduced by Senator Van Buren requiring five out of seven for such invalidation, a bill seriously debated for weeks. The fly in this ointment, of course, was that it would have given any three Justices as much power as a majority of the Court previously had and would have involved all the evils of the two-thirds vote in the Senate. It would have meant minority-controlled judicial decisions, and yet it was revived periodically whenever Congress was angry with the Court, only to go down each time to well-justified defeat.

All this storm over the Court was, however, a gentle summer breeze compared to the blizzard that raged in the late 1850's, after the Dred Scott Decision held that (1) Negroes were not regarded as citizens in the Constitution's intent; (2) slaves could not be citizens and (3) Congress had no power to exclude slavery from the territories. The more hotheaded members of Congress were ready to abolish the Court altogether, and as a matter of fact any corrective would have had to be radical—for it was not a close decision, there being seven in the majority and only two in the dissent. The mood of the critics was not helped by another decision upholding the Fugitive Slave Act, and soon state courts, prominent individuals and respectable organizations were announcing intentions to ignore the Court's decision. "A judicial Vatican," the Court was called, and "a gowned conclave, gravely setting aside statutes and constitutions of states . . . prompting its ministers to mayhem and murder." Speech after fiery speech in Congress threatened the Court with every imaginable reform, and the press poured kerosene on the flames. But even the struggle that shortly was capable of bringing the nation to civil war and blasting it into two armed camps could not prevail against the institutional standing of the Court, and nothing happened.

Although institutionally the Court has remained unchanged since its position was established by the Constitution and asserted by John Marshall, it has not escaped entirely from the effect of political forces. Its composition—although the debate in 1936 led many to believe otherwise—has been changed six times, and other changes were frequently suggested. Some of the six effected changes were largely nonpolitical, but some of the increases in the number of Justices and the two decreases were purely political in motive. Indeed "court packing" is no innovation of modern times. The first change in the Court occurred in 1801 when a lame-duck Congress cut the number of Justices down from the six originally established by the Judiciary Act of 1789 to five. The bill, providing that the next vacancy on the Court should not be filled, came on the eve of Jefferson's inauguration, and the President-elect—the first non-Federalist in the White House—was convinced it was to deprive him of the chance to make an appointment—although a more obvious political consideration was that the same bill created six Federal circuit judges whom John Adams spent his time appointing in the interval between Jefferson's election and inauguration, getting the last of them confirmed the day before he left the Presidency. A year later, before any vacancy on the Court occurred, the new Congress repealed the bill and the Court remained with six members. Actually the repeal of this act of 1801 was far more of a political move than its enactment and restored to the Justices of the Supreme Court the burdensome necessity of riding circuit.

In 1807 and again in 1837, the Court was enlarged, first from six to seven Justices and then from seven to nine. The act of 1807 provided for an additional Justice because of an increased volume of Court business stemming largely from the near frontier of western Kentucky, Tennessee and Ohio; and Jefferson, embittered as he was by the Court, nevertheless made a nonpolitical appointment. In 1837, on March third, the day before Andrew Jackson—who had had his troubles with the Court—was to leave office, Congress enlarged the Court from seven to nine, creating two vacancies. Jackson promptly made two appointments during his last twelve hours as President, but one man declined because he wanted to be free to indulge in political discussions. In spite of its nicely timed political implications, the increase of 1837 was really to help the Court get its business done. But Justice Story—who served for thirty-three years and knew the Court well—said that the increased number made the Court both less facile and less rapid: "I verily believe that if there were twelve judges, we should do no business at all."

During the Civil War Congress raised the Court to its greatest numerical strength, creating a tenth Justiceship, to take care of additional circuit work in California and Oregon. In the midst of war and sorely beset by political problems, Lincoln chose a Democrat for the job, the Chief Justice of the California Supreme Court. But the thoroughly amoral Thirty-ninth Congress summarily reduced the Court to seven in 1866 to prevent President Johnson from making appointments and to punish the Court for not bowing to the Congressional brand of military control of the defeated South. This crudest partisan tampering with the Court in our history was solely a Congressional stratagem. President Johnson nominated the Attorney General of the United States and a highly qualified lawyer, Henry Stanberry, on April 8, 1866, to fill the vacancy caused by the death of the aged Justice Catron. The Senate failed to act on the nomination and, in July, passed an act reducing the Court by three members, thus disposing both of Johnson's nominee and of any future appointments by him. One month after Johnson's term expired, the Congress raised the membership again from seven to nine, for Grant was regarded as a safe President, subservient to the Congress. Grant made the mistake, however, of appointing E. R. Hoar, then Attorney General of the United States and formerly an able judge of the Massachusetts Supreme Court, who was politically repugnant to the Senate. Hoar was not confirmed. But meanwhile, on December 15, 1869, Justice Grier resigned, his resignation to take effect the following February. Grant, eager to be congenial, couldn't wait for the effective date and on December 20 nominated the politicos' darling, Edwin M. Stanton, Lincoln's irascible Secretary of War and Johnson's relentless enemy, who was confirmed immediately and dropped dead four days later. Mr. Justice Grier had the odd experience of attending his successor's funeral before relinquishing his seat to him. Finally, Grant filled the two vacancies with nominees suggested to him by the rejected Hoar, and the Court was constituted of nine men again.

The last attempt to alter the Court was made by Franklin Roosevelt in February 1937, after the overwhelming victory of his New Deal program at the polls in 1936. Roosevelt frankly felt that the Court was hopelessly out of harmony with the times, the Congress and the people. He felt it was applying a narrow construction of the Constitution to blot out vitally necessary legislation. Neither attracted to nor skilled in institutional politics, Roosevelt made the mistake of appealing to Congress to increase the size of the Court on the ground that it was unable to handle the great volume of work—particularly the men on the bench past seventy. This was faulty reasoning, bad observation and a hasty recommendation, particularly since the oldest man on the Court, the great Justice Brandeis, then eighty-one, had been most tolerant of New Deal legislation.

After his message to the Congress stirred up a hornet's nest, Roosevelt went on the air and declared in effect that his complaint was not with the Court as an institution but with its current personnel. The public—even Roosevelt's devoted followers—sensed an uncomfortable dilemma. The President sought a broad institutional change to solve a transitory incongruity of judicial personnel. It looked dangerous. The Court could number anything from nine to eighteen Justices, depending on whether none or nine were over seventy. Moreover, politics and not age was the real trouble; and the President said so: "I will appoint Justices who will act as Justices and not as legislators." Was legislation then a preoccupation of the elderly and judicature of youth? The whole issue was hopelessly confused. No one welcomed the cure, and Congress emphatically defeated it when it came to a vote.

Roosevelt's mistake was to attempt, perhaps under the compulsion of the greatest electoral victory in our history, to speed up processes better left to political evolution. But, as he correctly pointed out, he did not act without precedent, the most solid specific of which was furnished by the Congress itself seventy years earlier. The only difference was that the people were by 1937 far more politically alert, and Roosevelt's best defense against the theory that he had them in uncritical submission was his worst defeat.

VIII

In its most oppressed periods the Supreme Court has had one charge brought against it over and over again—that it has appropriated to itself the final vote on the policy of the nation by deciding ex cathedra what laws are Constitutionally valid and what are not. The charge is superficial and belittles the process of Constitutional amendment. Actually, so long as the Congress and the state legislatures and the people can amend the Constitution, this republic is not in ultimate fact subject to judicial supremacy. For by this process the Court's decision that a law is invalid because unconstitutional (and the Court cannot otherwise declare it invalid) is subject to reversal in effect on address of the Congress and three fourths of the States, who in approving an amendment automatically make it Constitutional. Franklin Roosevelt was right in calling this a long and difficult process, but it is far more desirable that fundamental changes be long and difficult, so long as they are still possible, than that they be fast and easy. Else the nation would find itself operating on a different body of basic law with each change of administration, each change of national circumstance and each change of popular mood. Moreover, the essential folly of Roosevelt's complaint that Constitutional amendments are too difficult to pass was that if they were any easier there might as well be no judicial review at all. Consequently his proposal overtly directed at the personnel of the Court was nevertheless essentially against its institutional standing, for if the Supreme Court has any value or any meaning at all, both would be gone if additions to its personnel or changes in it were accepted as a reasonable alternative to Constitutional amendments.

But Constitutional amendments are nevertheless possible, and the difficulty sometimes surprisingly limited. An intriguing example is the Sixteenth Amendment, sponsored by the Republican administration of William Howard Taft, which empowered the Congress to levy taxes on incomes. Such a tax was first levied by another Republican Congress, in 1862, to help finance the Civil War and was ruled Constitutional by the Supreme Court in 1880, eight years after it ceased to be operative, on the ground that it was not a direct tax and therefore not subject to the Constitutional requirement of apportionment among the states according to population. In 1894, however, when a new income tax act was confidently passed by Congress, the Court reversed itself, held that it *was* a direct tax and therefore unconstitutional. This apparently killed any prospect of such a tax bill ever being introduced again, but in 1907 Theodore Roosevelt urged Congress to pass an income tax law, and by the campaign year of 1908, popular demand for such a tax was so high that both William Jennings Bryan and William Howard Taft favored it—although the latter was careful to add that his approval was "in principle" and apparently not necessarily in application. After Taft's inauguration, he called a special session of Congress to "reform" the tariff, and a Democratic Senator added a rider to the tariff bill providing for an income tax. The administration and its leaders in Congress were disturbed to find not only Democrats but liberal Republicans rallying to its support. Taft and the Congressional leaders went into emergency conference and brought forth a molehill that turned into a mountain. They would remind the Congress of the Court's invalidation of the last income tax law and both kill the new bill and retain support of the tax's supporters by proposing a Constitutional amendment to legalize income taxes. Everyone knew how hard it was to get an amendment ratified, and besides none had been passed since Reconstruction days. The supporters of the income tax, however, would have to agree to the amendment or fly in the face of their own principles. It was all very neat—almost foolproof. Almost, but not entirely. Before Taft left the White House, the states, contrary to expectations, could hardly wait to ratify the amendment, and it was the law of the land. Today the master legislative strategy—predicated on the hypothetically insurmountable difficulty of the amendment process—haunts the minds of all good Republicans even as its lesson seems to have sailed far over the head of as good a Democrat as Franklin Roosevelt.

Everyone adulates Lincoln, but nobody wants to bother reading what he said. If his counsel, wise in understanding and skilled in politics, were followed, there would be very little conflict over the Supreme Court in this republic. In his first inaugural he pointed out that decisions of the Court were addressed to specific cases and were not pronouncements of the fixed and final policy of the country. And if he did not concur in one of its decisions, he would not resist it but do what he could to have it overruled later. Otherwise he would resort to the Constitutional amendment. "Law must be stable, and yet it cannot stand still," Roscoe Pound has said, and the Court has on the whole deeply realized this antinomy and met its challenge. Where it could not, the amendment process has solved the problem. And there is perhaps in all our political history no single force that has done more to build a fluid and vigorous democracy on a solid Constitutional foundation than the Supreme Court—even though it may have seemed from time to time exclusively preoccupied with the foundation.

And on the whole also—despite its very extraordinary powers comparable to those of no other institution on the face of the earth—the Justices have kept in mind the words of Holmes: "We must remember that we are not God."

Yet the Court is charged with a godlike function. Aloof from the people, institutionally immune to political reckonings, surviving changes in parties, Congress and Presidents, it must be the perpetual adjudicator between tradition and progress, reconciling the new with the old, accommodating, within the Constitutional framework that is in all sober fact the guardian of our liberties, the requirements of new times, new problems and new intricacies. All this the Court, fallible as it is and as all the institutions of men are, has done.

It was Holmes also who wrote, "It is a pleasure to see more faith and enthusiasm in the young men; and I thought that one of them made a good answer to some of my skeptical talk when he said, 'You would base legislation upon regrets rather than upon hopes.'" But we owe it to the Court that we may look back on our legislative history and therefore our political history as hopes realized rather than regrets made irrevocable. For democracy flourishes on moderation and is driven to death by extremes. The Court has not been alone in furnishing this spirit to our nationhood, but it has been the expression of this spirit of moderation and has kept it as a political ideal, undramatized and frequently unrecognized by the people, but nevertheless so deep a part of their political nature that, for all the shouting, innovations are not seized on with hasty relish nor old values thrown over without forethought.

Nor is this all. The Supreme Court has evolved in the United States as an importantly and usefully creative organism—in some ways as creative as the Presidency or the Congress. The Court has in fact created a political morality which has made the selfish political leader pause and the careless one think twice. It is almost enough simply to know that it is there and, by popular will, unassailable.

Part Two

THE REALITY:

POLITICAL EXPERIENCE IN AMERICA

---

*The two parties which divide the state, the
party of conservatives and that of innovators,
are very old, and have disputed the possession of the world ever since it was made.
This quarrel is the subject of civil history.*

—RALPH WALDO EMERSON

Chapter Five

The Basic Conflict

WHAT THE BASIC CONFLICT IN AMERICAN POLITICS HAS BEEN
ABOUT, AND HOW IT IS VERY OLD AND NOT NEW AND WHY,
DESPITE THE OCCASIONAL INTENSITY OF THE CONFLICT, OUR
MAJOR PARTIES ARE MORE SIMILAR THAN THEY
ARE DISSIMILAR

I

EVERY year, in Washington and in the large cities throughout the land, some of the most conservative business leaders of the nation join the most conservative politicians at expensive dinners in memory of a man who once said, "Labor is prior to and independent of capital. Capital is only the fruit of labor and could never have existed if labor had not first existed. Labor is the superior of capital and deserves much the higher consideration." That comes from the patron saint of the party of Herbert Hoover, Thomas Dewey and Robert Alphonso Taft, who customarily join in paying tribute to the wisdom of Abraham Lincoln each February. Eight weeks later such assorted dignitaries as James A. Farley of New York, James Michael Curley of Boston and Martin Kennelly of Chicago foregather to ponder the greatness of their party's founder, Thomas Jefferson, who gave utterance to the words: "The mobs of great cities add just so much to the support of pure government as sores do to the strength of the human body."

There is less of the paradox in these somewhat incongruous events than would appear on the surface. Most Republicans who worship at the shrine of Abraham Lincoln each year have not read much more than the Gettysburg Address and possibly the Second Inaugural, both of which contain high and broad principles to which both Vermont farmers and Pittsburgh industrialists can equally subscribe. And most Democrats are vaguely aware that Jefferson stood for certain antioligarchic standards and wrote a major document of high principles called the Declaration of Independence, to which both the Lowell millworker and the Southern landowner can equally subscribe. But neither Republicans nor Democrats as such want to probe the heritages of their traditional heroes for particulars, since these not only have no place in the party but might seriously disrupt it. For an American political party is not a band wagon but a big tent. There is room for everyone—which is what distinguishes a party from a faction.

Parties do not exist in the political processes of small towns, because every man can go to town meeting, state his own position and conduct his political affairs on his own behalf. If enough of them act in common, they might form a faction. In larger towns there are apt to be committees representing various groups of citizens who subscribe to some specific proposition, such as building a new school, and they will pool their energies and pin their hopes on the policy and activities of their committee, which might also become a faction. But in a large nation, over sixty million voters could not, without making themselves so diffuse as to be ineffective, conduct their political affairs individually. Nor could a hundred separate committees formed for a hundred separate purposes. Consequently, the political party evolved as a natural condition of democratic life when extended to hundreds of thousands of people, its identity being established by its pronouncement of certain broad principles for political action and its effectiveness being commensurate with the number of voters hospitable to those principles.

The major purpose of a political party in a democracy, of course, is to elect its candidates. In order to do this, particularly in a country involving sixty million voters, it is usually necessary for the party to attract a majority of the voters, which means it must be capable of accommodating hundreds of factions and millions of individuals. This obviously cannot be done if the party is too narrow in the scope of its principles or too restricted in the area of its interests. A party devoted solely to eradicating the boll weevil, for example, is unlikely to have much room for automobile mechanics. But a party devoted in general to a higher degree of prosperity would not only be apt to attract the mechanics but also, since elimination of the boll weevil would contribute to prosperity, the victims of that predatory and politically useful insect. Similarly, it is all right for a party to declare itself for tolerance, which even the Ku Klux Klan claims that it favors, but it would not be good for any party to say that its sole purpose was to admit Negroes to Washington hotels. Party principles are useful in inverse ratio to their precision.

This is neither as ridiculous nor as cynical as it seems. The party is courting the majority and has to in order to justify its existence at all. Moreover, the opposition party is courting the same majority—not a different one. Necessarily, therefore, the broader the principles of the party the more people it is likely to attract or, what amounts to the same thing, the less it is likely to repel. Moreover, in view of the fact that the major parties must in general rely on swaying the same body of voters and not different bodies in order to win, it is not probable that they will ever be vastly different in their stated principles or widely divergent in fundamental issues. Consequently we have in this country two great parties both of which are basically and primarily for freedom and growth. No party has ever been against either. The party conflict has revolved around differences, to some extent, as to what constitutes these ends and, to a much greater extent, as to what methods are the most appropriate and least dangerous for attaining them.

The only major exception to this absence of differences on a really fundamental issue was the conflict over slavery. There the differences were not limited to how slavery could best be abolished, as the differences over government spending are really limited to how best to promote the prosperity of the country. There the conflict was basic and fundamental, as though it were over the question of whether there should be any prosperity at all. And our political processes were unable to resolve the conflict, declaring their bankruptcy in a civil war.

Nor is it at all likely that in the face of another such basic conflict our political structure would be able to accommodate the battle. To guess the outcome one has only to imagine what would have happened in the early 1930's if one of our major parties had been flatly and fully for unemployment and the other flatly and fully against it. But both were against it, and three Presidential campaigns and six Congressional campaigns were waged, not on whether to beat it or not, but on the best methods to beat it. Similarly, Hitler, who was stupefied that we had a Presidential campaign at all during the war, was baffled to find that in two campaigns both major parties had the same basic anti-Hitler tenets and yet took the elections quite as seriously as any other. This very breadth and near identity of basic principles are what make it possible for political parties to alternate in power to a very considerable extent in this country, what allow Congressional control to shift twice in a two-year period and what have made it impossible for any Presidential candidate to win more than three fifths of the vote or win by a margin of much more than 25 per cent. The similarities of our parties and not their dissimilarities are responsible for the health of our two-party system.

Nevertheless, there is a deep and real political conflict in

America, and has been from the beginning, which has developed inevitably into a partisan conflict. The issue has been a very broad one, for the reasons indicated above, and it has also been primarily one of method rather than of aim: conservativism versus progressivism, caution versus experimentation, adherence to what is proved versus adventuring with what is not, suspicion of innovation versus impatience with the outmoded. This is the basic conflict in American politics, but it is important to note that it is neither exclusively American nor exclusively political. The faculty of every university, the board of every corporation, the membership of every profession is apt to be involved in more or less degree in a similar conflict. Similarly the conflict knows no geographic limit, is peculiar to no nation. British, French, Latins, Orientals are not without a continuing experience in the same basic conflict. The ecclesiastical world has been characterized by it, culminating in the Reformation. The worlds of art and letters, of philosophy and even science have been similarly characterized. Moreover, a man who is a traditionalist in another field is apt to be conservative politically, and a man who is an experimentalist in another is apt to be progressive politically.

The conflict is thus largely a human one and the parties through which it expresses itself in the area of American politics are merely serving broad human interests and interpreting human compulsions politically. We can see the extranational nature of the conflict very clearly when we note that many American Republicans find themselves more closely attuned to Mr. Winston Churchill than to a man so thoroughly steeped in the American tradition by family heritage, education and associations as Franklin Roosevelt. And we can see the extrapolitical aspect of the conflict in the fidelity of the conservative to the old ways in education, for example, and his aversion to innovation, and in the congenial reception given to the experimentalist in art by the progressive and his somewhat impatient boredom with the traditionalist.

The economic determinists, who are fond of by-passing every factor contributing to political alliances except the economic, have loudly proclaimed that this basic conflict is nothing but a battle between the haves and the have-nots. Politics has very seldom been so paradoxically complicated by such an over-simplification. It is fully as reasonable to assume that a man who is naturally conservative will become a man of property as it is to assume that all men of property naturally will become conservative. Both theories have some truth in them. A man who has acquired considerable assets, whether by work or heredity, has more reason to distrust experimentation than a man who has not, for the simple reason that he has more to lose. He is, therefore, probably a more consistent human being than he would be if he were interested only in experimentation for its own sake and did not care whether he lost his assets or not. Even progressives are reluctant to try new campaign methods when the old have brought in many contributions. But perhaps the instincts which made the man a conservative in the first place are those also which made him a man of property. He would naturally put a good deal of store by the independence, solidity and certainty that property brought, and by the support which it would permit him to give to the maintenance of traditional institutions. Thus a man who is seriously pained by paying a million dollars in taxes and takes it as a conspiracy directed at his destruction might cheerfully and voluntarily give three million dollars to a university, hospital or public endowment, regarding it as his social responsibility.

On the other hand, further to confuse the Marxists, the man of property is sometimes peculiarly allergic to conservatism and the man born in relative poverty is peculiarly allergic to progressivism. As nice an example as we can find in American politics are the four Presidential campaigns of 1932, 1936, 1940 and 1944. The man of property, Franklin Roosevelt, who knew more of opulent living than most of his critics ever surmised, was successively and successfully the champion of progressivism against Herbert Hoover, Alf Landon, Wendell Willkie and Thomas Dewey, all of whom sprang from pretty restrained family fortunes. But can anyone assume that if he had been born the son of a poor tenant farmer, Roosevelt would have been a great conservative? The truth is that he was a natural progressive, with all the extraeconomic attributes of the progressive character—"sanguine in hope, bold in speculation, always pressing forward, quick to discern the imperfections of whatever exists, disposed to think lightly of the risks and inconveniences which attend improvements and disposed to give every change credit for being an improvement." Lord Macaulay thus characterized the progressive over forty years before Franklin Roosevelt was born, and it is not insignificant that his words would be useful also in describing Theodore Roosevelt, whose political complexion was no more tinted by his economic origins. But how useful—even though these men had never campaigned for the Presidency—would they be in describing the humbly sprung Hoover, Landon, Dewey or even, despite some refreshing qualities that gave him trouble in his brief political career, Wendell Willkie?

Moreover, property—whether the economic determinists find it destructive to their theories or not—simply does not enter largely into the conservatism of many Americans who are politically conservative because they are conservative in everything else. On remote farms and in small towns generation after generation of citizens are ingrained conservatives and will even vote against their immediate economic interests to assert their conservatism. Two of the poorer per capita states in the Union, Maine and Vermont, are traditionally and inalterably conservative. This is unquestionably due to their inhabitants' innate suspicion of change, because change does not characterize their own lives very much or their communities'; and they consequently distrust it for its strangeness. And they would be equally as suspicious of a free-thinking sculptor with a red beard, beret and a predilection for drinking wine with his meals as they are of political progressives. Similarly, more than an occasional Indiana farmer, whose economic lot has certainly not been injured by political progressives, will remain a steadfast conservative because he always has been and because the cities, which he does not trust, from never himself having got over feeling strange in them, are too often progressive. He trusts predictability, conformity and a pattern of certainty—and these are conservative virtues often lightly held by progressives.

Society, in its limited sense of community standing, is also a determining factor in the line-up of the basic conflict; and its sense is very limited indeed. Southern Bourbons who despised everything the New Deal stood for stoutly supported Roosevelt at the polls, because to vote Republican, which would have been much more congenial to their real feelings, would have involved a social stigma comparable only to that of breaking forth with the "Beer Barrel Polka" in the Episcopal church during the bishop's visitation. On the other hand there are towns in New England with these social values so reversed that the best young men in town are members of the Young Republican Club, while only the taxi drivers and grocery clerks can be found in the Democratic ward clubs. Social preferment is sought by belonging to the right party as it is by living on the right street.

Related closely to the social factor, of course, is the hereditary influence. Just as most children don't choose their churches, many don't choose their side in the conservative-progressive conflict either, unless they are rebelling against that along with everything else. But the rebels are usually in the minority, and the more stable young people of the community are fairly sure to go along with their heritage. This is especially obvious among families of leadership position: second and third generation Adamses, Harrisons, Lodges, Hyde Park Roosevelts, Oyster Bay Roosevelts and Tafts do not occur in parties different from those of their forebears, and there is little reason to suppose that the less articulate issue of the political noted, such as the sons of Hoover or Coolidge, renounce their political heritage.

Religion, or more properly religious affiliation, is also a determining factor in the choice of sides in the basic conflict—sometimes sufficient to outweigh all others. In Boston a Catholic Republican is a rarity and the Democratic clubhouses are not jammed with Protestants; and the cleavage is fairly common throughout the Northeast, particularly in New England, where the two strongest Protestant states are inclined to political conservatism and the great Catholic strongholds are inclined toward progressivism. In the South, of course, economic, social, hereditary and environmental considerations have all been tossed overboard in a political conflict because of a single religious factor, as was well demonstrated in the Smith-Hoover election of 1928. In parts of the country, on the other hand, the religious basis for political association is cast aside in favor of some other determinant. In many industrial towns of New England the citizens of French-Canadian lineage, who are Catholics, are stout Republicans because the citizens of Irish descent, who are also Catholics, are stout Democrats. The Franco-American groups know that they have little chance of political importance in a party where they would be so vastly outnumbered, so they team up with the waning and numerically weaker Protestants. In general, however, almost all immigrants and their progeny have associated themselves with progressive units, because they had little for the conservatives to conserve for them. Their hopes lay along untried ways.

II

All these nonpolitical factors explain the continuity of party labels in the United States in the face of a total absence of any continuity in party principles. The basic conflict of conservative versus progressive has continued, but at times which party was on which side has been so completely confusing that Mexican revolutions have been far more understandable. There is not much doubt today that the Republicans form the conservative party in the United States and the Democrats the progressive party, but a superficial glance at the record might be disturbing to both parties.

The Republicans, and not the Democrats, introduced the income tax. The Republicans, and not the Democrats, introduced the regulation of big business. The Republicans, and not the Democrats, introduced the active participation of the government in private business, with the Reconstruction Finance Corporation. The Republicans, convinced that the Democrats are out to wipe away personal liberties, went down defending the noble experiment of Prohibition—the only outright abridgment of personal liberty in our history.

And consider the Democrats. They who urge on the electorate the wisdom of expanding the scope of the national government have been the State-rights party from the beginning. They who decry legislation preferential to the mercantile class introduced the protective tariff system as far back as Jefferson's day, in 1816. They, who brought undying fame to Andrew Jackson's administration by the destruction of the second Bank of the United States, chartered it in James Madison's. They who abhor the *status quo* preserved it stubbornly during the one decade in our history, 1850-1860, when it was most nearly fatal to do so.

Little wonder that Lord Bryce compared party labels in

America to the labels on empty bottles! And yet the parties go on—the only political instruments in the basic conflict.

If Washington had had his way, this conflict would forever have remained one between individuals—as it was in his own Cabinet—and would never have become partisan. In his Farewell Address, the last resort of every orthodox isolationist because of its caution against foreign entanglements, Washington wrote an even more serious warning against political parties, which has been appropriately forgotten: "The common and continuous mischiefs of the spirit of party are sufficient to make it the interest and duty of a wise people to discourage and restrain it. It serves always to distract the public councils and enfeeble the public administration. It agitates the community with ill-founded jealousies and false alarms, kindles the animosity of one part against another. . . ." But Washington was no political philosopher and did not see the inevitability of partisanship, though it had its origin during his first administration in the conflict between Hamilton and Jefferson—both highly gifted political geniuses—of which every subsequent political conflict in the nation's history has been a variation.

The first nominal partisan expression of the continuous conflict was in the alignment of Jeffersonian Democrats (first called Republicans for no very good reason except for their sympathy with the new French Republic) against Hamiltonian Federalists. It is patently ridiculous to assume that either of these parties had a monopoly on virtuous aims, for both concentrated their very great energies on the building of a strong, vigorous and free nation. But each had a distinctive road to strength, vigor and freedom. Hamilton believed in a strong federal government and, being a political realist of the first order and having an advantageous position as Washington's Secretary of the Treasury, was more interested in creating it on the very real level of finances than in merely theorizing about it. The

$56,000,000 national debt was a logical beginning, and he had it funded by recognizing and paying the par value of all outstanding obligations. But more important to the advancement of his theory of nation over states was his insistence on the new nation's assuming in its own name the debts which the separate states had incurred during the Revolution. This was a major precipitating cause of the partisan conflict, since some of the states had already paid their debts and did not relish the notion of now paying, through the Federal Government, the debts of the other states. The Hamiltonians further founded a national bank, passed excise taxes and extended in general the authority of the National Government along Constitutionally latitudinarian lines that left no doubt that this nation was to be a nation in fact and not a confederation of states.

Of all this, Thomas Jefferson, Washington's Secretary of State, took such a negative view that, after the President was thoroughly irritated at the rift in his Cabinet, he resigned and devoted his political talents to building a party to combat the Hamiltonians. He was quick to see that nearly all their measures were directed to a strengthening of the mercantile classes of the young republic and not particularly considerate of the interests of the yeomanry. Devoted as he was to the idea of an agrarian democracy, Jefferson regarded the whole Federalist program, with some justice, as conducive deliberately to the creation of an oligarchy, the rule of a propertied few in the interests of a propertied few. Not yet himself administratively experienced, Jefferson saw no cure for this but an emphasis on State rights and a narrow construction of the Constitutional powers of the Federal Government. If this seems strange coming from the founder of the party that subsequently, through Jefferson himself, Jackson, Polk, Cleveland, Wilson and Franklin Roosevelt, depended on the extension of national authority and a very broad interpretation of the Constitution, it should be remembered that the extrapolitical conditions of the early days—the lack of communications, the provincial values, the absence of a national spirit and of an identity of the people with the new nation—all these inhibited the guarding of the interests of the common people on a national level. To be close to them and to protect their interests looked to be impossible if the determining agency in their political destiny were far removed from the scene of their daily lives. Jefferson consequently felt that only by reserving a great body of rights solely to the states could the interests of the people be protected. There was, therefore, no essential contradiction in his historic position as the founder of the Democratic Party and his overt defense of State rights against national encroachment.

Under the surface of all this there was an undercurrent—indeed, a main current—of deeper conflict between Federalist and Republican-Democrat. It was, as both Hamilton and Jefferson knew very well, as to whether this nation would best move forward under the control of the few who were in positions of propertied leadership (and therefore theoretically the most responsible group) or could be entrusted to the control, direct as possible, of the mass of the people; whether measures designed to promote the welfare of the few would filter down to promote the welfare of the many or whether the many must assert themselves or be left to the wolves.

Nor did this main current of the conflict ever disappear. For it has not merely recurred in our political history; it has been a continuing debate. This very continuity would suggest that honesty of conviction has not been an exclusive characteristic of either side, although selfish interests have attached themselves from time to time and in one guise or another to both. Just as the man who cares nothing for the welfare of his nation so long as he can profit from a position of advantage might attach himself to the conservative forces, the cynical political boss who

cares only for perpetuating his own power often attaches himself
to the progressive forces. But political parties do not endure for
decades and generations because they accommodate such miscarriages. More accountable for their endurance is the readiness
with which the natural springing into being of the two major
parties of the United States has furnished hospitable organisms
for the political expression of the two fundamentally divergent
attitudes and characters that human beings bring to their group
efforts: the sense of caution, devoted to the proved methods of
the determined past on the one hand, and the sense of daring,
alert to the challenge of the undetermined future on the other.
The former is politically manifested in men genuinely less
trustful of a huge body than of a small group who have won
leadership privately and, since we live in a business civilization,
usually in business. The latter not only is genuinely more trustful of the great body of people but welcomes something which
the conservative profoundly suspects—the intuitive willingness
of the masses to play it by ear instead of according to precedent.

From the beginning the conservative-Republican forces in
this nation aligned themselves with the Hamiltonian school—
the Federalist-Whig-Republican line of descent. And the pro-
gressive-Democratic forces have aligned themselves with the
Jeffersonian school—the Democratic tradition. The majority
has shifted from one to the other—though frequently for by-
reasons not directly associated with the basic conflict—with the
very great disruption coming of course with the slavery dispute,
the harshness of the Civil War and the cynicism of Reconstruction, which interrupted normal political alignments in general
for a generation and in some particulars up to the present. Nevertheless the orthodox Republican today still has more in common
with Alexander Hamilton than he has with Harry Truman, and
the Democrat (to whom it is impossible to apply the adjective
"orthodox," for reasons that we will see in another chapter) has

more in common with Jefferson or Jackson than he has with Mr. Hoover. And the continuous debate is renewed every four years, with only the personalities in each Presidential campaign frequently obscuring the basic conflict and with such occasional anomalies as a Theodore Roosevelt, among the Republicans, or a Pierce or Buchanan, among the Democrats, sometimes throwing the whole pattern askew. Normally, however, the defenders of the past—of which a version acceptable to them is getting increasingly remote—are the Republicans, who seem to lose their fear of innovations when they are no longer new; and the devotees of the new are the Democrats, who seem to alarm many good men by being particularly jaunty about it.

III

From all the preceding, it might well appear that the sole function of the political party in America is to take one side or another in the basic and continuing conflict of conservative versus progressive, devoting campaigns to the applications of the respective principles to the particular issues of the time by the particular personalities involved. Since the party is the only mechanism for nationally mobilizing and crystallizing political opinion, this is indeed one function of the party. But it is only one of several functions, many of which have become quasi-Constitutional, some of which are peculiar to the majority party and some to the minority party.

In a functioning democracy, perhaps the most important function of the political party is its use as a vehicle of compromise. We have seen how, in the ancient democratic experiments, persistent adherence to one's own interests and points of view brought about collapse, for there was, when the test came, no common ground for action.

The Romans, sensing the danger of the political deadlock

when no faction will yield an inch on its demand, practiced the art of legislative compromise, weighing the demands of all factions and attempting to please each in part. Now in modern America there are far more factions, each with its own values and its own demands, than there ever were in the ancient democracies. If each of these retained its factional identity in political life and had no broader affiliation, the country would be hopelessly submerged in a maelstrom of persistent and very narrow demands. We would have a separate political entity for farmers who wanted subsidies, another for those who did not; one entity for those who cared neither way but wanted protective tariffs and another for those who did not; one entity for those who favored Federal aid to education, another for those who did not—and so on until there was a distinct political entity for every shade of thinking on each conceivable issue. The political party absorbs these factions and attempts so to interrelate their demands that a broad principle of governmental action emerges that will advance, even if never fully satisfying, the interests of each.

Moreover, since to keep all factions which comprise it reasonably happy the party must never become too narrow in its principles, the necessity to compromise all the factional demands within it has a tendency to keep the party an instrument of a great body of the people rather than of a special group. It also keeps the party that has any intention of surviving in a healthfully flexible condition, for the weight and gravity of the factional demands made on it are always shifting. When that flexibility is gone, political sclerosis sets in and the party is apt to be chronically out of power. But when it is reasonably healthy, it has no difficulty in adjusting itself to very grave changes in economic, social or political conditions and in compromising the resultant shifts in factional demands.

This compromise function of the political party is so primary that a party's strength and vigor in America are commensurate with the ability to execute it. This has long since been manifest. Twice one of our major parties has approached danger of extinction because of a total inability to execute it: the Democrats at the time of the Civil War and for a generation thereafter, and the Republicans at the time of the Depression and for what is fast reaching a generation thereafter.

In the first case, of course, both political parties failed, because neither was able successfully to contain and compromise the demands both of abolitionists and slaveholders. But the Democrats, who visited upon the United States two of the most ineffective Presidents in history during the eight years immediately preceding the war, became the villains; and the Republicans, who couldn't wait to bury Lincoln's policies with his body, became the heroes. The Republican Party also grew in strength, because it succeeded astonishingly in compromising the demands of widely divergent elements within it, from the strict moralists of New England to the avaricious carpetbaggers, from the founders of giant businesses to the great mass of working men of the North, from the shopkeepers of the East to the Midwest farmers. Whatever the shortcomings of the Republican Party during this period from Grant through McKinley, it flourished in the fulfillment of its compromise function.

But when the party became inflexible, when it was felt by the factions of industrial workers and of farmers and of shopkeepers that something was wrong (which is to say simply that their changing interests were no longer effectively advanced by the party's old general principles, which represented rather the views of one powerful faction than the compromised views of all the factions)—then the Republican Party went into a steady decline, while the Democratic Party, faced with the much more impossible task of reconciling the Southern colonel with the Detroit union agent, blossomed.

The conditioning of the strength of political parties by their degree of success in fulfilling their compromise function was never more astonishingly demonstrated than in 1948. The personalities of the candidates, decisive factors in the Roosevelt campaigns, the Jackson-Clay or even the Smith-Hoover campaigns, played only a small part, for neither Mr. Dewey nor Mr. Truman was among the most colorful candidates in history. By all external appearances the Democrats should have lost. Roosevelt's death had left them without a strong leadership. Victory in the war had already been achieved. Both parties were in accord on the peace, both supported the United Nations, both agreed on a foreign policy. These major issues were therefore lost to the Democrats in their campaign. Moreover, superficially it appeared that the Democrats had lost also that great gift of effective compromise with which Roosevelt had held widely divergent elements of the party together. Here was a party apparently without that indispensable ability to compromise the interests of the factions comprising it—the *sine qua non* of party health. And it was on this breakdown that both the confident Republicans and the prophets depended.

But the fact is that no one—with the possible exception of Mr. J. Howard McGrath, the Democratic National Committee's chairman—probed the difficulty below the surface. In the first place, the entire history of political parties in America teaches the necessity to distinguish between a party's inability to compromise the views of factions within it and the inability of the factions to submit their views to party compromise. In the latter case, the usual result is an abortive third party, which is ordinarily not a party at all but a faction with a name. In 1948 two such factions were unable, through nothing more profound than a lack of political maturity, to submit their views to compromise within the Democratic Party: the far-to-the-left Russian apologists whose major political value was faith in the good intentions

of Communism, and the far-to-the-right Southern irreconcilables whose major political value was the ability to sit on a
streetcar without another human being of darker hue occupying
the adjacent seat. Both of these exoduses from the Democratic
Party had really little relevance to its essential health, for the
party continued successfully to formulate a platform of principles and a program that represented a very effective compromising of the interests of the Massachusetts millworker and the
Iowa farmer, the Eastern office clerk and the California ship-
builder.

The Republicans, as since 1932, were still less a political party
than the Democrats, but now in even more serious condition;
for where the party's health had been drained by losing the
ability to compromise and represent in general principles the
views and interests of many factions, it was now facing the
prospect of listening only to itself, of losing entirely that variety
of factions which alone keeps a party healthfully flexible. In
1948, the Democrats lost not the ability to execute the party
function of compromise but only two factions who refused to
submit to compromise and who did not in the end count for
much anyhow. But the Republicans, in almost as desperate a
condition as a political party can get, lost the need to fulfill the
compromise function at all.

IV

A related general function of the political party is the sim-
plification by a party stand and the codification in a party platform of the several issues confronting the voter. The number of
such issues, their complexity and very often their interrelation-
ships would in their raw state be very likely to overwhelm the
voter and offer him no clear alternatives for his choice. The
party serves to arrange such alternatives in a body of general

principles, so that the voter generally sympathetic with it can make his vote count most by aligning himself with a vast number of citizens, unknown to him, of the same general persuasions. For all the sometimes guarded language of platforms, this is a function successfully executed in the main by both major parties. The effectiveness, however, consists in sensing the degree of generality and of specificity that the times demand in the substance of the platform. Moreover, the usefulness of such a codification is proportionate to the extent to which it is supplemented by the party's propaganda, for no party can hope for success without constantly informing the public, keeping it aware of major problems of the government and alert to impending actions by it. Despite the heavily weighted rendering of this service, which is always balanced by one party's weighting it one way and the other's weighting it the opposite way, the party here serves an urgent purpose, for it makes the voters far more alert to what their government is all about than they would otherwise be. And this works both ways, for the channels and facilities of the party also serve to inform the public servant what the people are up to and what their problems are. Through this upward filtering, in fact, come ultimately the specific policies of the party and therefore possibly the policy of the nation, as for example woman's suffrage, which first became party policy and then national policy.

v

A final and the most dramatic function common to all parties is the selection of candidates for public office. Theoretically, the essence of a political party being the compromised will of millions of individuals and hundreds of factions, the choice of candidates is the final strictly partisan step towards the execution of that will. The duty of the candidate is to persuade as many people as possible during the campaign that the principles and methods advanced by his party are best for the country and to put them into practice if he gets into office. But in practical politics the tail frequently wags the dog; and a parallel to Hughes's statement that while we live under a Constitution, the Constitution is what the judges say it is, suggests itself: we live under a system of parties but the parties are what the candidates say they are. No one would insist for example that the Republican party of Alf Landon was in all specifics the same as the Republican party of Wendell Willkie or that the Democratic party of Andrew Jackson was the same as that of James Buchanan. A strong candidate molds his party's principles while a weak one simply reflects what was already there. Because of this propensity, and probably also partly because, to the extroverted American character, personalities are more interesting than issues, the selection of candidates is far more important to the party than the forming of a platform, while in England a party stands on its principles and regards the candidate as incidental. (An interesting digression here might be to speculate on what would have happened had the magnetic Winston Churchill been seeking re-election in the United States instead of in England in 1945. Does anyone suppose that the relatively subdued Mr. Attlee could have defeated him?) Nevertheless, there is an essential identity of the candidate with the platform and ordinarily a man strong enough to win a nomination in a party not deadlocked at its convention is strong enough to have able representation on the committee composing the platform.

Functioning at its best, the party nominates candidates fairly devoted to its principles and vigorous enough to press them. But just as in the evolution of those principles, the element of intelligent compromise enters importantly in the nominating process. When that breaks down, the choice is apt to be such a political abortion as Warren Harding, and it is destructive of nothing so much as the party's own interests. Yet this has happened repeatedly in American politics, and invariably because of the ignorance of major blocs of delegates of the compromise function of the party or of a willful neglect of it. If a party finds itself split with 45 per cent of the delegates supporting one candidate and 45 per cent supporting another, it obviously makes no sense for it to resolve the situation by agreeing on any one of five candidates dividing the remaining 10 per cent among them. This is not compromise but escape and evasion, and it has been happily on the decline since 1920 and 1924—happily because such bankrupt choice of candidates is exactly the thing which the party system should avoid. The service which the nominating function of the party renders to democracy is that it operates very strongly against the possibility of a man with a minute plurality of votes achieving office. Without parties, this would be a very likely possibility and a very grave threat to the survival of democracy. If every voter were to cast his ballot for his individual choice, it would inevitably result in fifty million votes being split among as many as five hundred contenders—and the man who commanded anything over one five-hundredth, or a hundred thousand, of the ballots could win. The effect of the party system is to make millions of voters, of common general purpose, unite in advance on one candidate and combine their strength to bring about his election.

This is without question the greatest single contribution that the political party has made to advance democracy in practical operation in America, and it has virtually annihilated the major obstacle to the use of democratic methods by any political organism too large to meet in one room.

VI

When the votes have all been counted, the erroneous prophecies explained away and the post-mortems concluded, the governmental functions of both the victorious (majority) and the defeated (minority) parties continue, but in differing capacities. Broadly it is the function of the former to organize and conduct the government and of the latter to watch and criticize it, and in England the acceptance of these distinctive roles is so established that the majority party is actually called the Government and the minority is called the Opposition. In America the cleavage is less certain, because we not infrequently have a President of one party and a Congressional majority of another and sometimes even a majority of one party in the Senate and of another in the House. In the event of the joint Congressional majority being of one party and the President of another, the nation is required to suffer the experience of both parties playing the conducting role and both playing the critical. During the tenure of the Eightieth Congress, and the last two years of Mr. Truman's first administration, the Republican Congress conducted the government by enacting new legislation, and President Truman spent a good deal of time criticizing it. At the same time the President was also conducting the government through the execution of his Constitutional and statutory functions, and the Congress spent a good deal of time criticizing him. In the elections following such periods, party responsibility is far easier to establish than normally, because both parties have a record to justify. In 1948, for example, for the first time in sixteen years, the Republicans had one, which as it happened did not sweep the electorate off its feet. But when the Senate is of one party and the House of another and the President necessarily therefore divided in his attitude toward Congress, the Constitutional imperfection of our government is most intolerable and the subsequent responsibility of the parties at the polls most confused. Not infrequently the voters will respond to the governmental inertia created in such a situation by effecting a complete house cleaning.

Since the President is the irremovable leader of his party while he is in office, it is logical to assume that his party's responsibility for his administration is completely inescapable. That is not, however, always the case, because the Presidency is a highly personal office inasmuch as all the aides, from Cabinet ministers and ambassadors down, are personal choices and neither accountable individually to the party nor necessarily even belonging to the same party. Thus the Republicans were able in 1924 successfully to shake off any particular responsibility for the shenanigans of the Harding administration, which were all charged up to personal and not party failings. And from 1841 to 1845 the nation had a President who was not even a member of the party that elected him—John Tyler, the Virginia Democrat, who was nominated as Harrison's running mate on the Whig ticket to attract dissident Democratic votes and who served all but a month of Harrison's full term. Had Willkie won in 1940, there might have been the same absence of party accountability for his administration, for he had a habit all through the campaign of addressing Republicans as "*you* Republicans" as though he himself were still a Democrat—which was exactly the way the Republicans treated him four years later. Moreover, even in the case of more orthodox partisans who get to the White House, there is only one President and he is—as Cleveland insisted—the President of *all* the people. Consequently, once he has achieved some poise in the office he may break through party confines, as Jefferson, once he saw the practical aspects of the Presidential office, virtually abolished his previously vehement insistence on limiting the power of the Federal Government—a tenet which was the major principle of the party he founded. And at his re-election Jefferson was much more assayed for his personal achievement than his party was for its achievement.

With the Congress, however, party responsibility is much clearer, for it is essentially a partisan body both in organization and in the conduct of its business. The majority party holds all committee chairmanships, steers legislative affairs, elects the Speaker and the President Pro Tempore of the Senate, appoints the chamber officers and generally assumes responsibility for introducing and passing a legislative program involving every aspect of the national life. The minority party, sitting on the other side of the center aisle, both through its minority memberships in committee and its actions on the floor, devotes itself primarily to watching how the majority is running things and criticizing it vigorously as the occasion appears to demand. The minority is usually more vociferous than the majority, because it does not have to frame a program but merely subject the majority's to modification or critical review. Individually, however, the member of the minority can be as much of a creative and constructive legislator as he may desire, and in every Congress there are members of the minority who distinguish themselves beyond many of the majority.

There is no area of the government in which the partisan nature of our political processes expresses itself more forcibly than in the Congress, for here the partisan alignment is formalized and continuous. Moreover, the Senate, like the Supreme Court, is a perpetuated body, there never being an entirely new one at any one time. Thus, far more than the Presidency, the Congress serves to keep party principles active; and there is never a danger that the entire Congressional delegation of a party will repudiate it, as Tyler did the Whigs and Andrew Johnson and Theodore Roosevelt the Republicans. Indeed, were it not for the acknowledged and quasi-Constitutional partisan role in the Congress, it is very likely that no party could survive a long period of being out of power. For the nation has long recognized the critical role of the minority in Congress, and the supporters of the majority have come to prize it. In the 1920's Republicans as well as Democrats valued the investigations of Senator Thomas Walsh into the scandals involving the Harding administration. And in 1937 Democrats, who had three months earlier voted enthusiastically for Franklin Roosevelt, welcomed the critical reception given by the minority to the Court reformation message of the President. Similarly the duty of the majority party to steer necessary legislation through the Congress is not limited by partisan boundaries, and no majority has yet suggested that most routine legislation is not either non-partisan or bipartisan. The partisan organization of the Congress and the implied functions of the majority and minority parties, then, have in the main been highly beneficial to the nation. It is only the party hack, who doesn't belong in the Congress in the first place, that has sometimes made the party an obstacle rather than a means to a legislative end.

Although the parties have fulfilled their organizational and functional roles in the Congress, party government has never evolved in America along the strict lines that tend to create party responsibility. Some observers have seen this as a major threat to our political health, but it should be obvious that no mechanism to inspire such party responsibility can be created out of thin air and succeed. If it is to work, it must evolve, and to evolve it must first be surrounded by conditions both political and nonpolitical that are hospitable to the idea and conducive to its growth. Such conditions have not existed and do not now exist in the United States. Constitutionally the Executive and Legislative branches of the government are clearly divided, and party responsibility is impossible when the Executive and the Legislature are not incontrovertibly associated in a single pro-gram. For example, how could there be any reasonable party accounting for the Supreme Court Bill of 1937? A Democratic President proposed it, and a Democratic Congress rejected it. Moreover, the further Constitutional independence of the Judi-ciary, particularly since it has the power of judicial review, would further tend to minimize party responsibility. Can a party be held responsible for the collapse of a legislative program that the people might want but that the Court held unconstitutional? There would certainly be no advocates of the extension of party responsibility to the Supreme Court.

Aside from the Constitutional deterrents to the idea of party responsibility, practical politics in America have not so developed, due primarily to the geographic extent of the country, that they would necessarily respond to the accountability of parties. Members of the House and of the Senate are not really elected by parties at all but by districts and states respectively, frequently on nonpartisan bases. The late Republican Senator George W. Norris of Nebraska, for example, could hardly have been associated with any responsibility involving the Republican Party during the Hoover period, and conversely the Democratic Party can hardly be held accountable for the distraught activities of Congressman Rankin. Indeed, even when the administration is involved in overtly disastrous conduct, it is impossible to pin the responsibility on its party. The corruption attending both the Grant and the Harding administrations, for example, left the Republican Party blissfully unanswerable for the events, and Democrats who suggested a degree of responsibility were considered to be untutored fellows and unsportsmanlike to boot, hitting below the belt. And there is something about the American temperament that supports this view.

Along with a greater amount of party responsibility, in any case, the nation would have to be prepared to sacrifice a considerable amount of political stability and of intraparty freedom—both of which have made very real contributions to the growth of the nation. For party responsibility to have real meaning, it would be necessary to establish some chain of responsibility—possibly the President responsible to the Congressional majority and the Congressional majority responsible to the people. This would inevitably involve the unpredictable collapse of administrations with all its attendant evils. Within the Congress it would mean strictly partisan division on legislation, with no liberal Republicans joining Democrats on some votes and no conservative Democrats joining Republicans. Inevitably this would make for government by extremes, for only straight party men would survive in either party and the moderation and flexibility necessary to party health would disappear.

The probable result of all this hypothetically increased responsibility would be a multiparty system, for a new party would have to be evolved to take care of members of Congress who, though nominal Republicans or Democrats, did not see fit to vote with their party on particular legislation. There would follow the whole line of political confusions that have dogged and sometimes rendered ineffective the democracies of Europe: government by coalition or combine, the exaggerated importance of the "large" party that can command only a quarter or a third of the vote, the precarious balance of power in the hands of fringe parties that manage to stay in existence by winning a handful of legislative seats. For all its limitations with regard to party responsibility, the looser and broader bipartisan structure of the present is more compatible with the real interests of this nation.

Chapter Six

Democrats

THE ORIGIN, EVOLUTION AND PRESENT STATUS OF THE DEMO-
CRATIC PARTY AND THE ROLE WHICH IT HAS AT SOME TIMES
ASSUMED AND AT OTHERS HAD THRUST ON IT IN THE GROWTH
OF AMERICA, AND ITS SIGNIFICANCE

I

DESPITE all the campaign oratory and shrieking editorials to the contrary, both major political parties in
America have been devoted to a system of free capitalism from the beginning, and all minor parties that have set
up a different economic objective have come to early and ineffective ends. Unless this is understood at the outset, the entire
historic development of the major parties is without meaning,
for both owe their survival under one name or another to their
broad identity with the American character. Because it has been
molded by experience and not by philosophy, that character
responds best and best realizes its potentialities under the capitalist impulse. Moreover, the peculiar genius of the American
people asserts itself most often in the material fields, and the
only system that freely accommodates this kind of genius is a
free capitalism. Devotion to it is the monopoly of neither party,
and contributions to its essential vitality have been deciding
factors in the success of either party at the polls. Indeed, the
substance of the partisan dispute in America has never been
whether to keep a free capitalism or abolish it, but rather how
best to keep it alive and most attuned to the common interests
of the people. In the last decade at least the conflict has not even

been whether justly to regulate capitalism or not, but rather what constitutes just regulation; and many a legislative innovation that was erroneously and solemnly said to spell an early end to capitalism has been afterward accepted by the same alarmists as necessary to its continued existence. Stubbornly the broad identity of purpose of American political parties persists below the surface, and stubbornly the nature of the basic conflict as one of differing means rather than of different ends manifests itself.

Nevertheless, political reverses obscure the judgment of partisans and tend to exaggerate their fears of methods with which they disagree. Moreover when either party is out of power very long, it seeks its salvation in alarming the people—which is best accomplished by ascribing to the opposing party in power ends that are known to be uncongenial and even repellent to the majority. Consequently, it is assumed—though with little demonstrated justification—that it is easier to defeat the party in power by saying its purpose is to destroy free capitalism than it is merely to challenge its methods of continuing it.

During the long Republican rule of laissez-faire capitalism (which by the way, as we shall see, was first a principle of Jeffersonian democracy), the Democrats announced over and over again that capitalism was being run into an early grave. Its death was pronounced again when Cleveland entered the White House, really believed by many when Theodore Roosevelt was there, proclaimed anew during the Wilson New Freedom program and became an alleged certainty during the Hoover administration. Similarly during the present Democratic period of regulated capitalism, we have been treated by many good men who know better to Dantean visions of how the doom of capitalism is rapidly being sealed. That no huge majority wanted to see that doom effected is obvious or Mr. Wallace would have walked away victorious in the 1948 election; the warnings were valued as an outright scare device. But the people, suitably pausing, sooner or later found out that 1948 corporation earnings were up sixteen billion dollars over 1932, the last year of free capitalism in the eyes of some partisans, and that stock dividends mounted from two and a half billion in 1932 to nearly eight billion in 1948. Obviously capitalism was neither destroyed nor seriously weakened, even though a party misleadingly referred to as anticapitalist had been in power for sixteen years and not by any very slim margins.

Actually both major American parties are so deeply rooted in capitalism that true socialists gave them both up long ago. And by now the conflict is simply this: the Republicans think that the more government leaves capitalism alone the more it flourishes, although they have welcomed such government interventions as the protective tariff, the patent system and the Reconstruction Finance Commission; and the Democrats maintain that unless it is constantly adjusted to social, technological and economic changes, it may perish of its own inflexibility. Both attitudes are as old as this republic.

II

The United States had its national birth in a period of profound changes among the institutions of men all over the Western world and in one unlimited in its promise of greater changes to come. Soon afterward came the even deeper reshaping that resulted both in and from the Industrial Revolution. And through it all was the changing spirit and the violent material alterations peculiar to a nation of expanding frontiers, in which the very premises which motivated political action were remade overnight. Later still there followed the shift from a predominantly agrarian nation to a predominantly industrial one, from a population primarily with independently derived incomes, however limited, earned by farms and shops and small factories, to one primarily dependent on being paid by someone else. Never in the world's history had one nation in a matter of decades undergone so many and so radical changes. The political agency that evolved to adjust an inherent capitalism to those alterations was the Democratic Party.

This practical basis for the founding of the party by Thomas Jefferson has been lost in the interest created by the volume and freshness of his legacy of political theory. The party was created in response to the Federalist tendency to strengthen the Federal Government and to use its strength to bolster the mercantilism of the seaboard, for the Hamiltonian idea was that prosperity at the top meant prosperity at the bottom. Jeffersonianism took the opposite view that only a free capitalism geared to protect the inland farmer and the frontiersman would insure common prosperity. And he was convinced from what he saw in a Federalist Cabinet that you could not look to a strong Federal government for such protection. The stand of Jeffersonianism against the extension of Federal powers must, therefore, be related to the fact that all the extension had thus far been made by the Federalists and in conformity to Federalist values. The historic identity of Democracy with State rights later assumed an unjustified doctrinal importance due to a neglect so to relate it, for the theory was introduced by Jefferson as an expedient to protect the small man of the inland against the giants of the seaboard and not as a fundamental philosophic tenet of Democracy. And indeed the first Jeffersonian Democrat to abandon the theory in the Presidency was Thomas Jefferson. "What is practicable must often control what is pure theory," he wrote after his inauguration.

Already changing realities marked the beginning of the end

of Jefferson's dream of a happy land of enlightened farmers, and Jefferson was quick to recognize the signs. And his first taste of administering national affairs not only converted him to the idea of a strong national government but also tended to convince him of the desirability of a strong Presidency. Since Jefferson was the party, his views became party views, and the party soon was standing, in practice at least, for many of the things that had previously outraged it. It availed itself of every strong agency of the government that Federalism had established over its protest and put them to its own use.

Jefferson's purpose was to promote in general the economic opportunity of the common man (who was the man of the land instead of the man in the countinghouse) and, as a first step, to divorce the government from mercantilism. He sought equal opportunity for the landed farmer, the frontiersman attempting to hack out an economic future, and the craftsman. Mercantilism ended anyhow during his party's rule, for the Embargo Acts restricting foreign trade during the Napoleonic Wars and the War of 1812 brought about a shift in Northeastern efforts from trading to manufacturing. As Jeffersonian Democracy continued through the Madison tenure in the Presidency, it evolved into a fumbling but finally successful effort to adjust the nation to the changes brought by the War of 1812. With the declaration of war, only promotion of the new manufacturing ventures could insure paying for it; and Jefferson's party was also forced to charter a second Bank of the United States, the graven image of Hamilton's bank against which they had stormed, in order to manage financially at all. Soon, since Jeffersonian Democracy—still called the Republican Party—was as much for a free capitalism as Federalism was and since by 1820 it even adopted the methods of Federalism, it absorbed Federalism altogether. In the brief period of a single generation, that identity of ends which has always characterized major American parties had broadened even farther to include identity of means; and when the distinguishing characteristic of American parties, a divergency in means to reach a mutually desired end, no longer existed, the nation faced its first and only period of one-party government.

The least disastrous thing that can happen under one-party government is the ascendancy of personal politics, which was fortunately what happened in the United States in the 1820's. The old party issue of nationalism versus State rights was gone at least temporarily, for not only had the Napoleonic Wars taught all men that prosperity which depended solely on trading with other nations was precarious indeed but they soon saw also that in order to construct a self-sufficient and independent economy, the approach had to be national. The methods employed also had to be national, for they necessarily involved a national currency, a national tariff and a national fiscal agency and the use and disposition of the vast public lands which, since Jefferson came to office, had tripled the size of the nation and the acquisition of which was closely followed by the problems of migration.

As the new lands opened up, state versus national power became less than of academic interest to the migrants, who were beginning to think more boldly of the future than at any time since the Revolution. The area of political interest broadened immeasurably, as property qualifications began to disappear in one state after another. Men everywhere lost all party designations, becoming Clay men or Webster men, Calhoun men or Jackson men, rather than Federalists or Republicans or anything else. And the new partisan alignment that followed was based on issues individually sponsored by these great names and not by any parties.

In such an atmosphere, as the importance of the Presidency

underwent a sharp and inevitable decline, the importance of the Congress rose. Men who did not know whether Madison, Monroe or John Quincy Adams was in the White House, knew all about Henry Clay's "American System"—a unique scheme to protect the manufacturers of the East with a high tariff and benefit the farmers and frontiersmen by spending the money, thus raised, on roads and canals. Despite its smoothness, Clay's plan represented the most positive statesmanship of the era, but it left the South, which had enough natural waterways, cold; and the new West, which suspected its patness, chilly. The immediate benefit was all in favor of the manufacturers, and even Eastern shipping interests were against it.

In the absence of a positive issue, the political stage was set for a positive personality, and it was found in that hero of the near frontier, Andrew Jackson, who asked flatly, "Do you think that I am such a damned fool as to think myself fit for the Presidency?" But, all through the 1820's, the lack of any real national policy had left the mass of people foundering in depression conditions and suspicious of the old type of political leadership, which was fast becoming no leadership at all. They responded enthusiastically to the name of a man who had led a motley mob of yeoman-soldiers to victory over the disciplined British army at New Orleans. Having no idea of what he stood for, except that he was not associated with the old political survivals, they rallied to his support, and in 1824 he captured a plurality of the electoral vote, ninety-nine compared to the eighty-four of his nearest contender, John Quincy Adams, while Clay trailed in fourth place with only thirty-seven. No candidate receiving a majority, the election was deadlocked and thrown into the House where Clay swung his support to Adams, who subsequently named him Secretary of State. The Jacksonians were furious, and at that moment the Democratic Party of today was born.

III

Capitalism in America was flat on its back when the honest
upright and incredibly nonpolitical John Quincy Adams lef
the White House four years later in 1828. Nobody was happy—
not the manufacturing or shipping leaders, not the millworker
or the yeomanry, not the landowners or the prospecting fron
tiersmen. In the midst of the general discordance Jackson se
about the construction of a program, congenial to the growth
of a liberal capitalism, that finally set the nation out on the mair
road of its subsequent development.

Nothing is more erroneous than the notion that Jacksonia
Democracy sprang solely and full-blown from the rebellion o
the masses against moneyed interests. Much the product of th
knowing Martin Van Buren, the first skilled practical politicia
in our history, the party was a unification of local interests int
a national pattern. In it were the "plain" men of the North
plantation men of the South, farm and woods men of the Wes
Adams Republicans and what was left of non-New Englan
Federalists. Behind it all was the great equalitarian principl
that the government existed to serve all the people, which mean
in material terms an equality of economic opportunity. Thi
sparked the two great conflicts fought by Jackson: the destruc
tion of the Bank of the United States, the private depository c
the national funds, which epitomized the Jacksonian struggl
against privileged monopolies and for the liberation of cap
talism; and the anti-Nullification crusade, which resisted th
notion that individual local economic interests could nullify th
economic policy of the land.

It is ironic that the identity of Jacksonian Democracy wit
the rights of the people has obscured its other essential cor
tributions and corrections to the American destiny. As Dani
Webster of the opposition noted, it replaced monopoly wit

competition, paving the way for the building of the whole structure of business enterprise in America. It replaced devotion to
an impoverished, uncertain and unpromising *status quo* with
a zeal for new enterprises, for every man was to have a chance.
It modified the extremes of a propertied aristocracy, well in-
vested by Federalism with protective measures, and a non-
propertied working class, by creating a climate favorable to the
growth of a giant middle class. It insisted on equal protection
for all and privilege for none, thus establishing a dynamic capitalism where industry counted for more than influence. Before
Jackson left office, the mold had been stamped for the future of
the nation: it would be neither an oligarchy nor an agrarian
state, but it would be big and energetic and overwhelmingly
middle-class, being renewed from what was below and renewing what was above.

By now the fundamental role of the Democratic Party was
beginning to establish its own pattern of paradoxical but not
contradictory conservative-progressivism. Twice already and
thrice later, it came to the relief of threatening pressures against
capitalism, saving it by minimizing its abuses and extending
its impulses to an increasing number of people. But the role was
not fulfilled unaccompanied by an overhauling and strengthening of the partisan structure and a broadening of the partisan
function. When Presidential electors ceased to be chosen by
state legislatures and popular votes determined the outcome of
elections, the influence of the leaders who got themselves
elected as members of Congress or as electors on grounds of
personal rather than partisan strength rapidly declined. Political destinies were no longer controlled in the halls of the
Capitol or in Eastern drawing rooms or among the gentry of
the South, but were shaped by the man on the prairies of the
West and on the city sidewalks and on the struggling farms.
To them the party was an indispensable instrument for political

expression—a fact which Jackson and the astute Van Buren knew very well. Jackson established the Presidency in a position of new strength for partisan leadership; he established a system of partisan dispensation of appointive offices; the party convention was first used in the Jacksonian period to nominate Presidential candidates, previously chosen by Congressional caucus; party discipline, *i.e.,* regularity, became an active political concept. Moreover, a distinctly American quality was attached to the party for the first time in our history, its membership swollen by the non-English migrants of the early nineteenth century. Both in composition and in practice, it became the first peculiarly American party.

Before the issue of slavery, which, as we have seen, was far too fundamental to admit partisan solution at all, shattered the Democratic Party to bits, it won six of the eight elections between the defeat of Adams in 1828 and of Frémont in 1856. But through all these years—through the Whig-Democrat alternating in power in the forties, the Congressional rule in the fifties and the bankruptcy of politics in the sixties—the development and natural growth of political parties was suspended. There was not one Democratic Party but two and sometimes three, each having a separate ax to split to smithereens the trunk of which they were branches. Indeed, despite the fact that, for eight of the twelve years immediately preceding the outbreak of civil war and immediately following the expiration of Polk's term, Democrats occupied the White House, Polk was the last until Cleveland, thirty-six years later, to promote perceptibly any major principle of Democracy. He advanced the frontiers of America through Texas to Mexico on the south, through California to the Pacific on the west and through Oregon territory to Canada on the north, and revised the tariff—all in four years—and then left the White House aged far beyond his fifty-three years, to die exhausted four months later. But the party—

dependent in considerable measure since Jefferson's day on the support of the agrarian South—was already badly mangling the issue of slavery. Concessions made to the South disrupted the party in the North, and factions in both North and South disrupted it further. Meanwhile all partisan processes in the opposition broke down, too, and factions rather than parties were formed of the splinters. Out of the wreckage a six-year-old minority party called the Republicans and an ex-Congressman from Illinois named Abraham Lincoln emerged victorious in the dark year of 1860, when it was far too late to avert civil war.

IV

One of the most astonishing and least appreciated facts in our political history is the recovery of the Democratic Party after the Civil War. Burdened by identity with the proslavery and compromise elements before the war, tainted with defeatist elements during the war, stripped of any major influence in Congress and enervated by its own discordant postwar survivals, the party should by all precedent have been doomed to extinction—a fate which had been visited on other parties for infinitely less reason. But the party rose phoenixlike in unbelievably short time.

Toward the end of the Civil War in 1864 the Democrats dropped to a low of 24 per cent representation in the House, but four years afterward it had a 62 per cent majority in the House and retained a majority for three successive Congresses, and after a Republican interlude, for three more. In fact, of the twelve Congresses between 1874, when the abnormalities of Reconstruction were over and partisan values returned, and the end of the century, traditionally though mistakenly regarded as a period of Republican monopoly, eight Congresses had a

House with a Democratic majority. Eleven years after the war the Democrats won the Presidency with a popular majority exceeding the Republican vote by a third of a million, though the Republicans took the office by assuming a one-vote electoral margin in a dispute over Deep South returns.

During the long Republican control of the Presidency from Lincoln through Taft, interrupted only by Cleveland's two administrations, the Democrats accumulated total popular votes, in the thirteen elections, of nearly 58,000,000 to the Republicans' 64,500,000, or some 90 per cent of the Republican vote. To understand the meaning of this in terms of the strength of the Democratic revival, it has to be compared with the Republican situation during the post-Depression Democratic control of the Presidency. In the five elections from 1932 to 1948, the Republicans accumulated a total of only some 99,000,000 popular votes to the Democrats' more than 127,000,000, or only some 77 per cent of the Democratic vote. Yet for all its comparative health in the number of voters it continued to attract, the post-bellum Democratic Party was floundering and flaccid, and the vote it received was less a tribute to its merits than a commentary on the high-riding Republicans' faults.

The emergence of the only strong leader of the Democrats between Jackson and Cleveland was dependent far more on the cynical corruption of the Grant administration, the unholy alliances between immoral Congressmen and predatory speculators and the retroactive salary grab of the Congress than on any newly inspired virtues in the Democrats. The Democratic governor of New York, Samuel J. Tilden, an experienced politician of no Galahad purity, gave those who could no longer stomach the politicos in Washington a strong leader to fight Republicanism in the campaign of 1876. The depression of three years earlier created a climate favorable to the Democrats, for thousands had lost their fortunes, while in Washington Grant sat hopelessly inept in the White House and the Congressional cabal lost all sense of responsibility. Tilden was portrayed as a great reformer, and the nation was both in need of and in the mood for reform. But the portrayal could not stick for the duration of the campaign, for all the stock-market riggings that Tilden had perpetrated, all the manipulation of railroads, all the profitable dealings with Tweed, Fisk and Jay Cooke came to the surface. This apostle of reform, nevertheless, led the Democrats to victory in popular votes over Rutherford B. Hayes, the Ohio Republican, who actually was a saintly character compared with the highly questionable Tilden. After a disputed electoral vote, however, the election was awarded to Hayes; and the Democrats lapsed back into a not undeserved obscurity until Grover Cleveland.

What had happened in the Tilden-Hayes campaign of 1876 was that the Democrats and particularly their candidate had no identification with the main stream of their party's history, addressed themselves *ad hoc* to the situation of the moment and were merely trusting that the Republicans had been sufficiently brazen in their corruption to be thrown out of office. Under the leadership of William Jennings Bryan twenty years later, the Democratic Party returned to its historical premises and advanced them apace. Garfield had won the intervening election of 1880 for the Republicans by a scant ten thousand votes; and as the war receded in the public's feelings the two major parties approached unprecedented parity, and with more than superficial reason. Both the old Federalist and the old Whig parties had been for an identity of the government with concentrated capitalism, and both Jeffersonian and Jacksonian Democracy had reacted with a call for a divorce of business and government and for a liberated capitalism. As the 1880's began, the historic position of the conservative party—the Republican heirs to Federalism and Whiggism—was modified. The government could best serve the concentrated interests by leaving them alone, and so Republicanism too was for a liberated capitalism, a divorce of business interests and government actions—the traditional position of the Democrats. Moreover, the country itself was feeling its strength, raw, undisciplined, speculative and ethically undemanding. There is little wonder that, in the gilded interlude, the political parties approached parity so closely, for there was no longer between them any difference about the methods best employed to attain and preserve Utopia. Democrats and Republicans were simply two factions in one great big party, even lacking any very strong factional purposes.

In consequence, to satisfy those opposed to the state of things, there was an epidemic of third parties and mugwumps, who bolted the major parties all through those years. Only three factors prevented the rise of a new major party. First, the mugwumpery was too diffuse and unpredictable to be of positive use. Secondly, the nostrums of the third parties were so specialized that they could seldom cut across regional boundaries. And finally, a nominal and curious Democrat, Grover Cleveland, stepped in twice to interrupt the nominal Republican rule—which gave the appearance without the substance of a healthy two-party system.

The name of Grover Cleveland, a gruff, conscientious and honest man, held a magic spell over the Democrats long after he was gone. The major ostensible reason was that he was the only Democrat between 1856 and 1912, the only one in fifty-six years, to become President—a position which any Republican who alone wins the office between 1928 and 1984 may equally expect to occupy in his party's traditions. Yet not only did Cleveland not restore Democracy to power but he also did not even restore it to its own main principles and *raison d'être*. Woodrow Wilson, who knew something about the Democratic Party, once said, "You may think Cleveland's administration was Democratic. It was not. Cleveland was a conservative Republican." It was not quite so simple as that, but in effect Wilson was right. During his first administration Cleveland was a cautious Democrat. During his second, after the Harrison interregnum, he was a Republican, neither more nor less than typical of his era. To understand his limitations and, more important still, to understand his failure to revitalize Democracy, it is necessary to understand his background.

The child of a village manse, Cleveland inherited from his cleric father a high sense of moral duty, a quality which never deserted him. After his father's death he was left at sixteen to care for himself and drifted to Buffalo, where he studied law. Buffalo became his world, and he was pleased with it and it with him. He served awhile as sheriff, won a circle of friends among the local Democrats, and by 1881 was satisfied with his situation as a reasonably prosperous lawyer. Neither contemplative nor profound, he had no interest in political theory and not much, beyond an ex-sheriff's horizons, in politics. But four years later he was in the White House, having been first drafted to run successfully as mayor of Buffalo and then chosen as compromise governor of New York, in both of which posts he achieved a rather odd fame for prolific use of the veto.

An accidental Democrat, Cleveland had no particular concept of the political stand of the party but knew very well what he stood for personally: honesty, directness, fairness. In harmony with this credo, he saw the Presidency as the people's agency for the prevention of abuses, corruption and yielding to special pleaders. Creative statesmanship was no part of his talent or intention, and even those things which fanned a faint flame in the low-burning embers of Democracy during his first administration were negative rather than positive: the stands against the tariff, against veteran-pension raids, against preferential legislation for any specific interest or group.

Cleveland had also a blunt suspicion of the way capitalism was drifting and feared for its health when he saw its benefits restricted to a smaller and smaller and increasingly powerful group. But his suspicion was short-lived, and he lacked the imagination to see what could be done about it anyhow—and in this respect more than in any other he failed to participate measurably in the Democratic tradition. For it had been the historic function of his party, in Jefferson's and Jackson's day before him and in Wilson's and Roosevelt's after him, to apply the correctives when capitalism went awry. But Cleveland thought that it must be let alone and he subscribed to laissez-faire capitalism when laissez-faire had ceased to be the cure and had become the curse. Four years later, when he returned to Washington after spending the interlude in Wall Street, he drifted completely from the Democratic views and became in effect a routine Republican of the Gilded Age. And he left the Democratic Party as he found it—indistinguishable from the Republican.

v

The vacuum left by the political merger in all but name of the Democratic and Republican parties could not go on forever, and in 1892, when Cleveland was running successfully to succeed his successor, it looked as though the void would be filled. The Democratic Party having abrogated its function, more and more people who had looked to it futilely for aid turned to the new Populist Party, which sought a correction of the abuses of capitalism and an extension of it to the small businessman, the independent tradesman and the farmer. It was more than a ripple, winning twenty-two electoral votes, twelve seats in Congress and many more state offices. But like most third parties, it lacked the moderation which Americans instinctively demand even in reform programs. Nevertheless, it had the strength and the logical position on the political scene to shake the Democratic Party out of its long coma, when it joined forces with William Jennings Bryan in 1896.

In his unpolished, unthoughtful, emotional and glossingly superficial way Bryan resurrected the Democratic Party by an intuitive appreciation of its fundamental purpose, to broaden opportunity in the land and to create conditions favorable to the development of the small businessman, whether he was the farmer seeking to make a profit on his produce, a factory worker seeking to make a profit on his labor or a merchant seeking to make a profit in his store. This is what Bryan saw as the purpose of the Democratic Party, and giving expression to it was the sole constructive achievement of his long career.

But he had no more mature notion of how to go about accomplishing it than a child. For intellectually Bryan was a child, and he depended on a kind of loud, emotional and somehow debasing political evangelism to impress the voters. An ignorant, unread, imperceptive and unreasoning man, he stormed around the country giving dramatic voice to the hopes of the mass of Americans and suggesting absolutely no thorough or thoughtful program to realize them. With a bland and naïve confidence, he offered instead one nostrum after another, reducing his party on the practical level to the dimensions of a faction. Nominated for the Presidency three times, he never lost his completely emotional obsession with free silver, never grew an inch in real political knowledge, never got below the surface of a single issue, never remotely approached Presidential-candidate, let alone Presidential, stature.

Yet this patent-medicine man of politics, with his genius for the vulgar and his parochial mentality, made the Democratic Party mean something again. And after the succession of Seymours, Tildens, Hancocks and even Clevelands, that was no small contribution to the political life of the nation. When he entered his political decline, there was no doubt left that the Democratic and Republican parties, except for the anomaly of Theodore Roosevelt, marked different roads to fulfillment of the nation's potentialities.

Bryan was, like Chautauqua and the stereopticon, a passing phenomenon, which could have happened only at the time that it did; and it was inevitable that politically more mature figures would rise to give leadership to the Democratic purpose again. The return of the Republican Party to its historic identity with the interests of the few, after the Theodore Roosevelt departure, furnished the occasion for a basic shift in political forces. After the Taft administration, the laborer began to sense the Republicans' limited concept of capitalism and to drift away from the party to which he had earlier given support. He had shared in the past in the view that the Democratic stand against the tariff would so open the American market to the products of cheaper labor abroad that his very job would be in peril, and long before that he had been led to believe that the ancient agrarian tendency of the Democrats would operate against his interests. Now, however, the laborer was doubtful that the Republican notion of a free capitalism was sufficiently inclusive and impartial to consider his position, and he began to identify that position less with his boss's than with that of the small farmer. He continued his basic belief in capitalism, for American labor never swarmed into radical political camps and was never converted en masse to socialism. But he questioned whether the benefits of a capitalism adjusted exclusively to the demands of a top few would ever trickle down to him. For he was a capitalist, too, offering his labor for sale at, he hoped, a sound profit, even as the small farmer and the village storekeeper were. He began to think that maybe the benefits of capitalism should spring equally from below, that perhaps the government, as it had manifested interests in the problems of those at the top of the industrial kingdom, should manifest some in the problems of those at the bottom. Knowing that with Theodore Roosevelt out of the party he could expect little in this direction from the Republicans, he began to look toward the Democrats.

But the men at the top had anticipated him and started looking for another Grover Cleveland to head the Democratic Party, so that at worst the voters would be confronted with a Hobson's choice at the polls. Heads, the concentrated interests would win with Taft; tails, they would win with a nominal Democrat of Republican persuasions. The House of Morgan offered, in a burst of public service impelled by Theodore Roosevelt's bolting of the Republican Party, to pick and groom the Democratic candidate.

They picked and groomed the wrong man, the dignified, respectable and solid president of Princeton, Woodrow Wilson. Because he had the scholar's skepticism of the Populist movement, because he had the sane man's contempt for the theoretical claptrap of Bryan, because he had the political scientist's suspicion of the extreme cure, Wilson was considered safe. What the manipulators overlooked was the fact that, in an entirely different way, Wilson was the only thoroughly balanced man since Lincoln to aspire to the Presidency.

Erudite in the political history of America, at home in comparative politics, perceptive in the forces and counterforces that accounted for the organic growth of domestic parties, Wilson knew very well that capitalism had to be guided down either the suicidal street of privileged interests or up the broader avenue that gave impetus and equal protection to all the people, and that there was not then and never had been in our history any essential conflict between capitalism and anticapitalism. "It is rather," he had said, long before being tapped for political office, "between capitalism in all its larger accumulations and all other less concentrated, more dispersed, smaller and more individual economic forces." This was in essence a return to the principles of Jefferson and Jackson—capitalism renewing itself through extension rather than concentrating itself through accumulation. He feared and hated "centralized and corruptible control," and he applied the phrase equally to private groups and to socialism. He saw the practiced function of government to be, not only the protection of the people from such control, but the creation of conditions conducive to the advancement of the interests of all the people and not just a few.

One year as governor of New Jersey, which constituted the inspired political grooming of Wilson, was enough to give his discoverers ground to suspect their own judgment. And all remaining doubts were dispersed during the three-cornered campaign of Roosevelt, Wilson and Taft in 1912, when the electorate found Wilson's way to a liberated capitalism somewhat more promising if less vociferous than Roosevelt's. It gave him 6,000,000 votes to Roosevelt's 4,000,000, with the Republicans trailing wearily behind.

Wilson, in office, held that capitalism thrived on free competition and was being constantly subjected instead to a brazenly manipulated competition, with any business at the bottom suffering from restricted credit and murderous underselling, due to the overlapping control of banks and to its big established competitors. In the most skilled direction of legislative processes and the shrewdest handling of discordant legislators by a President in all our history, Wilson brought about the remedial legislation he had promised: the Federal Reserve Act, giving public control to banking and credit; the Clayton Act, revitalizing the almost dead Sherman Anti-Trust Act; the Federal Trade Act, creating a commission to wipe out unfair competition and illegal trade practices; a child-labor act; an eight-hour-day act for railroad workers; and an act to extend Federal credit to farmers. This was Wilson's "New Freedom"—prototype of the New Deal and designed to restore freedom of opportunity and freedom of competition—the real and classical virtues of capitalism—to the people. Wilson believed that his program was merely the minimum adjustments necessary to preserve capitalism and its related institutions, and he was unquestionably right. But the circles remained who were opposed to any adjustment at all and took over the whole stock of laissez-faire clichés. With Roosevelt now entirely forgotten, they pinned their hopes to Republicanism.

The First World War occupied the second administration of Wilson, and the struggle that followed over the League had no appropriate or fundamental part in the partisan conflict, being rather in part a manifestation of the old Congressional jealousy of Presidential treaty powers and in part a manifestation of the insular mentality and incredible shortsightedness of Senator Lodge. (Perhaps the informed efforts of A. Lawrence Lowell of Harvard, a confirmed Republican, in behalf of the League are the best key to the nonpartisan nature of the struggle. The only partisan element was not doctrinal but simply a matter of following the leader. Lowell afterward said, "Probably a majority of the American people then desired some method of preventing the recurrence of war. Probably a majority of Republicans would have favored heartily a League of Nations for this purpose if presented by their leaders.")

The return to Republicanism and laissez-faire in 1920 was short-lived, and a decade later the doctrine that capitalism worked best when left alone was assigned a permanent place in the nation's folklore. Among the Republicans, only Herbert Hoover, a stubborn survival, and Alf M. Landon, an odd and obscure political anachronism of the mid-thirties, ever attempted to revive it, Wendell Willkie and Thomas Dewey wanting no part of it. The relegation of the doctrine to the political museum seemed again to leave the nation deprived, as it was between the fall of the Federalists and the rise of Jackson and during the post-Civil War years, of a rational party cleavage. But before laissez-faire was suitably buried, the Democrats had in 1924 nominated John W. Davis, probably with Wilson and Jefferson the most erudite man to run for the Presidency but one who, by associations and training, might have very well served the Republicans as a Democrat, just as Grover Cleveland in his second term had done; and no one will ever know how much that progressive governor of New York, Alfred Smith, was swayed toward the dying laissez-faire principle in his later years by conviction or by resentment of the Presidential incumbent.

At any rate the laissez-faire principle was dead as a partisan issue, and the man who presided over its burial was a traditional Democrat, Franklin Roosevelt.

Roosevelt took over *in toto* the accumulated content of implications of Jeffersonian, Jacksonian and Wilsonian Democracy—the rescuing of capital from itself. He came to office, however, during a time much more critical than any faced by his party predecessors, when the economic structure of the nation was tottering, and the Republican vacating the White House had said in total defeat that there was nothing left to do to save it. If Roosevelt had been of a basically radical rather than a basically conservative nature, he could have revolutionized the entire economy without popular resentment. But his views—for all the shoutings of his opponents—were the same as those of effective Democracy from the beginning: the extension of the benefits of capitalism to the many and the liberation of capitalism from the tyranny of the few.

He pointed out that "our economic life is dominated by some six hundred-odd corporations who control two thirds of American industry. Ten million small-business men divide the other third. . . . Put plainly, we are steering a steady course toward economic oligarchy, if we are not there already." And, later: "Private enterprise is ceasing to be free enterprise and is becoming a cluster of private collectivisms." The cure? With good Democratic orthodoxy, "adapting existing economic organizations to the service of the people."

Less skilled in building a legislative program than Wilson and less knowledgeable, Roosevelt improvised as he went along, trying first one thing and then another, always playing it by ear, always testing expedients. He kept recovery going as a juggler keeps six balls in the air, gave the tired economy a second wind and made sure that it would not be permitted to get so tired again. But the major fact is that the economic structure did not collapse, and none of our institutions toppled. Personal liberties were not destroyed, free enterprise was not destroyed, business did not go bankrupt. The body of New Deal reforms even lacked originality, for government regulation of business was as old as the Sherman Anti-Trust Act of 1890; independent regulatory commissions were as old as the Interstate Commerce Act of 1887; labor legislation was as old as the Clayton Act of 1918; regulation of the currency and credit was as old as the Federal Reserve Act of 1913; the income tax was as old as the Civil War acts of 1862-1872. Without resort to nationalization, even of the railroads, private enterprise was strong enough, after nine years of the New Deal, to win the war of production, and in the nine peace years of the Roosevelt era there was no epidemic of bank closings, no mass wiping out of investments, no string of bankruptcies of great businesses.

Indeed the Roosevelt myth that needs critical revision is less that he ushered in a new order, which he did not, than that he sought the destruction of free enterprise and the capitalist system.

The capitalists (both those who accrued the major part of their worth since 1932 and those who still held theirs of earlier origin), who died a little each time Roosevelt's name was mentioned, were like drowning men who, having been hauled out of the water, despise their rescuer for having pulled their hair. Never—not even in the comparable hatred of Lincoln and earlier of Jackson—was informed estimate so blandly neglected for the indulgence of an attitude. Yet we have to ask how much of that attitude was in truth directed at Franklin Roosevelt. One suspects that it was directed rather at the irrevocable but not unprecedented end of an era and that, as Lincoln became the villain-image for those who dreaded to see the end of slavery and Jackson for those who could not accept the end of private control of the currency, so Roosevelt—the conciliatory and essentially moderate improviser—has become the villain-image of those whose major complaint was really their own inability to reconcile themselves to what was nothing more than a new phase of progressive capitalism.

Although this was a normal reaction, it was not without danger, for it confused an effect with a cause. Republicans were shocked to find that in 1948, even without the becharmed or bedeviled figure of Roosevelt stalking the election, the Democrats won with a relatively undramatic personality. The point they missed was just that it was not Franklin Roosevelt who won for a fourth and then for a fifth time, but a political party that was for a principle attuned to the demand of the time— progressive government action to keep capitalism on the side of the people. Until the Republicans hit upon something that seemed more important or a better way of doing it, their prospects were not bright.

But just as the Republicans, during their entrenchment in power after the Civil War, made virtues of their evils, there is reason to suggest that the Democrats, entrenched in power after the Depression, can make evils of their virtues. For sound progress also requires knowledge of when to stop or, more precisely, when to shift the course—a knowledge that is not promoted in political circles by long retention of power.

The critical problem that confronted the Democratic Party when it acceded in 1932 was to create a degree of security and of opportunity for the people that would not be antagonistic to traditional economic institutions. The achievement of twentieth-century Democracy was to do this in a legislative program that gave some security to the aged and unemployed, insured bank deposits, regulated stock transactions, established minimum wages, protected farmers from vulnerability to risks that no amount of industriousness and prudence on their own part could avert, and brought relief to home owners whose mortgages had been so numerously foreclosed that many banks had gone into the real estate business. Since the Willkie and Dewey campaigns it is obvious that all this has passed out of the area of a partisan program into the realm of nationally accepted principles of modern democracy, partly because they have been recognized as conditions and not deterrents of a free capitalism and partly because they destroyed none of our institutions, in spite of all the warnings and recriminations.

But where does the Democratic Party go from here? If it continues to emphasize the amelioration of the imperfections of capitalism and the creation of conditions designed to extend its benefits while minimizing its abuses, then it will renew itself with a continuing application of its major tradition to changing demands. But if it shifts its political emphasis from the creation of such conditions to the creation of substitute benefits, then it confesses the bankruptcy of that tradition and is embarked on a new one no more consonant with its own historic development than with that of the Republicans.

Chapter Seven

Republicans

I

AN OUTSTANDING truism of American political history is that Americans are basically a conservative people; but even a conservative people can be divided on how to conserve its institutions. We have seen in broad outline how there has come from below, *i.e.,* from the mass of small people, a periodic and effective demand for progressive government action, or else a similar response to leadership which promised it, to insure the survival, extension and readjustment to changing realities of those institutions. But a great body of citizens, only on four occasions less than 40 per cent and on eleven occasions more than 50 per cent of the whole, has been inclined to believe that those institutions would best survive if left relatively alone. This belief, and its corollary that what was good for the concentrated interests was good for all down the line, has however obtained a majority concurrence only when natural complications did not challenge the *status quo.* Consequently, the history of the less progressive of our major parties (always excepting the fundamental digression from partisan values in the Civil War) has been on the whole less of a constructive than of a holding nature. It has been in power when there has been no popular recognition of trouble or impending trouble, and as a result has confused its usefulness with its tolerance. It has seldom been a political instrument of the people, although it has often been an instrument of those whom the people were willing to leave in charge. Its historical function has been to check progressivism, the importance of which function can be too easily underestimated, and its predominant nature has been critical and passive as the Democratic nature has been predominantly creative and active. It is always on the defensive, whether in power or out, because it has to go before the voters as an instrument for governing when it is attached to the idea that the less governing there is, the better. It is therefore negative rather than positive, but it must be remembered that democratic processes, like electrical processes, cannot exist without both.

Although it has from time to time claimed a line of political descent from the Federalists, Republicanism inherited most of its surviving tenets from the anti-Jacksonian Whig Party, and it has appealed to Hamiltonian thinking mainly in order to reconcile its politico-economic philosophy with the origins of the republic. The cornerstone of Federalism was a strong and active centralization of power in the Federal Government, and it was laid by broad Constitutional constructionists who saw in the Constitution no inhibitions to the growth of Federal power. At this cornerstone, although sympathetic with the purposes of the Federalists in planting it, the Republicans have been systematically hacking away for years. It has thus been characterized more by being against things than by being for them and has therefore not fulfilled nearly as completely as the Democrats the major partisan function of serving as an arena of compromise, for it is easier to compromise the aims of men than it is their fears, and it is both impossible and unnecessary to compromise fears at all when they get to be identical. And the Republicans inherited from the Whigs a rich stack of fears.

The Whig Party was born in 1832, the year of Jackson's second election, lived for some twenty years, during which time it elected two aging generals as Presidents, both of whom died in office, and then was succeeded by the Republicans in 1854. It was primarily the creation of the Great Compromiser, the perpetual Presidential aspirant, Henry Clay, who in 1832 headed the anti-Jacksonian factions in a political catchall called the National Republicans and compromised himself right out of the Presidency. Clay's "American System" was dead when Jackson went into office four years earlier, but Clay refused to bury it. It reappeared in the campaign of 1832—a mass of particulars, with something for everybody, but incorporating no broad principle that gives a party direction beyond the moment. To this multicolored kite Clay in a lapse of political prudence tied a tail, the endorsement of the Bank of the United States; and Jackson won the election in a walk. Clay was defeated so badly that there was no opposition party left. Moreover, the Bank of the United States seemed permanently contrary to the will of the people after 1832, and there was really no other national issue on which to oppose Jackson. But there were plenty of regional issues, and the opposition became a conglomeration of regional complaints and regional interests, and each of these was the special platform of one of several rising factions, many of which mistook themselves for a while for political parties: State-rights Democrats, who were against Jackson because of his strong nationalism; National Republicans, who were against Jackson because his nationalism was not the kind they wanted; Antimasons, who were against Jackson because he was a Mason; and any other group who was against Jackson for any other reason. So diverse were the real interests of all these elements of the new Whig Party, with only anti-Jacksonianism as a common bond, that they nominated four different Presidential candidates in 1836, all of whom were defeated by Jackson's protégé, Martin Van

Buren, a political strategist of first ability who had few qualifi-cations for the Presidency.

During the next two decades, however, great changes were taking place all over the country, shaping new political forces; and—even though the Democrats won four out of the six elections during the inclusive years 1836 to 1856—the agency through which these new forces were to express themselves was the Whig and then the Republican Party. The reason was obvious: the country was in its adolescence, beginning to feel its strength, creating new values, forming new alignments. New England, the majesty of its shipping days over, was embarked on a great manufacturing period; the prairies and all the Ohio Valley, in Jackson's day the frontier, were fully developed, with growing cities, vigorous newspapers and positive political values of their own; the South, wholly dependent on cotton, forged strong commercial links with the New England manufacturers, who made the thread and the cloth, and with the expanding West, who bought it. The railroads were knitting the country together, technological revolutions were just beginning, the young were seeing a new and more opulent future, and men everywhere were looking for a party which would do nothing to upset the applecart, which would preserve the *status quo,* limiting its active phase to the protection of manufacturing, which would protect also the worker in his job and the cotton grower on his plantation, and to the development of internal improvements. Despite the fearful shadow of slavery hanging over the land, there was an optimistic flexing of the national muscles. And the Whigs were an optimistic party: they were for a tariff, for internal improvements, and hoped successfully to straddle the disruptive issue of slavery, which the nation also hoped indefinitely to straddle. But this was not enough to give the Whig Party the vigor and vitality necessary for its endur-ance, despite the amazing regularity with which it attracted the men of the new West, like the young Abraham Lincoln, who were to form the rising political leadership.

The Whigs elected the ancient general, William Henry Harrison, in 1840, and that tired old warrior was completely baffled by what he was supposed to do. He wrote a long, rambling inaugural address full of allusions to old Roman military heroes, which Webster took over and edited liberally, saying afterward that he never killed so many Roman generals before in one session. The aging President, however, caught a severe cold at the inaugural proceedings and was dead three weeks later. The first Whig Presidential term thereupon fell to the Democratic John Tyler, who had been nominated to the Vice-Presidency on the Whig ticket to attract the Democratic voters fearful of the strangely irresponsible leadership of Van Buren. Tyler treated the stunned party to an independent-Democratic administration, pleasing no one. Thereafter the Presidency alternated between both parties, with only the Democratic Polk of a clear mind as to what he intended to do with the office. By the time his term was finished, the Whigs had elected old General Zachary Taylor, who died to leave the office to Fillmore, and then the Democrats availed themselves of the irresolute spirit that prevailed in the country on slavery to put two ineffectives of their own, Pierce and Buchanan, in the White House.

Through it all the country existed only because of the series of compromises effected in the halls of Congress, but it was really an armed truce and there was no man who did not sense a whistling in the dark. Slavery was too fundamental an issue to be handled by partisan processes, largely because—as we have seen—the successful party compromises the aims of all the factions within it and crystallizes them into an operable pattern of proposed action. But you could not incorporate a proslavery or antislavery feeling into the broad principles of a political party as you could convictions about the tariff or the building of canals with Federal funds. Consequently both the Whigs and the Democrats, without declaring themselves flatly for or against slavery, took Constitutional dodges on the question, the Democrats saying that there was no Congressional power to break down domestic institutions, and the Whigs saying that the nation could be half-slave and half-free forever so far as the competence of the Congress to compromise went. It became obvious that if any party ever flatly came out against slavery, it would have to be created for that purpose. Such a party was born in Ripon, Wisconsin, in February 1854, and it styled itself Republican.

II

The Republican Party was not, as the Federalist, the Democratic and even, to a lesser extent, the Whig parties were, the creation of a great leader like Hamilton, Jefferson or Clay. It sprang into being to accommodate in an effective whole the less wealthy elements of the defunct Whig Party plus those whose great purpose was to stop the extension of slavery to the Western territories. To the party flocked homesteaders who favored free dispensation of Western lands, temperance fanatics solely interested in combating rum, Know-Nothing alumni who were against foreigners, disgruntled Democrats who were for defeat of the Democratic Party, laborers who could see nothing for them in the old agrarian party, farmers who feared its proslavery tendency, and radical abolitionists. Many of these factions were mutually contradictory in their demands, but all of them were against the extension of slavery. And after they had undergone one abortive Presidential campaign (having inherited from the Whigs the practice of nominating generals instead of politicians, the new party nominated John Frémont in 1856), Abraham Lincoln, bred in the tough politics of the prairies, led this combination to a plurality victory in 1860.

Lincoln faced a stupendous task, which might very well have been impossible had not the depression of 1857 completed the discrediting of the fumbling Democrats then epitomized by the ill-equipped Buchanan in the White House. For the new Republican Party had lacked, aside from a sufficient identity of broad interests among its components, the measure of respectability necessary to success in a society which prized respectability, and many an Eastern voter whose instincts directed him to the new party turned from it because the leaders in his community were against it. Only an issue of immediate danger could sway these voters, for political parties are postulated on principles but thrive on events. The event of depression brought to Lincoln the support he needed from those who had to be jarred from aping the respectable. In 1856, the business leaders, the manufacturers, the bankers and the shippers not only would not go near the Republican Party, but they actually feared it as a mob of irreconcilables, ten times worse than the old Jacksonians, who might very well wreck the Union. As Emerson tartly observed, "Cotton thread holds the Union together," and the manufacturer dependent on it for his mills and the shipper for his carriers were interested only in avoiding a rupture in the highly profitable relationship with the South. Moreover, the Western flavor of Republicanism, with its homesteading element, was repellent to the industrialist, who saw his workers drifting away to the West and a new agrarianism with its inevitable votes in the Senate springing up on the Western prairies. Furthermore, the new Republicans had strategically omitted any reference to the tariff in their platform of 1856. But the depression of 1857, not unjustly ascribed to the Democratic administration of Buchanan, gave the laborers of the East reason to question the wisdom of their manufacturing leaders and, respectability or not, they were drawn to the Republican fold.

Thus Lincoln faced the country in 1860, the candidate of what was really a farmer-laborer party, with the abolitionist, nativist and alien factions incongruously included. The greatest conciliator in political history, he proceeded to find an issue acceptable to all these elements and repugnant to none. And that was the extension of slavery.

Legend, which finds the political field fertile, identifies the origin of Republican ascendancy with the abolition of slavery. Except for its minor content of abolitionists, who were not happy at Lincoln's nomination and who were in the party simply because there was no place else to go, the Republicans exhibited virtually no moral attitude toward slavery and not much moral interest. Well after his election and deep into the Civil War, Lincoln himself had no desire for abolition and finally issued the Emancipation Proclamation only as a military stratagem. And during the campaign of 1860 he had far too much political sense to make concessions to the abolitionists. He restricted the issue to the extension of slavery and he was persuasive on a coldly practical level: if slavery were extended to the territories, thousands of white settlers would be deprived of farms and homes on land appropriated by a new slavocracy— which impressed the farmers; and if slavery were extended to the territories it could be extended to the free states, either re- placing the factory worker with a slave or making the worker himself a slave—which impressed the laborer. By such skilled marshaling of arguments in the three-way election of 1860, with the two Democratic candidacies of Douglas and Breckinridge canceling each other out, Lincoln won about 40 per cent of the popular vote and victory. When the Civil War followed, the partisan conflict was suspended, and a new Republicanism emerged afterward.

The Republican Party of Abraham Lincoln was actually a latter phase of Jacksonian Democracy. The business community was not identified with it; farmers and laborers and a minority of progressive idealists who had no purpose but abolition were its components; and its function was the old Democratic one of liberating capitalism from the grip of the few and extending its benefits to the new territories of the West and to the rising labor classes of the East. This was the appeal of Lincoln and the implied objectives which won him victory. After the war was over and Lincoln was dead and after the quarrels of Reconstruction, during the era when Andrew Johnson alone fought for the principles of Lincoln and was tried in impeachment proceedings by his own party for his pains, the Republican Party retained only a nominal tie to its first victorious candidate and no tie whatsoever to his purposes. Its first act was to revert to the old Whig practice of nominating a general, a particularly naïve version of which they found in Ulysses S. Grant. Its first purpose was to promote business prosperity from above, the mechanism for which purpose was an alliance with the highly concentrated interests that were the real rulers of the nation both politically and economically. And here the Republican Party settled into its major and enduring phase.

Few things constitute a greater obstacle to an understanding of the Republican partisan role in our history, and therefore their dilemma in our present, than the superficial conclusion that it was merely an alliance of strong and predatory interests and weak and misguided politicians to exploit the masses. It was no such thing. It was an organic expression of political values that seemed at the time to make very good sense. Although often stupid and usually shortsighted, it was neither malicious nor avaricious. It defined its own code, which—

contrary to present opinion—was related to honest conceptions of the national welfare, and even in its most incredible acts was true to those definitions. It participated strongly in the national character of the time and it was itself participated in by many radically different exemplars of that character. It was neither an anachronism nor a throwback but more than anything else the creation and the reflection of post-bellum America. It did not even lower the moral standards or abase the aspirations of its time but merely approximated those that already existed and flourished on them.

For what had happened in America that gave rise to a degree of Republicanism which even Republicans now prefer to forget simply took politics along with it, and the lonely and confused souls, the men apart, were the reformers and not the politicos. Although the nation had just been bathed in the blood of the Civil War, the historic effect of which was an affirmation of the principles of union and freedom, principles formed no major part of postwar life and no part at all therefore in the parties that were its political instruments. The accumulation of money as fast and furiously as possible was not only the sole criterion of success; it was the sole criterion of usefulness, of morality and of the fulfillment of life, at once both the means and the end of living. All the old values were dead, and yet the nation—the issue of slavery at last settled once and for all—was possessed of unheard-of resources and in no mood for marking time until new values arose. It plunged ahead, and the natural wealth of the land was to the gangling republic like candy in the hands of a child: it gorged itself until it was ill. But like the child it had a good time doing it.

And everyone, including the Democrats, joined in the fun. The President of the United States, sitting in the box of the notorious swindler, Jim Fisk, at the latter's private theater, dazzled and did not disgust the public. Oakes Ames, the blueblood

Congressman from Massachusetts, passing out bribes to his fellow Representatives to forestall an inquiry into the construction of the Union Pacific, blandly admitted doing it as pretty sound business practice and insisted that he could see no wrong in it. Neither could most of his associates and the press. As Ames pointed out, if you wanted to get things done in business, you made some judicious distribution of stock shares, and he could see no reason why you shouldn't do the same thing with the Congress. And the nation admired getting things done, the outward sign of which was making a fortune. The factory worker was not critical of his boss's methods, because he hoped to be a boss himself someday and would want to use the same methods. The farmer was not critical of the financial practices of business leaders, because they were successful men who practiced them and his son might be a successful man someday. And the nation, admiring the men at the top and sparing criticism of their methods, wanted a government that did the same. The Republican Party accommodated them, and if it had not the Democrats would have.

It was thus the historic misfortune of the Republican Party to have flowered during a period that was essentially an era combined of collapsed values and somewhat immature wishful thinking. It necessarily geared itself to the advantage of the concentrated moneyed interests, because they were the object of admiration and emulation of the people, and men devoted to principles of honesty and justice were so scarce as to be for all practical purposes nonexistent. The big names in politics were those of the type of Benjamin F. Butler, Roscoe Conkling, James G. Blaine, James A. Garfield, Nelson W. Aldrich—whose principles were to make money and to make it fast and whose principles were approved by the people. They *were* the Republican Party, and they guided it through its confident phase as the chosen party to realize the potentialities of the new industrialized America. They admired and obliged the fortune makers and sought to protect their interests—and, as Oakes Ames seriously suggested, one way to make them conscientious protectors of the manipulative capitalists was to give them a little manipulated stock of their own to protect.

In this period also was formed the basic composition of the Republican Party—which was the traditionless middle class, unused to wealth but convinced that it was the key to the full life, admiring material success because it recognized no other kind, idolizing the self-made man without caring very much how he got that way. Its heroes, and the men it wanted to see in charge, were not the occupant of the White House, whoever he happened to be, and the leaders of the Congress, but the Cookes, Carnegies, Armours, Goulds, and Rockefellers—men of humble origin who had made their mark and whose names meant far more than those of Rutherford Hayes or Benjamin Harrison. They could do no wrong nor could the party that served them, for they would certainly not undo the country that had made them. Consequently, behind the newly rich titans at the top were all the lesser merchants, manufacturers, shippers, professional men, native workers and farmers who made up the body of the party.

Conspicuously absent was any aristocracy, and most of the old landed families of less flashy and less gigantic wealth were identified with the Democratic Party, having little in common with the barons of the new fortunes. Conspicuously absent also were the immigrants of the Northeast, for the simple reason that the Democrats were smarter about taking them in and holding them. Deprived of the mellowing influence of the old and the freshness of the new, Republicanism took on all the confusions of its middle-class components and reflected them faithfully in all its tolerances; and it also and inevitably became rather stagnated in power, neither creating nor giving direction to the public policy of the time but merely going along with what was visited on it or at times simply with what was dictated to it. At no time in history was America with less of a government than in the post-Civil War years or closer to anarchy. Never before were both the Presidency and the Congress simultaneously so undistinguished.

But conditions were on the side of the party and the nation. The frontiers, both economic and geographic, were truly limitless and so accommodating to the crude and undisciplined forces of the time that disaster was far from likely.

Moreover, the era of excessive tolerances did not last forever, and there arose within the party men who, though of no great strength, were honest and perceptive and who checked the tendency of the government to follow along in the tradition of the spoilsman of the Grant period. Rutherford B. Hayes was one such, and probably at no time between Lincoln and Wilson did such an intrinsically good man sit in the White House. In his one term he brought the despoliation of the South to an end, created a semblance of jobs-by-merit in the government service, and took a stern and sober view of the Presidency as a position of high trust and responsibility rather than managership for the fortune makers. Such phrases as "judicious control of capitalists" occur in his writings, and he knew that the structure of the nation could not stand an endless concentration of wealth and an endless toleration of abuses. But he lacked both the talent and the support to do anything about it, and the party was not pleased with his views and did not nominate him for a second term. The party rejected also Chester A. Arthur, the New York machine politician who succeeded on Garfield's death, for Arthur, utterly untested for fitness to hold any office, took the Presidency as seriously as Hayes did and attempted one reform after another. A natural majesty asserted itself in his character once he made up his mind about the responsibility of the Presidency, and he knowingly committed political suicide by refusing to compromise it. Like Hayes before him, though of far less intellectual caliber, he pushed through what reforms he could and accepted his undeserved fate.

After the debacle of Blaine and after the singularly inept administration of Benjamin Harrison, and since the Democrats won two elections with Cleveland, it became apparent that the temper of the nation had changed, that the day of surrender to natural forces was over, that the common interests of those who made up the great middle class and those who controlled the nation's economy were not so common after all. The West was disgruntled, strikes were occurring among the laborers, the rumblings of the Populist movement and the political evangelism of Bryan were stirring the rural areas. The danger of Republican solidarity being split by classes in the East and of a geographic split between East and West forced the Republicans to a degree of political activism, for they could not survive either split.

But they averted both, no doubt in part because of the general inadequacy of any opposition that had to depend on Bryan for leadership but more especially because of the constructive politics of Mark Hanna and William McKinley, both men of insight, both skilled politicians, both aware of the new challenges of the times, yet both of the genuine persuasion that prosperity was best achieved by guaranteeing it to the top, whence it would filter down to the rest, but both of the unique opinion also that business had to operate in harmony with the interests of all the people and not ride roughshod over them. Hanna and McKinley were in fact the first modern Republicans, and they were also the last ones.

IV

The year 1896, when William McKinley defeated Bryan for the Presidency, brought the Republican Party into closer attunement with the natural conservatism of the American people than it was before or since, for McKinley's was in some ways a Lincolnesque political mind and certainly no one else since Lincoln had so combined political talent of a high order with an incisive knowledge of the people. Moreover, McKinley was a serious politician who represented a departure from the servant-of-the-interests type and the coming of a new servant-of-the-people variety. Studious and broad-minded, he was also experienced and mature. In a day when strikers were lumped indiscriminately with anarchists and revolutionists, he served as defense counsel for strikers accused of that most feared of offenses, the destruction of industrial property, and served them well. Genuinely concerned then and all his life for the welfare of labor, whose leaders regarded him as organized labor's first President, he was backed by his political patron, the Ohio millionaire, Mark Hanna, who had always taken an impatient and scornful view of antiunion industrialists. "A man who won't meet his men half way is a God-damn fool," Hanna had said of Pullman, who had refused to arbitrate before the great Pullman strike—which, incidentally, the Democratic President Cleveland broke with Federal troops. From Samuel Gompers down to the bench worker, the labor movement consolidated its alignment with the Republican Party at a time when there seemed to be a permanent rupture imminent, and this was to a very great degree the personal achievement of McKinley and Hanna.

Moreover, both were known to be obstinate opponents to the theory that justified political corruption as only an extension of accepted business practices. As a young Congressman, McKinley had sat admiringly at the feet of Hayes, when that good and lonely man occupied a White House carefully and significantly shunned by his Republican colleagues. And a Wall Street firm was shaken to its foundations one pre-election morning when the Chairman of the Republican National Committee, Mark Hanna, with characteristic bluntness, sent them back their campaign contribution of ten thousand dollars. McKinley and Hanna were shifting the party's practical politics from privileged conservatism to popular conservatism, and they made no bones about it.

Nevertheless, neither McKinley nor, certainly, Hanna was in any sense a reformer, even on a party level. They had no basic complaint against the tenets of Republicanism and brought no new principle to its fundamental philosophy. But they probably represented that philosophy, for whatever it was worth, at its purest, and they unquestionably did the people a service beyond the not negligible one of keeping Bryan out of power. They created a true conservatism that had at heart the interests of the many and not the few, and it was no accident that McKinley was the most loved President in American history. All his Congressional career, and long before, an informed and searching student of the protective tariff and never a blindly partisan devotee of it, he went before the people—much as Lincoln had on the extension of slavery—and interpreted the tariff in terms of the welfare of the nation, the worker and the consumer. Nor was this simply a propagandist apologia. No towering intellectual, McKinley may have been wrong on the whole historic effect of the tariff and its contemporary economic consequences; but he honestly regarded it as beneficial to the laborer whose job it protected from cheaper labor abroad, to the consumer for whom it was graded downward from highly competitive to noncompetitive imports, and to the taxpayer who was relieved of paying the revenue its repeal would wipe out. These were all political and not economic arguments, but the job of the campaigner is not to diagnose theory but to interpret and justify, if he can, policy.

There was in McKinley Republicanism another important

element, representative of a major milestone in American politics and accounting for a peculiar persistence in Republican thinking. The party today relies primarily, in the face of repeated defeats on the issue, on its stand against socialist tendencies, which it reads into the program of the opposition even when they do not exist there. Oddly enough, this stand is frequently expressed by spokesmen of the party who are more exercised than precise in their addresses against "paternalism"— a concept of governmental function that originated with the Whigs and flowered in the McKinley era of Republicanism. For in the late 1890's, the Republicans held, and the nation accepted, the theory that the government should do all in its power to aid, protect and advance the interests of the business community. This was considered the aim of domestic legislation and the point of departure for foreign relations. Protectivism, the sole continuous issue in American politics for as long as a century, was nothing but the employment of government powers to shelter from harm private parties, whether individual or corporate. It was a major assumption of the McKinley doctrine that, in so doing, the paternalism of government was also directed to the people in general, for their prosperity was dependent on, even if not always commensurate with, that of business. The significance of the McKinley triumph lay in the popular choice of that paternalism in an age when socialism and quasi-socialist Populism were much more seriously and less timidly considered as alternatives than they have been in the twentieth century.

America turned away from socialism at the turn of the century, and it was the accomplishment of McKinley Republicanism, which offered a paternalism more acceptable to the American character. The subsequent conflict has been more about the level to which that paternalism should be directed than about whether it should exist at all, and no Republican ever suggested that the tariff was an unwarranted injection of governmental processes into the affairs of private business. But it is necessary to remember, particularly so for the Republican Party, that the popular appeal of McKinley's policy, summarized by the tariff, lay in its having been related by him to the general welfare of the people, and in the failure of the opposition to combat it on that ground. It must be remembered also that the McKinley program was adjusted to the times, stated in specifics and not in slogans, and offered as a concrete principle of government and not simply as a political philosophy. The key to its acceptance was in its then demonstrable effects and not in selling the public the notion that it would otherwise be voting itself to ruin.

V

If the Republican Party today chose to revitalize itself and become a serious contender for the custodianship of the national welfare—a choice which it has been carefully avoiding for the last two decades—it would feast on the memory of William McKinley and Marcus A. Hanna, forgetting most of what went before in its counsels and all of what came after. For there is such a thing as a constructive and useful conservativism, flexible rather than rigid and imaginative rather than sententious. Such was the conservativism of the McKinley administration and, when weighed against the floundering, confused and very badly grounded progressivism of Bryanic Democracy, it was much the better electoral choice. Never before and never since has the Republican Party so fortuitously served in the primary capacity of conservativism, which is to check progressivism that is hasty, precipitous and sloppily charted—all of which was certainly true of the Bryan variety. Moreover, it was expressive of the national mood and at the same time responsive to it. In many ways, and in spite of the obvious contradictory aspects of the hypothesis, it may well have been the foundation on which the Republicans could have built a political party more closely related to the people than any since Jackson's day. Instead, Republicanism went into a decline which dated from the somewhat stagy rift of the Roosevelt-Taft era.

Theodore Roosevelt was an accident in Republicanism and really a political individualist who lacked the disciplined nature essential to success within the party mechanism. The really great Presidents have all been men keenly aware of the partisan role and protective of their party relationship. Roosevelt was something of a prima donna, who couldn't bear to pass up the great-man role for the great partisan politician's more difficult and deliberate task. He could not have been a skilled and enduring leader of any party, for he was too impetuous, in a sense too wild and always too impatient to deal with what is inevitably a great, slow-moving and complicated machine, when he could achieve a more dramatic if ultimately less lasting effect by tramping ahead on his own. It is not insignificant that, having dropped the Republican Party like a hot potato before the 1912 election, he dropped the Progressive Party like a hot potato right after it. Eager to stamp his vigorous personality on a party, he was reluctant to let a party do much stamping of him. And he fancied himself much more of a political innovation than he really was. Throw away his speeches and count his deeds, and you have a pretty temperate orthodoxy.

The essential trouble with Theodore Roosevelt was that, in his compulsion to be personally an institution, he did not have the temperament to identify himself with a national point of view. The great conservatives and the great progressives invariably represented the view of one segment or the other of the population and associated themselves with it. Franklin Roosevelt, unqualifiedly speaking for the forgotten man, and

McKinley, with equal directness identifying himself with the business interests, both framed programs reflecting not themselves alone but the forces with which they allied themselves. Theodore Roosevelt on the other hand played it alone, casting himself in the role of a referee. He would crack a big stick over the big corporations if he thought they got out of line, and he would trot out the Army with fixed bayonets if labor kicked up with too much fervor. He would send the Navy to take care of any foreign moves of suspicious intent, and he was perfectly willing to discipline the whole world if occasion arose. To the Presidency, his career as police commissioner followed him, and in a very literal sense he was the most forceful man ever to occupy the White House. He proposed to police the nation into what was good for it.

Roosevelt was the victim of his own conceits, and he made so much noise that the Republican Party was a victim of his utterances. Actually he was not nearly the fearful positivist that he liked to convey the impression of being, but he managed the appearance with such success that he turned out to be a costly visitation upon the party. He gloried in the strong word and was always, to a conspicuously irritating extent, going around shouting, "Bully!" and "Big Stick" and waving the threat of the Army, Navy or Militia around like a saber. His was easily the most vociferous stewardship in our history but it was far from the most progressive, and if its activities had been commensurate with its noise, it would have been by far the most turbulent. But as an administration it had no resounding effect on the destiny of the republic, and its only permanent memorial is the Panama Canal, which was far less of a political than an engineering triumph. Its permanent effect was equally lasting but less positive—to dislodge Republicanism from the line of its logical development.

The highly extroverted personality of Roosevelt prevented

him from assuming his appropriate role in the history of Republicanism—which should logically have been an extension of McKinley conservatism. By instinct himself a conservative and understanding much less the rising importance of labor than either McKinley or Hanna, Roosevelt subscribed to the theory, which was not without some sound aspects, that bigness in corporations could never be legislated out of the economic structure without defying economic evolution, and that they had therefore to be regulated carefully ("thoroughgoing control" was Roosevelt's more vigorous phrase for it) in order to protect the national welfare, rather than be dissolved. According to Hanna, McKinley, had he lived, would unquestionably have acted against the same trusts as Roosevelt, and William Howard Taft acted against almost twice as many in his one term as Roosevelt did in almost two. The regulating of trusts was a Republican measure and a logical implement of conservatism before Roosevelt, and yet Roosevelt made such a resounding commotion about it, as he did about everything else, that many a Republican businessman who didn't read very much thought that it was a Roosevelt innovation. Accordingly, Roosevelt acquired the reputation of being a red-hot progressive, and the party was somewhat relieved to hear that Taft was decided on to be the candidate in 1908. In its subsequent effort to keep away from a completely verbal and illusionary progressivism, the Republican Party thereafter kept away also from any genuine conservatism.

Since 1908 Republicanism has been without a sense of direction, badly confused and dedicated, as much as anything, to a do-nothingness rather than to a clear reactionism. The Harding-Coolidge-Hoover regime was, indeed, a later symptom and not the immediate cause of this negativism, and so were all the attendant oddities. As a matter of historical fact, it is quite possible to fix the Theodore Roosevelt era as the turning point and to discern a kind of retrogressive pattern. During the Taft administration, Republicanism rejected the enlightened conservativism, which was popular in intent though privileged in method; and the die was cast when the Payne-Aldrich tariff—a prime example of privileged conservatism which would have startled McKinley and Hanna for its brazen ignoring of popular interests—was crammed down the affable Taft's throat. This legislation, written in secret by a Senatorial cabal, presaged in method the return of the party to the Congressional-combine rule that disrupted the nation in the Reconstruction days, and it entertained the same contempt for the President as the sole elective official of all the people. The ruling cabal was bent not on conservativism at all but on retrogression.

Conditions within the party were ideal for the throwback to Grant's days. Taft, though by training and experience one of the most likely of possible Presidents, was by nature too weak and too disinterested in political processes, to stave it off or even to offer more than token resistance. Theodore Roosevelt, having chosen his successor and none too prudently, was off in Africa, brandishing his weapons in the jungle as he had in the White House. And the strong men in Congress, such as Aldrich and Lodge, were riding high. They were epitomized to the extent of caricature by the dictatorial Speaker Joe Cannon of the House. After Woodrow Wilson's domestic reforms, this kind of control of Republicanism reasserted itself with the nomination of Harding. The ensuing corruption, however individual in incidence, cannot be casually brushed aside as a few personal betrayals of the President, for it was all too close to the kind that afflicted Grant's administration. Apparently when you get a President willing to abrogate the strength of his office, you get an administration also that is not too resistant to corruption. The absence of recorded condemnation is not insignificant. Even if the entire Harding Cabinet was in total ignorance of the evils while they were happening, not one spoke emphatically in denunciation of them after they were common knowledge—not such men as Charles Evans Hughes, Herbert Hoover or the Vice-President and successor, Calvin Coolidge. In fact, Coolidge as President of the United States felt it was necessary to call in a third person, the Chief Justice, to ask Daugherty, the alleged defaulter, to resign from the Cabinet as Attorney General. This behavior, particularly in view of the fact that the great majority of the Cabinet unquestionably deplored the ethics of the Fall-Daugherty element, suggests very strongly something more revealing than a mistaken gentlemanliness: it suggests the view that the corruption was regarded as, though not an ordinary part of politics, an ordinary risk of political administration.

During the Coolidge administration, the positivism of McKinley had descended completely to a principle of do-nothing and, by the time of Herbert Hoover, to a conviction of can't-do-anything. The real victim of this was Hoover himself, who was forced to preside over the greatest emergency since the Civil War on a legacy of government impotence. This solitary and dedicated man, unschooled in politics and utterly unimaginative in statecraft, surveyed the wreckage around him and confessed defeat. "Save the surface and you save all" had been the Republican conviction, and now there seemed no way even to patch up the surface.

VI

The amazing fact of American politics since 1930 is not that the Democrats have shown such consistent strength but that the Republicans have shown any strength at all. For the Republican Party still shows no essential understanding of the proportions and of the impact upon old political values of the Depression— far less indeed than the people have seemed to have intuitively.

This would be comparable to the situation of the Democrats after the Civil War, if the Democrats had minimized the importance of that conflict and systematically denied that it had altered the ante-bellum values for good. For what the Civil War affirmed was that the Union was superior to the states, and it was an affirmation that came by ordeal even though from the days of John Marshall and later of Jackson it was inevitable. Similarly the Depression and its aftermath affirmed a principle whose origins dated from Jefferson, that any government program was risky which sought to protect and advance the interests of the strongest group and trusted that all would be well with the weaker ones; and it also was an affirmation by ordeal. The Republican Party needs to accept that, even as the Democrats after the Civil War accepted the fact of the Union's priority, as a point of departure and not as a point of conflict. Only in this way can the party come abreast of the people, who know very well that this nation is not on the road to statism simply because it has effected a program to protect the people, not only employees but investors and small independent businesses, from the disastrous effects of a laissez-faire capitalism. It might as well be said that the dietician regulating the use of food is out to destroy the benefits of food, as that a party committed to the regulation of capitalism is out to destroy its benefits.

Moreover, in politics—particularly in an age of speedy and direct communications—you cannot for long fly in the face of evidence, and more than one observer has been struck with the paradox of businessmen, whose volume has increased steadily since 1932, agreeing among themselves that a free capitalism, freedom of competition and freedom for business to grow have been all but extinguished in this land. Similarly, when the elder statesman of the Republican Party solemnly declares that the economic jig is up, one wonders what the followers of his party in the automobile industry alone can be thinking when the same month they hit a new high record in both production and sales. And the statism argument wears thin when an entire generation sees unemployment and old-age insurance, the regulation of security sales and of credit, the support of farm prices and the protection of bank deposits and mortgages, all realities without anyone's sacrificing his personal liberty to the state.

The great political disservice that this alarm ringing does is that, if a real fire ever breaks out, no one will respond, and then the results may be really upsetting. It is now apparent that the Republicans will have to address themselves less in terms of pessimism and fright and more in terms of optimism and confidence in order to achieve a majority vote of the people. To do this they will have to accept the present and build on it, for the energies of the American people cannot be accommodated by a treadmill, much less by an escalator thrown into reverse.

Nor can the Republicans look to issues of a foreign policy for salvation. For in the absence of imperialism as an issue, any foreign policy of the nation is bound to be bipartisan in intent and—in the present world of outright conflicts and obvious dangers—largely bipartisan in method. Indeed the virtue of the Republicans in supporting the Truman foreign program since the war is somewhat akin to the virtue of a citizen supporting the fire department right after he has seen the most damaging conflagration of his life not far from his own house. The avoidance of stupidity is not in itself inevitably a claim to political preferment.

From all this, it does not follow that the Republican Party is headed for extinction. Indeed a party out of power for a long time is in many ways in less peril than a party in power for a long time, for an appeal based on promises is always less easy to check than one based on performances—a major factor in the ability of the Republicans to gain Congressional power in

1946 and their failure to maintain it in 1948. But the old prescriptions of the Republican Party are now political anachronisms, and until they are replaced by a new set the Republicans are not much less desperate than the physician who spurns penicillin and fights pneumonia with the mustard pack.

Chapter Eight

Third Parties

I

A RECURRING phenomenon in American politics is the third party, a term which has come to include all parties other than the two major ones, and a device as destined to failure in aspirations in the United States as it has been to failure in performance on the European continent. In practical effect, the end of third parties—if they get anywhere—is multiparty government, and the end of multiparty government is instability. A coalition can perform effectively when its existence depends on unanimity in the face of a great problem, such as war, but when the problem ceases to exist the coalition is dissolved and there usually follows control by any minor party which chooses to upset the applecart. If anyone doubts that, despite the absence of a ministerial system, a third party could have the same effect on the United States, all he has to consider is the power of the State-rights Dixiecrats in the Congress.

Third parties in America are invariably one of two types. The first and less important is the single-issue party, whose very definition makes it in all but name a faction and not a party at all. The Prohibition Party, which is of the pleasantly uncomplicated persuasion that the secret to a permanent peace and a permanent prosperity is the barring of liquor, is a somewhat primitive example, and so also is the Vegetarian Party, which thinks that you could achieve the same Elysium by avoiding meats. The political strategy of such organisms used to be the rationalized relating of other issues to their main enthusiasms, much as the Prohibition Party will also stand foursquare for reading the Bible in public schools, abolishing ball games on Sunday and throwing cigarette smokers off the Supreme Court bench. Through this sort of expansion it is quite possible for a third party to grow numerically stronger, in much the manner that an assortment of fundamentalists, Sabbatarians and members of the Anti-Nicotine League might join forces with the Prohibitionists. Then the party can grow large enough to join forces with other factions and get its name on the ballots in national elections. It hopes also, from the multiplicity of its stands, to partake more of the nature of a party and less of a faction.

In the past this has worked, but in ways which almost defy historical analysis. For example, the old Prohibitionists (the oldest of current third parties, having been founded in 1869 and represented in every Presidential election since) adopted planks favoring woman suffrage, since it was assumed with classic impetuousness that women, by and large, would oppose liquor. By 1904, with a Presidential candidate inappropriately named Silas C. Swallow, it was able to poll over a quarter million votes, almost 2 per cent of the total. After both prohibition and woman suffrage became part of the Constitution, the Prohibition Party hit a low of 20,000 votes, or .05 per cent of the total, in the election of 1928, the first evidence of the frailty of its major purpose being its continued existence after that purpose was achieved. After repeal, presumably brought about with the concurrence of the women, the Prohibition Party started all over again, which is not unlike a proslavery party arising after the Civil War, climbing back to 37,000 votes in 1936.

Possessed of less tenacity than the Prohibitionists, other single-issue parties have chosen to adopt additional issues in an effort to grow large enough to enter and exercise their influence in a major party. This strategy was very common before the Civil War, and one third party after another arose to proclaim some cure-all and then expanded until it could march into a major party as a fairly imposing bloc.

The original strength of both the Whigs and the Republicans owed much to this tendency. The Antimasonic Party was started to spread the notion that Masonry was the greatest evil of the country in the 1830's, but by the time it was in the Whig locker in 1836 it had also by some strange concatenation concluded that related evils were low tariffs, regulatory taxes on banks, Andrew Jackson, the Democratic Party and the Unitarian Church. The course of Antimasonry was strange: its original premise was that Masonry was in league with wealth to exploit the poor; in about six years it was a faction of the party that stood for protecting the concentrated interests against violation by the rising masses.

This pattern of diverted evolution has been characteristic of many single-issue third parties, another classical example being the Liberty Party of William Lloyd Garrison, which was of course ardently dedicated to the abolition of slavery but ended up in the camp of Northern conservatism after a temporary identification with another third party, the Free-Soilers. A little later yet another third party, the Know-Nothings or Native Americans, obsessed with the idea that immigrants and the Roman Catholic Church were the major troubles of the day, was visited upon the nation, later to join the new Republican Party.

The third parties as single-issue entities had a field day between the end of Jackson's second administration and the Civil War, and some of their peculiar odysseys give the measure of their effectiveness as political instruments. As they were largely monstrosities, their intensity was usually matched by their shallowness; and they became impotent and lost factions, maneuvered skillfully by the opportunists within the major parties. Perhaps the clue to their confused role in political affairs lies in the post-Presidential career of Martin Van Buren, who ran for the Presidency (once successfully) three times between 1836 and 1848. The first two times he was a Democrat. The third time he was a Free-Soiler, candidate of the party succeeding Garrison's Liberty Party—so liberal that it originally thought the Constitution should be thrown out for not having declared itself against slavery. Here we have an ex-Democratic President who became the first candidate of a precursor element of the Republican Party.

After all the convolutions, the fact would seem to emerge that third parties devoted to a single issue, however much they attempt to bolster it by attaching themselves to other issues, are doomed from their beginnings. You have to have a very credulous people to convince them that the welfare and existence of the republic are dependent on one issue and responsive to one nostrum. And no substantial part of the American people, even in the most critical times, has confessed to such a degree of desperation, despite the fact that it is at just such times that the single-issue party becomes most evident. For Americans have inclined to the view that the political party is a practical agency for the carrying out of broad and basic principles of government and not the vehicle of a single specific, applicable to only one problem or to none at all. As will be seen, the major accomplishment of most single-issue parties which have made any political impression has been so to split the vote of the major party nearest their interests that they have managed to elect the major party

most remote from them. But the masochism of the zealot is not
a rare component of the single-issue temperament.

II

More closely related to the partisan structure of American
politics, though often no more realistic than the single-issue
party, is the third party which is formed by splitting from a
major party. These are usually extensions of the right or left
wing of the older party; they have characterized the histories
of both major parties; and they frequently spend themselves in
a single election.

The most recent example was the severance of the right-wing
State-rights Party and the left-wing Progressive Party from the
Democrats in 1948—although neither of these was typical since
both were really single-issue parties. The State-rights faction
were frankly so, their sole complaint being the Democratic
stand on civil rights, and they proclaimed their rebellion in a
formal platform which was easily one of the most amazingly
naïve documents in political history, wherein the Democratic
guarantee of protecting the Constitutional rights of everyone
was assailed as an attempt to replace the Constitution with
totalitarianism. The Progressive Party, although it ranged in
some hysteria all over the lot, was obviously intent on the single
issue of the Cold War, and for all the noise that it managed to
make was an overwhelming failure in every respect. The 1948
Progressives also had another common trait of the splinter third
party, the accommodation of a disgruntled or disappointed
leader from one of the older parties. Thus, the Progressive Party
of 1948 was as much a Wallace movement as it was a pro-Russia
movement, just as the Progressive Party of 1912 was a Roosevelt
movement. In both cases the candidate came first and the platform afterward.

One of the more rampant delusions among third parties is that they can easily become major parties by some process of political evolution. The truth is that every major party that has arisen in America originated as a second party—the Democratic Party to oppose Federalism, and the Whig and Republican parties, successively and not concurrently, to oppose the Democrats. Indeed the third party's very existence usually presupposed an impatience with evolutionary forces in politics and an unrealistic attempt to speed up the processes of history. (An inversion has to be noted here with regard to the singular States-rights Party in 1948, which was a denial of history and an attempt to pretend that nothing had happened since 1840, which was the campaign year the party chose to use in its platform to cite as historical authority for its antediluvian views. But it must be remembered also that the party had no faint aspect of a national organism but merely represented the passions of a sectional prejudice.)

In spite of the freedom with which it uses such words as *liberal* and *progressive,* the splinter party also tends to have little faith in the slower, surer pace of democratic action, for it usually suffers from a Messiah complex and the conviction that the voters are misled. None of them has yet adequately explained how they propose to rescue democracy when they have only contempt for the major parties which are democracy's creatures. The long process of trial and error, of slight gains and broad compromises, of balancing and counterbalancing, which is the essence of democracy, horrifies them, and therefore they are horrified by democracy itself.

In some degree the most useful purpose of the third party is to furnish a mechanism through which its supporters can blow off steam. Usually they are afterward back in the major party from which they split, hoping they have taught it a lesson but probably somewhat more aware of the lesson taught themselves. The third party is taken to be a political detour until the election, and afterward it is recognized to have been a dead-end street. There is nothing left to do but to get back on the main road.

Transitory, one-sided, politically immature and unrealistic as they are, the third parties have seldom had a determining effect on the destiny of the nation, but they have sometimes sprung from high corrective motives which, though seldom achieving their immediate ends, have had a salubrious effect on the major parties from which they split. But this role can be easily over-emphasized, for it is difficult to distinguish the artificial accelerations induced by such splits and the natural accelerations which would have come anyway. Moreover, there is probably no area of human activity where men are more anxious to justify their actions verbally and rationalize their errors than in politics. For this reason third parties are very apt to rise carefully after defeat, shake the dust from themselves and proclaim that they really won a moral victory because one of the major parties stole part of their platform. The documentation of their claims is another matter.

Probably the most justified third party in history was the Liberal Republican movement of the early 1870's, when many able men of the Republican Party were completely disgusted with the corrupt machinations of the Congressional cabal and the political nonentity Grant. The Liberal Republican movement attracted virtually all the honest intellects in the party, but the politicians who had a score to settle with the entrenched powers moved in and took the new party right out of their hands. The unhappy and inconsistent Horace Greeley was given the nomination, fought a hopeless and grueling campaign against Grant and the spoilsmen, and was in his grave three weeks after the election. Probably originally under more enlightened sponsorship than any third party, the split of the

Liberal Republicans from the Republican Party had absolutely no effect on the old party at all, and all the evils they protested continued unabated. Never was the imprudence of reform by a new party more obvious; instead of correcting the party from within, reshaping it and purifying it even if only minutely, the decampment left the corruptionists in complete control and more victorious than they would have been had there been no split at all.

The obligation almost every element feels when it splits from a major party is to go to doctrinal extremes that it would not have insisted on if it had risen to ascendancy within that party. There is probably some principle of being as well hanged for a sheep as a lamb in all this, but it is doubtless more intentionally done to attract attention and votes.

The Populists of 1890 involved themselves in such a fallacy and undoubtedly weakened themselves thereby. The only third party between the Civil War and Theodore Roosevelt's Progressives to garner an electoral vote, the Populists filled the role which the Democrats temporarily abrogated and offered the only meaningful opposition to pre-McKinley Republicanism. Under Benjamin Harrison's Presidency, the nation was sliding into a kind of servitude to concentrated interests that had about as much relationship to a free capitalism as prohibition has to temperance. Populism, since Cleveland's candidacy offered no relief from the Democrats, attempted an answer. But it furnished an alternative so extreme that to many people the cure seemed a little worse than the ill. It was at the height of the railroads' corrupting influence, but the cure offered by Populism was not remedial legislation but the taking over of the railroads, and the telephone and telegraph as well, by the government—although the government was hardly justifying itself at the time as the custodian of lesser matters. It was not enough to create some economic orderliness: national banks had to be abolished and silver coined freely; in addition and for good measure, the President could have only one term—a specific as popular with progressives when conservatives are in power as it is with conservatives when progressives are in power. So desperate for progressive action was the nation that even these innovations attracted nearly a fifth of the number of Cleveland or Harrison voters, and they carried six states and sent fifteen men to both houses of Congress. But in 1896, four years later, it was safely swallowed up and thoroughly digested by the Democratic Party, settling for the solitary expedient of free silver. Even the impassioned oratory of Bryan was not in itself enough to account for the abrupt collapse of Populism. It failed because it lacked moderation, the chronic shortage of the third party.

After Populism and until Theodore Roosevelt decided that his hand-picked successor, Mr. Taft, was a failure, the third-party movements were single-issue factions, Republicans opposed to the gold standard forming a splinter of Silver Republicans, and Democrats opposed to free-silver coinage forming a splinter of Gold Democrats—both of which metallurgical dissents got nowhere. But the split of 1912 was easily the most far-reaching third-party movement in history, even though it ended not with a bang but a whimper. Paradoxically, it was both bigger and smaller than a mere rift in the Republican Party. The progressive spirit flared all over the country during the first decade of the present century, fanned by a new breed of historian-journalist-crusaders whose persuasive and revealing writings were read eagerly in the popular magazines and in books. Lincoln Steffens, Ida Tarbell, Ray Stannard Baker, Samuel Hopkins Adams—all these were household names, and their work was far more than empty sensationalism. They knew what they were talking about and cited the evidence relentlessly. Not since slavery was the conscience of the nation so aroused; and in one spot after another it expressed itself in the political successes of reform candidates, first sweeping municipalities and then entire states—Wisconsin, California, Missouri, New York—stretching from one coast through the Midwest to the other. Moreover, the reform governments were getting things done, political machines were breaking down, the bargaining alliances were weakening, social advances replaced privileged protection as subjects of legislation. Originating in the heart of the country and cutting across class lines, the movement was as spontaneously American as the Declaration of Independence, and there was no stopping it by ascribing it to influences of foreign radicalism, disgruntled failures or ill-informed rebels. Familiar and respected names in politics, education, agriculture and the professions were associated with the movement. The achievement and reputation of Robert La Follette in Wisconsin spread across the country. And the movement had none of the limitations of a political faction but all the breadth and scope of an incipient political party. Its method, in fact, was to assert itself within the Republican Party and wrest it from the political grip of the machines. Democrats, Republicans, independents and those who had long before given up all hopes for any partisan politics watched it eagerly. It was larger than and prior to the organic split that came to the Republican Party in the convention of 1912, and its political strength under the indicated Presidential candidacy of La Follette was more promising than that of any new force since Lincoln's in 1860.

No movement of such dimensions could catch the major parties without warning. Careful calculations were made, and the interested powers behind Republicanism determined, since they could not hope to stop it with Taft, to stop it with that fire-breathing dragon of progressivism, Theodore Roosevelt, whose nostrils had once before exhaled flames and left those same powers unscorched. With his vehement campaigning for the Republican nomination, the Progressive voices would be drowned out even if it meant borrowing, at least temporarily, their words. Roosevelt went into the Republican convention with a slate of pledged delegates to absorb the expected revolt behind the name of La Follette. This he succeeded in doing, but the Taft-controlled National Committee refused to seat some of his delegates and steam-rollered through the nomination of Taft. Not graceful in defeat, Roosevelt and his delegates stamped out and started a party of their own.

Laying aside his big stick for the bellowing of the Bull Moose (which is what he said, accurately enough, that he felt like), Roosevelt proclaimed himself in favor of all the progressive legislation which during seven years in the Presidency he had done little to advance, including the eight-hour day—although he had once charged that agitation for a twelve-hour day was un-American and socialistic. Legislation outlawing corrupt practices, providing for primaries and the popular election of Senators, establishing conservation and a Department of Labor—for all these things he went crusading, bringing his enormous energies to the support of a progressivism which he had branded four years earlier as "fool radicalism." When it was all over and the ballots counted, he had broken Taft, leading him by over six hundred thousand votes. But progressivism found its real spokesman in Woodrow Wilson, who led Roosevelt by over two million votes. Five years later Roosevelt told Lodge that the Progressives were "an utterly hopeless nuisance" anyhow, and he refused to have any traffic with them in 1916. After one last gasp in 1924, under the aging La Follette, who adopted a hopelessly confused platform incorporating a few inanities, Progressivism as a third party was dead.

Third-party hopefuls are fond of pointing to the Progressive Party of 1912 and its eighty-eight electoral votes as evidence of the potentiality of the third party as an institution. In doing so, they misread history badly. The Progressive movement of that era was promising so long as it remained an insurgent and positive part of a major party. It was doomed from the moment that Roosevelt turned it into a partisan schism to promote his own candidacy. Its effect was simply to split the Republican vote between the Republican incumbent and his Republican predecessor. It was no more promising of the possibilities of a third party than the vote of Calvin Coolidge would have been in 1932 if he had decided to run against Herbert Hoover.

III

One of the most articulate and easily the most hopeful citizen of the United States is Mr. Norman Thomas, a man of considerable intelligence and gracious manner, who is equally at home on the university campus, in the drawing room, in the chancel and at a labor meeting. Since 1928 it has been the habit of this alumnus and honorary Doctor of Letters of Princeton to run for the Presidency, which he has done in a total of six campaigns— a record beside which those of the three-time losers, Clay and Bryan, are completely unimpressive. In 1932 for every eighteen Americans who cast a vote for Hoover, one cast a vote for Thomas. Mr. Thomas' curious standing as one of the most respected of citizens is matched by the curious position of the party he quadrennially represents, the Socialists.

Neither a single-issue nor a splinter third party and already surviving fifteen Presidential campaigns, Socialism in America has long since become an exercise in the refinement of radicalism; and since Woodrow Wilson and Charles Evans Hughes in 1916, the Socialist candidate, Mr. Thomas, has been the most literate of all Presidential candidates, with the possible exception of John W. Davis, the Democratic nominee of 1924. Moreover, while both the Democratic Party and the Republican Party have been getting progressively more liberal in recent years, the Socialist Party has been getting more conservative, and certainly Mr. Thomas' campaigning could serve as a neglected model of temperance for the major-party opposition. Nevertheless, Socialism has been so clearly on the wane that, if the present trend continues, it will be a more exclusive club than the Senate in a few years. It reached its peak during the Taft administration, when Eugene Debs received one vote for every four that Taft got and for every four and a half that Theodore Roosevelt mustered. Its percentile decline was steady thereafter until the Hoover administration brought about an upward trend in 1932, which has subsided ever since. If the Socialist Party were more given to politics than to theorizing, therefore, it would encourage the election of Republicans.

Only briefly, at its beginning, was American Socialism associated with Marxism, and that was in 1869 when the National Labor Union dispatched a delegate to the First International in London. Nothing much happened, however, until 1876, when the International broke up, and in the subsequent free-for-all there was a separate socialist party in America for every shade of opinion and every degree of loyalty or repugnance to Marx. The first American Socialist Party, which called itself Socialist Labor, to get anywhere at all was formed that year and was independent of the Marxians. By 1892 it managed to get thirty-six thousand votes out of some fourteen million for the Presidency. No one paid much attention to Socialism until Eugene Debs and Victor Berger split from this party in 1899 to form the Socialist Party, which soon outgrew its parent, although the Socialist Labor Party still appears on the ballot. For all practical purposes the Debs-Thomas Socialist Party has represented Socialism in America in this century. Its failure has been about as complete as it could be, and there is a pleasant air of unconcern about that failure even within the party. Mr. Thomas' political party simply has no taste for politics. Basking in the sun of its own idealism, it is content to sit on the shore, dabbling its toe in the political waters but never really diving in. In this reluctance to get into the maelstrom of politics, it displays less coyness than wisdom. Primarily an intellectual movement, it is scarcely a political party at all and treats such victories as the mayorship of Bridgeport as casually as it treats its overwhelming defeats. It rests its case on the spiritual appeal of Socialism and patiently awaits its acceptance by a people more given to competitive activity than to communal theorizing.

It will probably wait a long time. For all the experience of the years and for all the injections of new bloods, the Puritan compulsion to associate successful living with material evidence still remains strong in this country. This is something the European finds difficult to understand in the American character, for there is no fact of American life more important than the extrapecuniary appeal of the profit motive and the extraeconomic force of capitalism. Bishop Lawrence once said, in a much indicted statement, that riches and godliness were in league, and the bishop was being literal but neither foolish nor apologetic. In the New England and Virginia wilderness, the godly man worked hard to clear the land or to build ships. The visible measure of his worth and therefore of his "godliness" was his practical achievement, which soon became also the measure of his wealth. Except in the clergyman's study or the schoolroom, the man of contemplation or of art was a luxury in the community—tolerated, maybe, but neither rich nor godly. With conquest of the wilderness similarly the goal of westward-moving America for the next two centuries, material success meant the justification of life and the respect of one's fellows. Men would work to accumulate more profits long after they had acquired all they might need—as a matter of morality and public approval and not merely for material gain. Despite the taxes, they still do in America. And it is still the land of opportunity, however weary the cliché, for economic betterment.

Meanwhile the usual good sense of the majority of its people has turned to sources of correction at dangerous times, and the moderation of those corrections has left capitalism sufficiently flexible to provide the floors of socialism without the limitations of its ceilings. Moreover, for all its youth, America is one of the oldest of nations in the continuity of experience under a single political and economic structure; and if it has seen that structure shelter at times great evils, it has seen under it also the accomplishment of greater goods. It has stood always in greater danger of the unimaginative fears of those who would protect it than from the challenges of those who have assailed it. If it can be protected from its protectors, it will probably last far beyond any of its contemporaries across the world. Thus far it has been so protected, and the Socialist Party seems to know it.

IV

The importance of the 1948 elections to our political institutions was largely lost in the playful pleasure of the pundits in performing public penance, in the habitual charges that the death warrant of the republic had been signed, and in the triumphant assumption that had any other result obtained it would be headed back to the Dark Ages. It was an election held under the spell of no great national crisis—the first such since 1928—and sparked by no outstanding personality—the first since 1924. No emotional (except for the Southern defection), religious, chauvinistic or other extrapolitical issue was involved. It was the most dispassionate definition of choice in political values—made all the sharper by the two third parties, one to the right and one to the left—expressed by the American people in well over a generation; for in 1916 the issue was war, in 1920 and 1924 there was never a really clean choice between Cox and Harding and between Coolidge and Davis, in 1928 there were Smith's background and the Hoover legend, and from 1932 through 1944 depression and war. In 1948, on the other hand, the war had been over for three years; there was no cleavage on foreign affairs; the lunacy fringe was accommodated on the left by Mr. Wallace and his musical running mate and on the right by Governor Thurmond; each of the major candidates was smaller than his party and each appeared to be an honest representative of it. Clearly the election was neither a conflict between personalities nor a call for action in the face of crisis. Accordingly it had the effect of asserting the dominant political trend in America for our times and it also cleared the political air.

Formally, on the lesser side, the election proclaimed the independence of the Democratic Party from the support of the South—a condition which was mathematically deducible since 1932 but never politically emphasized. The Southern State-rights Party was careful to point out, in their platform, that in 1920 the Democratic Party won no electoral votes except in the South, but erred gravely in failing to note also that, in 1932, 1936, 1940 and 1944, the Democratic candidate would have won had the solid South to a man voted for a Republican or not at all, and that when half of their electoral vote went to Hoover in the 1928 election, in the first bolt of the South, the outcome of the election did not depend on it at all. In practice this means that the reactionary bloc of Democrats in the South are the great dispensables of American political life, and they haven't much choice except to adjust themselves to the enlightenment of the mid-twentieth century or to preserve a kind of sectional political aloofness that is for national electoral purposes all but useless.

A more important but still minor element of the political

climate clarified by the election of 1948 was revealed in the limited vote acquired by the other third party, the Progressive Party, which was smaller than that of the State-rights Party and only one fourth of what the venerable La Follette received in 1924. The sparseness of the Wallace vote was the final turning back of the nation from letting world affairs drift and its final assumption of maturity as a responsible and constructive force in the world. For the Progressive Party of 1948 was largely dedicated to the reversal of the nation's foreign policy; and its defeat, coming as it did only three years after a devastating war, was proof positive that there was no emotional retreat from unpleasant realities as there had been after other wars in our history. The fact that Wallace was friendly to the Soviet state was actually of secondary importance, for the possibility of any pro-Communist ground swell was so utterly inconsistent with the whole heritage and nature of America that even Wallace was aware of the liability of Communist support, though not very vigorous about repudiating it. Most Americans recognized Wallace as a latter-day Horace Greeley, whose idealism did not stop him from urging that the Civil War be called off when the going got rough, and one suspected that the similar confusions of Wallace were also more mystical than malicious in their origins. In a pitiable campaign his followers met with a kind of revival-meeting emotionalism that had not been seen since Theodore Roosevelt led those very different Progressives of 1912 in the singing of "Onward Christian Soldiers" and William Jennings Bryan was having America crucified on a cross of gold. The student of manners may in the future, indeed, find that the fullest meaning of the Wallace party was that it sounded the last fragmentary echo of the political age of evangelism, with the Presidential candidate preaching realities out of existence and his coadjutor, Senator Taylor, wailing folk ballads as a nunc dimittis.

Of far more importance than either the Southern revolt's completely predictable futility or the Progressives' staggering reverses was the death of the third party as a device for partisan realignment, confirming rather than dislodging a political tradition as old as the nation but one frequently underestimated. The partisan structure in America is more like a skyscraper than it is like a hangar. Political parties do not spread out on one level, including all on a level within them. They stretch up and down, each including in its following representatives of the business, professional, farming and laboring communities. In the greatest industrial nation in the world there is no great labor party, and in the most conservative nation in the world there is no nominal conservative party. Senator Wayne Morse, a leftish liberal, is not disowned by the Republicans, and the most Republican state in the Union, Vermont, produces as Senators the liberal Aiken and Flanders. One of investment capital's biggest operators, Joseph Kennedy, is a Democrat, and one of their best legal spokesmen, John W. Davis, was the Democratic candidate against a lower-middle-class Ohioan. Parties in America are inclusive and not exclusive. As more than one commentator has seen, that is the reason why the government could shift from one party's control to another at four and often two-year intervals with no serious repercussions. It is why a majority can shift from one party's support to another and why a Republican's able Secretary of State can become a Democrat's able Secretary of War. It is why also the third-party movement can be expected to add nothing constructive beyond an occasional jab, fore or aft, to the basic political conflict. Destructively, of course, it can prevent a major candidate from winning a state by splitting his vote; but once the anachronistic Electoral College is abolished, even that Pyrrhic victory will be deprived it.

Part Three

THE MECHANICS:

POLITICAL METHODS IN AMERICA

———

General propositions do not decide concrete cases.
—OLIVER WENDELL HOLMES

Chapter Nine

Conventions

THE CONSTITUTION NEVER MENTIONED NOMINATING CANDI-
DATES FOR OFFICE, AND SO THE CONVENTION EVOLVED—A
STRANGE AFFAIR INDEED AND ONE WITH GRAVE DANGERS
WHEN MANIPULATED BY UNSCRUPULOUS MEN AND YET NOT
ENTIRELY UNSUCCESSFUL

I

"THERE they smoke tobacco till you cannot see from one end of the garret to the other. There they drink flip, I suppose, and there they choose a moderator, who puts questions to the vote regularly; and selectmen, assessors, collectors, fire-wards, and representatives are regularly chosen before they are chosen by the Town." Twelve years before the outbreak of the American Revolution, John Adams so described the forerunner of the party convention. Over a century and a half afterward, Harry Daugherty, who had probably never read a word of Adams but who indulged in President making, said, "I think we can afford to take chances that about eleven minutes after two, Friday morning of the convention, when ten or twenty weary men are sitting around a table, someone will say, 'Who will we nominate?'" The wide chronological distance between the remarks, made in 1763 and in 1920, is significant. The smoky quality of the political convention, with its manipulations and its bargainings and its deals, has persisted in partisan procedures throughout our history. If most men have questioned from time to time what this cynical mechanism called a convention has to do with government by the people, there is little wonder. On the surface it would appear to be a device to limit the choice of the voters at the actual elections. And yet even the most radical parties have resorted to the convention as the ultimate implement of party action.

The American party convention is the product solely of a natural growth and has almost no theoretic background. It was born out of desperation, for there is no mention in the Constitution of how a Presidential candidate is to be chosen. The original electors, whom the Constitution makers hoped would be the most enlightened and stable citizens of the states, were simply to choose the best man available. Soon the Congressional leaders were discussing the most likely possibilities and eventually held caucuses to determine whom to support. The practice before long was referred to as King Caucus, for it created an autocracy that in substance told the people who was going to be President. Government was for, and neither of nor by, the people; and there was almost a chain of inheritance, with the office going to a survival of the old administrations—John Adams was Washington's Vice-President, and Jefferson had been his Secretary of State; Madison was Jefferson's Secretary of State; Monroe was Madison's Secretary of State; John Quincy Adams was Monroe's Secretary of State. Not until Jackson was the Secretarial succession stopped; and if it hadn't been for the rise of popular voting as a means of choosing electors, John Quincy Adams' Secretary of State, Henry Clay, would probably have succeeded his chief. Anyhow, four Secretaries of State in a row were elevated to succeed their appointers up to 1824. Since then none has moved directly to the Presidency, and only two former Secretaries of State out of forty-two—Martin Van Buren and James Buchanan—were elected in their later years. The death of the caucus, in fact, killed the Presidential prospects of Cabinet members, Herbert Hoover being the only one elected directly from the Cabinet in over a century.

By the time of the Jacksonian movement, when the people were no longer content to leave their political destiny to the control of the enlightened few, wide dissatisfaction was felt at the somewhat lofty and private way Presidential nominees were selected. But there was no legal force behind the legislative caucus; and though it had accounted for the candidacies and elections of four Presidents, from John Adams to James Monroe, it was relatively easy to discard. By the campaign of 1832, the party convention was born. The first convention was held by a third party, the Antimasons, who had foregathered in Baltimore in the fall of 1831, nominating for the Presidency William Wirt, for twelve years the Attorney General of the United States and, strangely, a Mason. The Antimasons never got very far as a political party, but they established the nominating convention for good. No other means has been used since to name Presidential candidates.

By 1840 the conventions assumed also the function of summarizing what the party stood for in a document known as a platform. This soon became an exercise in juggling, a kind of literary gymnastic taken very seriously by the drafters but not by anyone else, including the candidates. The actual intent of the platform, of course, is to have a little bit of something for everybody—a perfectly legitimate aim for a political party that hopes to court a majority—and it usually has all the objectivity and maturity of a soap advertisement, speaking of the party in glowing terms, the wonders that it has performed in the past and the rare and advantageous qualities it has for coping with the future. About the last place a political historian would go to investigate the principles of a party would be to its platforms, for it would be like reviewing a play by consulting its advertisements. Yet there is something consistent in this, for the convention itself has much more about it of the glaring advertisement, the trick publicity and the captivating but meaning-

less slogan than it does of political principle or public service.
And if anyone hastens to charge all this up to the effect of
advertising and commercial ballyhoo on the national character,
he would do well to remember that it had hit its permanent level
long before the development of either. "Tippecanoe and Tyler
Too" came long before "Hasn't Scratched Yet," and political
candidates were 99 44/100 per cent pure long before any soap
made the claim.

II

The convention in action is a carefully devised system to do
things the hard way, and it has actually only one thing to do—
to nominate a candidate for President—the platform being piti-
fully incidental.

Hypothetically this major function could be achieved with
eminent satisfaction in three or four hours in a remote and
quiet room by about a hundred informed members of the party.
In its period of finest flowering a political party may have three
or four representatives of almost equally high ability, leadership
and political attraction. In its less handsome periods it may have
no outstanding man and must consider the most promising of
those of lesser distinction. Usually it has one or two men who
might qualify. One would think that, if the party in each state
sent two of its best men to join with two each from the other
forty-seven states, the ninety-six could hit upon an average of
choices no worse than that realized by the convention. But
instead, every four years, from a thousand to over twelve hundred delegates, tens of thousands of spectators, hundreds of
political manipulators, scores of brass bands, novelty venders,
bosomy sopranos and hirsute basses, lobbyists and general hang-
ers-on converge in sweltering turmoil upon one of the larger
cities for from three days to two weeks. In the midst of the

resulting confusion of singing, shouting, parading, reheating of old feuds and creating of new, bickering, bargaining, jockeying for position and general contrivance, a man is named as the party's choice to be the President of the United States. How much careful thought, close analysis and judicial appraisal can go into the process can easily be deduced, and it doesn't take much to produce a Harding.

Yet the party convention cannot be called a failure, for the uncluttered reason that its purpose is not to seek the best candidate at all but to decide on the one most likely to win or least likely to lose—a corollary to the proposition that politics is the art of the possible and not of the ideal. Of course, if there are selfish, stubborn or cynical men in control of the convention or of enough votes, as there were in the Republican convention of 1920 and the Democratic convention of 1924, the party simply proclaims that there is something more important than principles and that is ambition or vengeance. Such occasions should proclaim also the time to give up the convention as a nominating device, but there is an artificially induced magic in practical politics and the most intelligent operative in the field can succumb to it.

Mr. Charles Evans Hughes, for example, was far too brilliant a man to believe that Harding was of Presidential stature; but he went along, however self-consciously, with the general persuasion that the convention choice was very wise, after the show was over. Presidential candidates do not win the nomination with greatness, but the magic lies in their somehow assuming greatness with the nomination. The persistent nomination of Bryan by the Democrats conferred on the old fundamentalist the appearance of a stature he never attained, and the half-ludicrous, half-pitiable efforts of the Republicans to make something of the suitably diffident Landon in 1936 convinced more than one knowledgeable journalist, who knew better, that the

Republicans had really stumbled on something. Much of this conversion is done simply by wearing the customers out, so that after enough sweating in the convention hall, inability to get taxis, putting up with noise and surviving other general nuisances, the good partisan will be unwilling to assume that any such concentrated effort by a thousand of his peers could possibly be abortive. He will go along with his party's choice, and he will also defend it.

To perpetuate this element of emotionalism in the convention that the leaders hope will keep the party united after the political band-aids have been applied to all the prenomination abrasions, it is necessary to make the convention last at least three days. This is done by the strategic employment of music, religion, speeches and formalities involving the organization of the convention. Every session is opened with a song and a prayer, and the entire first day is devoted to electing and listening to "temporary" officials. The latter, after their transitory burst of glory, are thrown out of office on the second day when the permanent officers are elected. Both the temporary and permanent chairmen come equipped with hour-long addresses, although theoretically they are not elected until a matter of minutes before they are delivering them. Meanwhile, two committees of some consequence have been meeting and return their reports.

The Committee on Credentials reports before the permanent officers are elected; and this committee, which deals in the hard mathematics of who is going to be recognized as a delegate and therefore allowed to vote, can stack the convention at the outset. (In 1912, when the Republican leaders observed the mounting progressivism within the party, the Committee on Credentials simply reported an authorization of Taft delegates and a challenge of Roosevelt delegates. The Taft delegates were seated.) After the permanent officers are elected and the permanent chairman repeats the import of the temporary chairman's address of the preceding day, the Committee on Resolutions reads the platform, which Wendell Willkie once called "fusions of ambiguity."

If it is anything at all, the platform is big enough for everybody to climb on, and is consequently more conspicuous for generalities than for precision. It must, and invariably does, contain violent blame for the opposition, high praise for itself and a sliver for everybody, from those interested in a united Ireland to those favoring more irrigation. It seldom says what the party will do if elected, for the Committee drafting it usually doesn't know. The candidate will take care of that, but the platform is drafted and accepted before the candidate is named; in 1948, for example, Taft, Dewey, Joseph Martin, Stassen, General MacArthur, Carroll Reece or Vandenberg would have run on the same platform. But they would not necessarily have felt that it meant the same thing, and they might not have bothered to read it at all.

From the usual platforms, indeed, it would be quite possible for the candidates of the major parties to exchange clauses (or planks) indiscriminately. There is everything to prove, so far as party platforms are concerned, that the Republicans are the prolabor party in America and the Democrats the proinvestor party. From the 1936 Republican platform you could prove that the Democrats caused the collapse of 1929, though they had not been near the White House for a decade, and that the Republicans were curing it. From every Democratic platform from 1920 to 1932, you could prove that the people really wanted the Democrats in power all the time, and from the Republican platforms from 1932 to 1948, that they really wanted the Republicans there. For the party platform takes a no less mystical view of the past than it does of the future. Thus, though the convention makes a great fuss about its platform (which it is careful to do before nominating begins, lest no one stay for it), everyone knows that it is largely wasted motion, that the opposition is not going to believe it, the public is not going to read it, and the candidates are going to make their own versions as they go along in the campaign.

But the platform, and not the candidate, is nevertheless the cohesive agent that holds the party together and gives the convention its *raison d'être*. It is because the principles that give a party its character and its unity, however, are necessarily so broad and so familiar that the platform itself, newly drafted at each convention, is not only frequently ridiculous but nearly always redundant. It is a little bit as though churchmen, instead of reciting the Apostle's Creed at their services, decided at each service to draft a new one, attempting to break the elements of their belief down in terms applicable to the moment. What might be far more useful for the Resolutions Committee to do would be to write a permanent statement of what the party believes in and what it repudiates, amending it each time the convention meets when the basic tenets of the party's philosophy change.

Most Presidential candidates, after saying in the acceptance speech that the platform is the best ever and the Committee should be congratulated on its work, take the same view of it that Mr. Willkie did, and ignore it. If they have to depend on it during the campaign, then they forget it afterward. It is hard to recall a platform quoted in an inaugural; and the party spokesmen suffer a kind of mass amnesia, as far as the platform is concerned, after election. Dr. A. Lawrence Lowell, who did not habitually make light of political institutions and was always willing to probe below the surface, used to tell a story about a Pullman porter who requested a passenger not to stand on the car platform. The passenger said that he thought a platform was made to stand on, and the porter corrected his impression, telling him it was made to get in on. For most practical purposes, the remark is true also of the party platform.

It is remarkable, because this is true, that the delegations of Alabama and Mississippi walked out on the Democratic convention of 1948. The presence of the civil-rights plank in the party platform no more ensured passage of acts by the Congress giving it effect than would a letter in the *New York Times,* nor would the absence of such a plank necessarily discourage such legislation. What the withdrawal of the Southerners meant was that they did not want to belong to a national party at all, because an emotional attitude was violated, and it happened to be a party plank rather than a candidate that did it. When the Dixiecrats composed their own platform, they defined their own limitations by writing a one-plank platform that said nothing but that they were terribly incensed with the Democrats and everybody else.

If the voters in America went to the polls on election day and were confronted with a ballot summarizing the major party platforms instead of listing candidates, they would be totally unable to make a choice on most issues. In 1948 both parties were for the Truman foreign policy, Palestine, civil rights, more housing, lower taxes, collective bargaining and the right to strike, increased Social Security benefits, adjustment of veterans' benefits, protection of farm prices and development of farm credit, stock-piling of strategic raw materials, development of natural resources, the promotion of competitive business and equal rights for women. They were both against Communism and inflation. It is tempting, in the light of all this, to suggest that something has gone wrong with the two-party system. Actually the similarity is much more indicative of its health than widely differing platforms would be, and it demonstrates that each party is ensuring its usefulness by going after the same majority. It also puts more responsibility on the candidates—

who are after all going to be doing the governing long after the platform belongs among political curiosa.

The party platform survives today for three reasons. One is the force of tradition, surviving from the days when issues were uncomplicated and clear-cut. The gold and silver platforms of the 1890's, the slavery platforms before the Civil War and the land platforms after it were frequently direct, unqualified, unevasive. It made much more sense, although it also involved more political risk, to say whether you were for or against the extension of slavery or the free coinage of silver than to say you are against Communism or inflation, which is a little like saying that you are against the pneumococcus. Moreover, people voted specific issues more in the past than they do now. Today they vote trends, and a political trend is more discernible in a party's record than in its platform. Nevertheless, the tradition continues, and rhetoric and politics go together; and the party platform is still worried into existence by devoted partisans, who seem completely unfazed by its limited role in the campaign.

Another reason why it continues is that, in a practical sense, it affords the party a mechanism for the conciliation of opposing factors or uncongenial elements within it. For example, some of the finest evasive literature in the language can be found in platform planks on prohibition before its repeal—essays to say two things at the same time but neither one too clearly. The platforms' purpose was, of course, to keep both wet and dry elements happy, and they succeeded a surprisingly long time in doing so. The platform can similarly be used to take care of groups seeking preferment in the choice of candidates but whose choice the party has no intention of nominating. It costs nothing to throw these groups a plank in the platform, which shows that they are not being ignored even though they are not being indulged.

Finally, the platform continues because, vacuous as it may be, it is still the only feature of the convention that is not solely concerned with the mechanics of politics and outright manipulation. It is supposed to be concerned with principles, and it is like saying grace before ripping into dinner. But no delegate has been known to stay at a convention only until the adoption of the platform, any more than he would stay at dinner only through the recital of grace.

III

The United States is the most pragmatic nation on the face of the earth, and nowhere is this more apparent than in the way its political representatives go about choosing a Presidential candidate—a pragmaticism that always seems and sometimes is merely abandon. On some Monday in June or July, every fourth year, from six to a score of men, some finely, some fairly and some very badly equipped for the Presidency, have serious hopes of leading a nation of a hundred and forty millions and, increasingly in effect, Western civilization. On the following Monday all but the chosen could walk into any drugstore in the land at lunch hour without diverting an eye from the club special. But the chosen is elevated to a prestige, however inappropriate he might be as a choice and however remote his chances of election, second only to the Presidential incumbent himself, and to an influence which may be completely disproportionate to his past achievements. The process that so selects a man and elevates him has no rules, no serious criteria, no predictable guides. It can happen to almost anyone. The process has puzzled men actively participating in it, and more than one foreign observer has found it difficult to explain how a mechanism that could conclude in 1916 that Hughes was a proper Presidential candidate could conclude in 1920 that Warren Harding was, or could choose Alf Landon in 1936 and Wendell Willkie in 1940.

The key to the puzzle lies in the one word "available"—

which is most meaningful in its very meaninglessness. It means everything and nothing. An available man is not simply one whom you can get to run (for that would qualify everyone); he is also one who can get the nomination, who might conceivably win the election, and who, without necessarily pleasing the majority of the party, will not displease any large minority. Extraneous qualities are more important at the beginning than more relevant political ones: he should not be Catholic, because the United States is still a non-Catholic country; he should not live in the South, because the North won the Civil War; and he should not be divorced, although illegitimate paternity is all right (Cleveland frankly admitted it in the campaign of 1884 and won the election), because the nation is still formally committed against divorce. Beyond these and such other obvious disqualifications as having served a jail term or insulted religion, there are no taboos.

But there are many practical considerations beyond these that contribute to the "available" catchall. Geographically it is helpful to come from New York, because the size of New York's electoral vote is worth courting, and there has not been an election since 1924 when one of the major nominees did not come from New York. The Republicans always had a better chance, however, with Midwest or Western candidates, the only exceptions being Theodore Roosevelt, who turned out to be dangerous anyhow, and Calvin Coolidge, who was first a successor to the Presidency as Roosevelt had been. With Lincoln, Grant, Hayes, Garfield, Harrison, McKinley, Taft, Harding and Hoover, they won—although Harrison, Taft and Hoover failed of re-election. With Governor Dewey of New York they lost twice, and they lost with Willkie of New York (reheating the Hoosier soufflé of his birth never worked), with ex-Governor Charles Evans Hughes of New York and with James G. Blaine of Maine. Until Truman, on the other hand, the Democrats won only with Easterners; in fact the only West-erners they ever nominated were Bryan in 1896, 1900 and 1908 and James M. Cox in 1920, both of whom lost. Of course, the geographic associations of these men are unjustifiably superficial reasons for their victories or their defeats, but "availability" is concerned with superficialities.

To be available for the Democrats is not the same thing as to be available for the Republicans. An available Democrat in 1928 and 1932, for example, had to be damp if not wet on the prohibi-tion issue, but available Republicans had to be dry. The avail-able Republican has to have no enemies in big business if he can help it, while an available Democrat is suspect if he doesn't have some. But an available Democrat can have some enemies in labor (Roosevelt had Lewis, and Truman created a few of his own), while a Republican who doesn't have a good many is suspect. Because, as we have seen, Democrats are in general active Presidents, and Republicans in general passive ones, a Democrat is more available if he is a man of force or strong leadership, like Al Smith or Franklin Roosevelt, while an apostle of negativism like Coolidge or Mr. Landon is attractive to the Republicans. All these generalities are, nevertheless, rel-atively worthless, for there is neither a pattern for choosing a nominee nor absolute requirements for the candidate.

Theoretically a major-party convention chooses a candidate in a sufficiently orderly way. When nominations are in order, the roll of the states is called and any state can respond by nominating a candidate or by yielding to another state farther down on the list which can't wait to nominate someone. Before the first ballot is taken, there is a healthy roster of candidates— some of them with no prayer of a chance to be selected, some of them favorite sons and some of them dark horses. Usually there are one or two strong candidates who gain strength on the second or third ballot and one is named as the party's nominee at some stage before the tenth. The favorite sons, having received the tribute of their own states' confidence in their Presidential stature, drop out—generally having arranged beforehand to throw their delegations to one of the principal candidates. But the dark horses, who are usually distinguished by the remoteness of their chances of being chosen and usually also by a lack of strong qualifications, may climb upward in strength if the principal candidates start slipping. Before 1936 the dark horse had a reasonable chance in the Democratic Party, because a nominee had to get a two-thirds vote and any man strong enough to be a principal aspirant was probably strong enough also to have slightly over a third of the convention against him. An affable dark horse, on the other hand, might have as few against him as he had for him.

When the nominating process operates simply, as it did in 1932 with Roosevelt or in 1944 with Dewey, the chances are good that the convention choice will reflect the opinion of the voters making up the party. There are enough states with preferential primaries and instructed delegates to influence the delegates in other states. Indeed a candidate who loses in a key state's preferential primary frequently eliminates himself from the contest, as Mr. Willkie did in 1944. If he doesn't, the delegates frequently will do it for him, as they did Mr. Stassen in 1948, after his reversal in Oregon. Stassen started to slip on the second ballot, which was far too early, and Dewey was nominated on the third. Taft, on the other hand, began to climb on the second ballot, and if Dewey's agents had not made some off-floor moves to line up the votes of favorite sons as they were released, the convention would have been deadlocked between Dewey and Taft—in which case a dark horse would have galloped away with the nomination much later.

Obviously to anyone attached to democratic processes there is something repugnant about the nominating processes of the convention breaking down and the consequent emergence of some

obscure dark horse as a Presidential candidate, and there is conversely less concern when the man entering the convention with
the largest vote, whether a majority or not, eventually wins.
Reasonably astute management can usually accomplish the latter, but when it fails it is usually due to the stubbornness, the
vindictiveness or the cynicism of men in positions of moral
leadership in the party. Unless they rise to sufficient moral
heights to advance the interest of their party above their personal or factional interests, there is no set of convention bylaws,
rules or voting procedures which could eliminate that smoky
characteristic of scheming and plotting that resulted in the
nomination of Harding in 1920.

IV

There is no method for the examination of party conventions
at work but the case system, for there is no continuous standard
of reference. The classic case of the convention as an utter failure is the one of which Harry Daugherty's prophecy was quoted
earlier. Daugherty went on to make a prediction—a dangerous
business with a dark horse: Harding, the Senator from Ohio,
who entered the convention with 39 votes (not even the entire
Ohio vote), would win. Harding did win, in a political mess
that was the creation less of the convention's institutional shortcomings than of the men who put them to dishonorable use.

Harry Daugherty was not, contrary to legend, the chief vil-
lain at all. He was merely a small Ohio politician, operating on
the ward level, trying to push his man ahead. He had no other
job at the convention and no other responsibility: he was purely
and simply a political manager. But he had the shrewdness to
bide his time and the mentality to seize on the opportunity
presented by the crude machinations of the most disastrous Congressional cabal since the days of Reconstruction, who were the

real nominators of Harding. They controlled the convention and they proposed to control the nominee. The *New York Times* observed knowingly afterward that, if it hadn't been Harding, it would probably have been someone worse.

The convention was opened with the engineered selection of the ringleader of the Senatorial Politburo, the viciously unprincipled Lodge of Massachusetts, as temporary chairman, who managed also to be named permanent chairman. Lodge set the tone of the convention by screaming against Wilson and for a return to nationalism in his address: "We must be now and ever for Americanism and Nationalism and against Internationalism" and "Mr. Wilson . . . must be driven from all control of the government and all influence in it." What was his larger purpose and that of such great statesmen as his colleagues, Smoot, McCormick, Brandegee and Curtis was confided to the young Republican journalist, Mark Sullivan: ". . . the man in the White House must not think he is bigger than the Senators . . . [we wanted] a man who was disposed by nature to seek counsel rather than act independently . . . a man in the White House who would more or less defer to the leaders of his party in the Senate . . . [we] think that the President should not send legislation to Congress to be passed but that Congress should send legislation to the President to be signed."

The cabal saw their chance in the prospect of a mutual canceling out of the strength of General Leonard Wood (a man of honor but an inept politician) and ex-Governor Frank O. Lowden of Illinois, each of whom had about a third of the delegates. Hiram Johnson was the leading runner-up, trailed far behind by Governor Sproul of Pennsylvania, Nicholas Murray Butler of New York and then Harding, with 39 of Ohio's 48 votes. The Lodge gang was further pleased when, by the fourth ballot, Wood had climbed from 287 votes to 314½ and Lowden from 211½ to 289. Obviously, the increases meant that one would neutralize the other. It was time to halt the proceedings and decide on a man who would "defer to" the Senators. Smoot, sitting on the platform, and Lodge, presiding, whispered in consultation, whereupon Lodge recognized Smoot for the purpose of moving adjournment and put it to a vote. There were a sprinkling of "ayes" in the hall and a mighty chorus of "noes," as the Wood and Lowden combined majority shouted it down. With his characteristic contempt for democracy Lodge declared the convention adjourned. The wife of a Republican Congressman and daughter of a Republican President, Alice Longworth, called the convention "wormy"—and was right.

Lodge hastened over to Room 404 in the Blackstone Hotel and, with his errand boy, Senator Curtis of Kansas, and Senator Brandegee, joined the renegade Democrat, "Colonel" George Harvey, at dinner. Harvey's only excuse for being there was his hatred of Wilson, who never recognized him as the great power he fancied himself, and his contempt for the League of Nations, which he had been spending his time raising money from people like Andrew Mellon to defeat. He was neither a Republican nor a delegate to the convention but was for obvious reasons the kind of character Lodge found attractive and useful. As the night progressed in Room 404, this assortment of statesmen decided that Harding was the man, and Charles Curtis was sent out to pass the word to the delegates, while at two in the morning Harvey, who loved the role, summoned Harding and somewhat naïvely asked that rumpled and baffled printer from Marion if there was any reason in his past life why they should not give him the nomination. One would think that he had the answer when Harding blubbered that he needed a little time to think it over. This completely escaped Harvey, who waited for ten minutes while Warren Harding wrestled with his soul in an adjoining bedroom and returned to proclaim his purity. The next day he was nominated for the Presidency. But Mrs.

Harding outguessed the cabal: "I can see but one word written over his head if they make him President, and that word is tragedy."

Senator Lodge, "the scholar in politics" who had neither the discipline nor the ethics of a scholar, must have been pleased with his work at the convention. What could even advanced scholarship make of Harding's double-talk on the League: "The League can be amended or revised so that we may still have a remnant of world aspirations in 1918 builded into the world's highest conception of helpful cooperation in the ultimate realization"?

Before the convention closed, Lodge had other business. Harding, the insipid Senator from Ohio, was safely nominated to the Presidency. It remained to nominate a Vice-President. The Senatorial cabal decided on Senator Irvine Lenroot, as they went into a huddle under the platform; and McCormick was assigned the job of putting the name in nomination, after which it was to be seconded in a planned steam-roller action. Lodge, his work done, went to his hotel and turned the chair over to a henchman, who recognized an Oregon delegate for the purpose, as he thought, of seconding Senator Lenroot. Fed up with the whole spectacle, Oregon nominated Calvin Coolidge, and the convention in open revolt unanimously nominated him. It was clearly a gesture to defy the Lodge Politburo, for Lodge had long ago walked out on the Massachusetts governor, who had ever since shown very little use for Lodge. The men were of different types: Coolidge, honest, shy and negative; Lodge, deceptive, arrogant and positive in his malice.

V

For all the bombast and razzle-dazzle of the convention as an institution, it is impossible to charge such travesties as the 1920 spectacle to its institutional deficiencies. The convention has the limitations of any democratic process, but it has also its advantages. Great and good men have come out of its proceedings as Presidential candidates. Its rate of performance easily matches in merit that of the several Congresses. But it is necessarily as vulnerable as the Congress to the control of evil men. Such men would abuse equally any other system of nominating candidates, and democracy cannot protect itself by making new rules. It has to watch constantly whom it lifts to power, it has to assume nothing, it has to undertake willingly the constant responsibility of alertness. Alertness came to the Chicago convention too late, and so the rebellion against the Lodge usurpation, obvious from the moment he ignored the vote against adjournment, came too late. No majority of those delegates wanted Harding; most had no more than heard of him. They did not choose him, but permitted him to be chosen for them. No institutional changes conceivable by the human mind can make democracy work in the face of such an attitude of irresponsibility and abandon.

And what of the leaders? If Wood and Lowden were hopelessly deadlocked, would it not have been the simple duty of the convention leaders to attempt by their influence to effect a compromise between the two forces? Or, failing that, to put their influence behind the best the party could offer? It was not the convention system that failed so miserably at Chicago in 1920, but the total moral bankruptcy of a party's leadership, epitomized in a phenomenon of malice which was not satisfied to wreck the prospects of world peace but conspired also to wreck the American Presidency. We have witnessed occurrences of similar bankruptcies in parliamentary democracies with their totally different system of selecting prime ministers from their legislatures.

Without abolishing the party convention, there is, however,

opportunity to bring it further from imperfection than it is now. The favorite-son gesture, for example, is time-consuming and always distorts a first ballot. A change in rules requiring endorsement by five or six states could eliminate that kind of nuisance. Extension of preferential primaries would seem a solution, but it might end with forty-eight favorite sons. A national primary has been suggested by both Wilson and Theodore Roosevelt, but some acceptable standard for inclusion of a name on the ballot would be necessary. More useful than either of these would be reforms preserving the convention but reducing its risks. Chastened by the marathon of 1924, the Democrats were able to abolish the two-thirds rule, and there should be a possibility of reducing the number of names on the convention ballots as the voting progresses, so that the choice finally boils down between the two leading contenders rather than by default falling to the least contender. For the purpose of the convention is to name a man devoted to the basic party philosophy and of proved achievements predicated on that philosophy. Obscurity and inoffensiveness are not the standards, when the choosing is tough, by which such a choice can be made.

The "smoke-filled" room has fallen into a permanent place in our political literature by now, and its implications are abhorred by most conscientious citizens. But its odor will linger to taint any other convention at any time unless those same citizens take the choice of their political spokesmen more seriously. The way to correct political evils in a democracy consists less in changing rules and customs than in keeping the Lodges, whether they go by that name or by Hague or Huey Long, in private life where they belong.

Chapter Ten

Campaigns

I

DURING one of William Bryan's three campaigns for the Presidency, he was to address a gathering of rural voters in a local politico's farmyard. The night before the rally, with the direct action popular in Bryan's heyday, some Republicans stole the wagon which had been decked up as a platform. Undaunted, Bryan stood on a near-by manure spreader and opened his speech: "This is not the first time that I have spoken from a Republican platform."

The story would have been more perfect if it had come from a candidate less given to a flavorsome brand of blather than Bryan, but it nevertheless characterizes a vast majority of political campaigns. The campaign itself did not come into existence until Andrew Jackson's day, but in the century following you can count on one hand the campaigns that made much sense. Indeed, campaigns are frequently noisy, exciting and memorable in direct proportion to their emptiness, and by far the most intelligent campaign speeches in American history—those by John W. Davis in 1924—are hardly remembered at all. Frequently the candidate who does the least campaigning wins, and the one who presses the campaign most vigorously loses. In

1940 Wendell Willkie conducted an extraordinarily forceful campaign and President Roosevelt made very little effort—although he regarded Willkie as more formidable than any of his other rivals. Silence can be golden. Coolidge won the campaign against Davis by maintaining silence, which Mr. Davis regarded as a somewhat overworked virtue: "No one can deny that the chief characteristic of the present administration is silence. If scandals break out in the government, the way to treat them is silence. If petted industries make extortionate profits under an extortionate tariff, the answer is silence. If the League of Nations or foreign powers invite us into a conference on questions of world-wide importance, the answer is—silence. The Republican campaign is a vast, pervading and mysterious silence, broken only by Dawes warning the American people that under every bedstead lurks a Bolshevik ready to destroy them."

The elements that go into a political campaign are many: the personalities of the candidates, the issues if there are any, the attitude of the press, economic groups, traditions, the opinion polls, and the party organization from the National Committee down to the precinct worker. The most obvious, though not always the most important element, is the personalities involved. Before Jackson, of course, when the caucus chose the President, the effect of personalities on elections was much more subtle, because none of the first six Presidents had to concern himself much about appealing to the crowds, although they had undoubtedly personal qualities that either attracted or repelled those participating in the caucus. (In 1820, when Monroe was re-elected for a second term, there was not even a miniature campaign within the caucus, because it was the era of good feeling and nobody wanted to oppose him. There was only one dissenting electoral vote, cast by a man who did not think that anyone but Washington should be elected unanimously.) In all American history there have been only two out of forty-one campaigns in which the personalities involved were the sole major factor. Although the two Jackson campaigns of 1828 and 1832, if only because Jackson was featured in them, involved to some extent his rugged personality, they were fought largely on issues—particularly the 1832 campaign with its preoccupation with the Bank of the United States.

II

The first campaign to involve personalities almost exclusively was the Harrison-Van Buren battle of 1840, in which, for the first time, all the stops were pulled out. Van Buren had been in the White House four years, having been designated by Jackson as his successor, and old General Harrison had fought the Indians at Tippecanoe and was nominated by the Whigs, lineal ancestors of the Republicans, who tossed the Vice-Presidential nomination to John Tyler, a Virginia Democrat. A newspaper opposed to Harrison suggested that he was too crude to occupy the White House and might better sit in a log cabin and drink hard cider. The remark was seized on by the Whigs, who paraded through the streets hauling log cabins and barrels of cider, printed Harrison's portrait over pictures of a log cabin and did everything to promote the notion that Harrison was the poor man's candidate. Van Buren was painted as an opulent aristocrat who had always lived in regal splendor:

> Let Van from his coolers of silver drink wine,
> And lounge on his cushioned settee,
> Our man on his buck-eye bench can recline,
> Contented with hard cider is he.

Actually, Harrison had been born in a famous Southern manor, the descendant of the great landed families of Benjamin

Harrison and Robert Carter, was educated at Hampden-Sydney College and chose the Army as a career because he liked adventure. Van Buren was one of the five children of an upstate New York tavern keeper and went to the village school until he was fourteen, when he went to work. Nevertheless, in a campaign hysterical with enthusiasms solely about the personalities involved, Harrison was hailed as the poor man's hero, the humble man of the cabin. There were log cabins on Boston Common, one big enough to hold hundreds in New York, log-cabin floats, log-cabin oases in village squares—and hard cider flowing like water everywhere. Vainly Van Buren tried to discuss issues, but no one wanted to listen, chanting in a chorus: "Van Van is a used-up man." There had been nothing before like it and there has been nothing quite like it since. "Tippecanoe and Tyler Too" was the campaign slogan—utterly meaningless, for the battle had taken place almost thirty years earlier, a fray involving a thousand soldiers under Harrison and an indecisive battle where Harrison's men were caught asleep by the Indians. But it was billed as a great victory—no one knew over what; and the pleased but confused old soldier won the election. It was solely a triumph of ballyhoo. Harrison had no idea what to do after he got to the White House and, perhaps providentially, died within a few weeks.

The meaning of the campaign of 1840 is paradoxical. One of the most insipid and yet noisiest in our history, it was a symbol of the shift of the source of political preferment from the leaders to the people and a final affirmation of the democratic right to do things wrong. The whole campaign was wrong: the mythical personalities conferred on the candidates, the outrageous myth of Tippecanoe, the outrightly mythical log-cabin origins of General Harrison and the strangely mythical background of aristocracy and wealth ascribed to the Kinderhook tavern keeper's son. But it was important that the nation win at that time the right to sit in the driver's seat, even if it did not know gee from haw. Democracy is a long, continuing effort in trial and error, and the people needed the kind of experience that will tolerate error without perpetuating it. There was hardly a less dangerous time in all our history for this adventure in political adolescence than in the 1840's.

The campaign of 1840, with its distorted personalities, its empty but rhythmical slogans and its launching for years to come of the log-cabin tradition, could happen only once, and it was the epitome of the campaign of personalities. Strong personality factors entered subsequent campaigns—notably those of the immediate post-bellum years—but there were issues also involved. In 1872 the contest of the seedy, inconsistent and pathetic Horace Greeley with Grant, the general who was so totally ignorant of either the ends or means of political action, was such a campaign, as had been also the hero-soldier's earlier campaign in 1868 against the moderate Horatio Seymour. Despite the closeness and bitterness of the contested election of 1876, the major factors in the campaign were not the personalities of Hayes and Tilden. Not until 1884, when James G. Blaine, the plumed knight of Republicanism, engaged Grover Cleveland in a political tilt, did the nation again witness a campaign dominated by personalities, and then it witnessed a masterpiece of vituperative and highly personal politicizing.

James G. Blaine had been Congressman from Maine, Speaker of the House during the spoils period, and Senator from Maine. His ethics were elastic, to say the least; while Speaker he threw a land-grant decision to favor the Little Rock and Fort Smith Railroad, in return for which he was made a bond salesman for the railroad. Personally he was good-natured, friendly and dramatic. He had defended himself with a terrible theatricalism against corruption charges on the floor of the House, and his personality engaged the attention of the public. His opponent in 1884 was the stolid, honest Cleveland, in comparison with whom Blaine was like an alderman to a child in experience in national politics. The spoils and profiteering background of Blaine made him a suspicious candidate, and the Republicans looked for something to pin on Cleveland to balance the campaign. They found a ten-year-old bastard son in Buffalo, and Cleveland told his managers not to deny the truth.

The conflict of 1884, then, was largely occupied thereafter with the debate as to whether Cleveland's personal morals were worse than Blaine's political corruption. Cleveland was alleged to have committed his ex-attachment to an asylum and to have kidnaped and hidden the son. He was accused also of dodging the draft, although Blaine as well had not served in the Civil War. Blaine, on the other hand, was ringingly proclaimed as "The Continental Liar from the State of Maine." When political leaders tried to get the Republican great man, Roscoe Conkling of New York, to give one speech for Blaine, he said quietly, "Gentlemen, I have long since given up criminal practice." The impurity of Cleveland was hard to sell over the dishonesty of Blaine. To add to the confusion, Blaine had been received by a committee of clergymen in New York. The group's spokesman, the Reverend Samuel T. Burchard, made a little address, in which he referred to Cleveland's party as that of "rum, Romanism and rebellion." The Democrats could hardly wait to print the words on handbills and the next Sunday they were distributed outside Roman churches. Not even an affidavit from the mother of Cleveland's son, attacking the candidate, could drown out the cries against the continental liar, and Cleveland won.

The 1884 campaign was the last outright and exclusively personal campaign. In the cases of the strong Presidents, Theodore Roosevelt, Wilson and Franklin Roosevelt, the personalities of all three played an important part, but it was more their theory of the Presidency and of government that drew attention than their personal characteristics. This was demonstrated to the surprise of nearly everyone in 1948, when the ideas of Franklin Roosevelt were a strong issue in a campaign after his death and the ideas, not their protagonist personally, won. In other elections, some aspect of the Presidential candidate's personality may have been a factor—for example, Al Smith's religious affiliation in 1928 or the Barefoot Boy of Wall Street characterization of Willkie in 1940, but the personalities involved in such campaigns have not been sole determining factors in the election. It is very questionable that America will ever again see a campaign devoted entirely to personalities. That sort is not characteristic of a very mature society, and events both at home and abroad have had an increasingly sobering effect on the political nature of the nation. The campaign of personalities is simply a luxury the people can no longer afford.

III

With the beginnings of the Progressive movement, which came after the geographic expansion of the nation had been accomplished and the predominantly industrial character of our society had been determined, the campaign issues moved into their present phase. Before Jackson the major issue had been the growing power of Federal government versus State rights; between Jackson and Lincoln it had been the extension of slavery; between Lincoln and Garfield, Reconstruction; between Garfield and Theodore Roosevelt, the tariff; and from Theodore Roosevelt to now, a laissez-faire versus a regulated capitalism. The campaigns through these years have revolved around the candidates' interpretation of these issues; and, in general, those candidates have won who have gone with the current of public opinion of their times, and those who have tried to buck that current have lost. The effective campaigner, therefore, has been the man who has been able to give articulate expression to that opinion and reasonable promise of heeding it once he is in office. And the ineffective campaigner has, on the other hand, set himself up as a dissenter, who is alarmed and who suggests correcting or altering the trends of his time rather than advancing them. In other words, the successful campaigner's talk is *of* the people, reflecting and perhaps clarifying their own thinking, while the loser's talk is *to* the people, correcting, amending and perhaps reversing what they are thinking.

It is for this reason that, in a very clear difference in the quality of candidates, the less qualified can frequently win. In the campaign of 1924 Davis was obviously a man of infinitely richer intellect, of far more penetrating insight and of generally more opulent personal qualities than Calvin Coolidge, who had a very provincial, shallow and limited mind. But Coolidge reflected the prevailing feeling of the time, which was simply to leave everything alone, and he won. Mr. Davis sought to impress on the people the abuses at home and the drifting abroad that bespoke trouble ahead, but it was no part of the people's thinking. They chose Coolidge.

Aside from its direct political function, which theoretically is to give the voters grounds for choice, the campaign serves another purpose. If the principals amount to anything as candidates, it contributes to the political education of the people. The campaign of 1860 was, for example, of the first importance because it served to stimulate thinking on the slavery question and the secession issue, and it accomplished a final alignment of forces on these matters. Similarly the campaign of 1912, though it was cluttered because of the Republican split, served to clarify the issue of whether capitalism in America was to be predatory with the government's benediction or serviceable with its guidance. Moreover, a good campaign serves as a desirable check on the party in power. If the party is moving too fast, it may be caused, by either the campaign or the prospect of one, to reduce its speed, or if it is moving too slowly, to accelerate. In this the party and the candidate that lose nevertheless serve a useful and real political purpose, and it is therefore reprehensible for a party to name a hopeless candidate just because its chances appear hopeless. The Republicans did great damage thus to have named Mr. Landon in 1936, and the Democrats to have named Mr. Cox—however towering he was compared with Harding—in 1920. In both years great and important issues were at stake, and they needed full and intelligent exposition. But in both years the less favored party simply abrogated.

IV

In every campaign the stands of the candidates involved are apt to have their appeal less to individuals than to groups, for man as a political being renounces his essentially solitary nature and acts in concert with others. Consequently a very important function of the campaign is to win over groups or, at least, to retain the support of groups already friendly, and possibly to inspire them to do some campaigning of their own. In a society more and more disposed to arranging itself in associations, this function of the campaign is more and more vital. In general the group can be divided into three categories: business, farm and labor. Of these, the least politically astute is business.

When Calvin Coolidge said the business of America is business, he was not making an effort to be talkative. But he could have gone farther to relate politics to business, an attempt that has been made more by progressive factions in America than by conservative ones. The businessman, perhaps hopelessly conditioned by the thirty-day balance sheet, seems unwilling to invest very much time in analyzing the relationship of political and business life and is for the most part content to perpetuate irrational attitudes, usually one of alarm when progressives are in power and one of relaxation when conservatives are in power. The ultimate effect of either kind of government on business is lost to the businessman, and he seems to be, even in the face of long experience, either indifferent or blind to anything but immediate effects. It is perhaps for this reason that owners and managers of businesses which are big and profitable now but which were small and even losing in 1932, can steadfastly and with a straight face maintain that Democratic rule has ruined business. It is a little bit like a man who was twenty years earlier in the bread line complaining later about paying a six-thousand-dollar tax on a twenty-thousand-dollar income. The important thing, which is that he has a twenty-thousand-dollar income on which to pay a tax, is lost to him in his immediate chagrin that he has to pay 30 per cent of it over to the government. And if you asked him whether he would rather have no income and therefore no tax liability at all, he is apt to look hurt, as though you were somehow taking advantage of him. The simple truth is that he is being romantic and not realistic about the whole problem.

Politically, American business is romantic and not realistic. It feeds on its past, but is inclined to view it with the air of an elderly Southern lady contemplating her lost youth. It is uncritical of its present, putting itself in the position of Don Quixote tilting with the windmill. It is fearful of its future, but in the sense that a healthy but romantic adolescent is fearful that she will die like Camille of tuberculosis. Business as a group is usually against things, and a whole generation has grown up now that associates business leadership with nothing but complaints and fears. Yet that same generation has witnessed no wholesale collapse of business and no epidemic of bankruptcies, and there is little wonder that it is not impressed by either the complaints or the fears. So business winds up by talking to itself, and politically it is so lacking in insight that it has almost ceased to be a political force at all. It lacks a constructive political imagination so that it has very little to bring to a campaign and can be as embarrassing to the party it favors as it is helpless to stop the party it opposes.

This is probably due to a basic oversight of what business and political parties should have in common—which is the desire and effort to court and win over the majority. The political party that does not understand the point of view of the majority is not going to win. Similarly the business community, as long as it separates itself from the values and aspirations of its customers, is going to isolate itself politically from them. This is not going to have any very serious effect on the life of the nation, however, simply because no business is going to give up. The average business goes right on selling, at a profit apparently, to the people whose views it holds to be highly dangerous. If this may put some in a contradictory position—the big city newspapers, for example—it does not seem to bother either the business or the customer. Consequently the role of business in politics may be said to have been reduced to virtual ineffectiveness in our time, and nobody seems to have suffered. The direct and immediate interests of business are still amply cared for by trade associations and lobbies, and its loss of the determining effect it had on national policy in the days of Grant or McKinley or Taft has been destructive neither of its own long-range interests nor of the national economy.

Before business emerges again as a political force of any real proportions, it will need to reconcile itself with the realities of the time. Following such reconciliation, it would be at least in a position to replace fear with confidence and regrets with adventure. Strangely, in private it really has such confidence and adventure, or not a new factory or a new product would have been built in the last seventeen years. The people are not unaware of this and therefore are less and less inclined to pay much attention to its public wails. The *sine qua non* of any revival of popular interest in what business thinks politically is more reasoning and less emotion in the formulation of the political principles of business. Until that happens, it is not going to sway the voters.

V

One of the more asinine of Communist charges against American democracy is that it is run by business. One reason why it is not—and a reason also for the limited political power of business—is that business in America presents no generally united front. It may favor specific things, but it often favors them in a restricted area. This is due to the fact that, when all the shouting is over, there is more internal conflict in business than there is external conflict with the government. For example, the trucking industry and the railroads both want low taxes; but the railroads, who have to maintain their own roadbeds, have always felt that the trucking industry, using the public highways, gets away with murder. And the great chain stores are disturbed at Justice Department activities which are reasonably pleasing to small, independent merchants. Compared with this division of interests, labor in America has presented a fairly solid and united front, despite organizational schisms, and is much more of a direct political power.

But the great fact about the political attitude of labor in America is that it has been more careful to see the point of view of business than business has been to see labor's, and the great fact about the political action of American labor is its reluctance to become in whole fact a political party. Despite the presence in the labor movement of the same kind of extremists and corruptionists as Gould was in business, the political attitude of labor has in general been far broader and more tolerant than that of business has become. The American Federation of Labor, for example, was for a long time consistently Republican, and labor also shared the enthusiasm of business for the high protective tariff. Moreover, labor has been more alert politically to get in step with the rest of the nation and to relate its interests to the national interests, with, of course, conspicuous exceptions. At the same time, it has been politically more flexible, making concessions to changing events and changing values. And it seems to have the ability to learn by experience.

The historic political identity of labor in the United States has always been with the Republicans and not with the Democrats, and the present alliance with the latter is less the result of innate Democratic virtues than of acquired Republican failings. During the period when organized labor was first feeling its strength in America, the prevailing wind of Republicanism was the popular conservatism of William McKinley and it was not inconsistent with the interests of labor. As it became gradually apparent that the political destiny of American labor lay less in any effort to become itself a political party than in the direction of an immense pressure group ready to exert its force on the established party, it should have occurred to the Republican politicos of the Taft era that here was the mightiest single force of voters that would remain as long as modern America existed. But the Republicans missed the boat and drove labor from their camp by the adoption of the political principle that, while there was much the government could do to protect the owners of industry, there was nothing it could appropriately do to protect the workers of industry. The Reconstruction Finance Corporation was the final touch: in the midst of the widespread human misery of the Depression, Republican policy indicated that direct

Federal relief to ownership was a moral duty and logical function of the government, while President Hoover asserted over and over again that it was morally wrong to extend direct Federal relief to unemployed workers. The total defection of labor from the Republican Party was then accomplished.

Without the emergence of Franklin Roosevelt, or someone else with the same convictions on the responsibility of the Federal Government, in 1932, there might very well have arisen from necessity a labor party in America. Roosevelt put his finger on the matter when he pointed out that it was time existent political institutions took account of new realities which were not temporary but permanent. Among these were the great changes modern industrialism had wrought on the social unit of the community. He emphasized that it had been traditional in America for the community to take care of those who were victims of economic distress. But thirty or forty people being dependent for relief on the community when a nineteenth-century woodwork shop met with disaster was a situation radically different from the problem facing a city of over a hundred thousand when half or two thirds of its working population were victims of the closing of giant textile mills. The industrialism that brought increased production simply brought with it increased social problems—beyond the power of the community to handle. You could not apply the reliefs of the era of local industry to the miscarriages of the era of national industry. Nor was this thinking new with Roosevelt. A generation earlier a very wise Republican, Elihu Root, had said, "In place of the old individual independence of life in which every intelligent and healthy citizen was competent to take care of himself and his family, we have come to a high degree of interdependence in which the greater part of our people have to rely for all the necessities of life upon the systematized co-operation of a vast number of other men working through complicated industrial and commercial machinery."

Labor knew this, not from theory, but from experience. The Democratic Party adopted this truism in national government, and labor would have been suicidal not to ally itself with the Democrats. Samuel Gompers had charted its political strategy a generation earlier: "One political party deals with our policies and rejects them; another deals with them and adopts them, that is, it expresses itself as being in agreement with us on these policies, and if we are to remain true to the principles and policies which we have urged upon the public, we necessarily must work with such party for the accomplishment of our object."

Although labor itself does not organizationally operate as a unit, and although the rift between the American Federation of Labor and the Congress of Industrial Organizations (C.I.O.) has often been deep, labor nevertheless recognizes a common interest. Consequently there has been virtually unanimous support of the Democratic Party in all campaigns since the Depression. John L. Lewis, who is far from being a characteristic labor leader politically, attempted to lead the miners into the Willkie camp in 1940, but all the coal-mining states went to Roosevelt, for American workers will follow their labor leaders in economic strategy, but in political strategy only if they agree with it. The reason for this is that the historic development of labor in America has been economic rather than political, for labor has always put more store by the effectiveness of its economic arsenal than it has put faith in political processes. Its political course and objective have been to seek a political climate in which its economic arsenal can be put to best use, and it will of course support no party that attempts to restrict the extent to which its economic weapons can be peaceably employed.

The backing of one candidate against another has unquestionably been the major political influence of labor in America, but a far more penetrating effect of labor's necessary concern with politics has been its "educational" activities, the C.I.O.'s

Political Action Committee and the A.F. of L.'s League of Political Education. As long as these organizations are engaged in informational activities, they should be healthful both to labor itself and to the working of democracy. It is important that the records of members of Congress be charted and available in convenient form, that legislation be reported in terms understandable to the laity, and that party and candidate principles be interpreted. But there is danger in these educational organizations, too, not because they have shown any tendency to operate as revolutionary cells as some nervous commentators have suggested, but because they tend towards the introduction of partisan political methods in labor's effort to advance its interests, at the possible cost of economic and pressure methods. Whether the supersession of the former over the latter would serve its real interests as well is highly questionable. Gompers was very much aware of the risks, the digressions and the complications that would beset labor if it ever sought to become a political party, and labor can ill afford to ignore him. Moreover, the weakness of labor as a party should be apparent. Allied with the Democratic Party, it could win against the Republican Party, but split from the Democratic Party it could have only some hopes of keeping the Democrats out of office. This would seem to be an objective not currently consistent with labor's major political purpose, which remains the improvement of the general chances of its economic weapons' working successfully.

VI

Forces that are not a part of normal political activity but that can account for the outcome of a political campaign seem to be on the decline in America. This perhaps is most obvious in the changes apparent in the political strength of the press. There was a day when one of the big questions of a Presidential cam-

>aign was which way the great papers would throw their
weight. In 1944, 87 per cent of the press threw its weight against
Roosevelt; and Roosevelt won. In 1948 the two biggest papers
n the nation, the *New York Daily News* and the *Chicago
Tribune,* threw their combined eight-million circulation against
Truman; and Truman carried both New York City and Chicago. And in all the elections since 1932 a majority of the press
has supported the losing candidate. Some observers in remark-
ing this have seen the disappearance of the ability of the press
to influence elections, which has undoubtedly happened, and
also a decline in the more general effectiveness of the press in
democratic processes, which has not necessarily happened.

Much was written after the 1940 election, for example, to
suggest that grave dangers imperiled the usefulness of the press
as an instrument of democracy. The grounds were that almost
80 per cent of the newspapers supported Willkie, even though
such news stories as the Gallup reports (then not discredited)
foretold the re-election of Roosevelt, and that less than a fourth
of the papers supported the winning candidate. The complaint
was that the election proved the "power of the press" to be at
a vanishing point and that the press either misrepresented public
opinion or did not represent it at all.

The fallacy of the complaint is obvious: newspapers are
neither endowed nor publicly supported but operated as businesses; and they participate in all the values, including the political values, of the business community. It was therefore no more
reasonable to expect that 70 per cent of newspapers would support Roosevelt than to expect that 70 per cent of brokers or
industrialists would support him.

The Secretary of the Interior, Mr. Harold Ickes, was nevertheless sufficiently alarmed to assemble a symposium on the subject
by 28 distinguished contributors. The storm was pretty much
a tempest in a teapot, for—James Bryce and Mr. Ickes to the

contrary—the function of a press in a democracy is not passively to serve as a weathervane of public opinion. Nor is there anything healthful in public opinion serving passively as a weathervane of press opinion. The alarming things about the 1940 election would have been a refusal of pro-Willkie papers to carry stories indicating a Roosevelt victory or a blind following of the electorate to the support of Mr. Willkie simply because the vast majority of the press advocated his election. The first would have indicated a concealment of news, a withholding of information, on the part of the press. The second would have meant an abrogation, on the part of the people, of that power to judge the press which Jefferson rightfully and wisely held to be a duty of the citizens of a democracy. Nothing would be more dangerous to a democracy than a press of such power that the elections were merely in effect an automatic, popular stamp of approval on the choices of the press for public offices. And when the press does achieve such power over the minds of the people, then we may as well do away either with the press or with elections.

When worrying about the power of the press, it is well to remember that the kind of power which is able to swing elections increases only as the ability of the people to exercise critical judgment decreases. An ignorant people or a haphazard one will depend on newspaper opinion to make up its mind for it. An enlightened people will read editorial opinions and then make up its own mind. It is, indeed, a far healthier symptom of the condition of a democracy to see a people exposed to such an overwhelming urging of the election of one man, and then go out and elect another, than it would be to watch any candidate with the most editors on his side ride into office. The power of the press, in short, should be a stimulative power and not a persuasive power. And the function of the press editorially, as Jefferson conceived it and as such recent history as that of the last sixteen years would tend to confirm, is to provoke criticism and to foster a critical attitude. Certainly that function is well fulfilled when the critical attitude of the people is sufficiently developed to enable them to criticize the critics!

Moreover, there have been fundamental changes in the American newspaper that alter its relationship to partisan conflicts. There was a century and a quarter of journalism in America when nobody's opinion graced a newspaper except the editor's. Today most dailies carry several columns of opinions that radically differ from the editor's and from one another. The diversity of opinion opens up a competition of ideas, and the man closest to the people or the most perceptive in detecting popular thinking will have more influence than the editorial page. Walter Winchell, for example, is totally indifferent to what the editorialists on the papers that use his column say; he makes up his own mind and says what he thinks; but does anyone imagine that his influence is not greater than all those editorialists' put together? Indeed, the columnist or commentator like Winchell—sensitive to what makes the people adopt one course against another, persistent in a certain unassailable independence and possessed withal of great and real talent for vigorous expression—is the real heir to that rugged journalistic tradition of Greeley and Dana and Bennett and Day, for the heads of newspapers have become businessmen and not journalists at all. There is a very striking example of the peculiar strength of the columnists in the *New York Mirror:* both Winchell and Drew Pearson write for the *Mirror,* which also has a standard Hearst-inspired editorial. Neither Winchell nor Pearson, however, shows the remotest political association with the *Mirror's* editorials; yet for all practical purposes they and men like them are the real journalistic influences in present politics. And while a century or less ago, names of great editors, like Samuel Bowles, Charles A. Dana, James Gordon Bennett or Henry Raymond, were familiar to every American, today most people cannot name a single one, although they know some thing about Winchell and Pearson, Walter Lippmann and Dor othy Thompson. The columnists *are* the newspapers so far as editorial influence goes; and because most papers have more than one, they bring a diversity of opinion to the press previously impossible.

This division of the editorial function of the paper is one of the healthiest developments of the role of the press in political campaigns. The present century has brought a great change to the personalities of newspapers. In the days when personal journalism in the United States was at its height, it was the editor alone whose personality became that of his paper. Not only the readers of the old *New York Tribune* but the entire nation always thought of Horace Greeley and the *Tribune* as synonymous. If you quoted the *Tribune,* you quoted Greeley; and if you said that the *Tribune* was guilty of a piece of folly, you meant that Greeley was off on a tangent again. Similarly, when the *New York Sun* lashed out at the *World* during the Cleveland campaign, everybody knew that Charles A. Dana was out after Joseph Pulitzer again.

If an editor was suffering from a delusion, as Greeley frequently was, then the paper was either useless or dangerous until he recovered. If he was by nature vicious and without principles, then there was not a principle to be found in his whole paper. As far as the health of the democracy went, such outright viciousness was not the worst thing that could happen, for the journal resulting from it could eventually be discovered and repudiated—and such journals always have been. But when the influence of a paper like Greeley's *Tribune,* perhaps the most influential single journal in all American history, was the printed personality of only one man, then the free press was really a danger. The *Tribune* and Greeley—inseparable as the two were—both had a liberal, humane reputation that exists, thanks to haphazard critics, to this day. What reason did the

American people have to question its purity of purpose, then, when the bitterness and the vanity and the personal ambitions of Greeley led the *Tribune* to advocate "letting the South go" in the Civil War whenever the going was rough and morale needed strengthening, to refuse to support Lincoln in the darkest days of the 1864 campaign, and to flatter the Congressional scheme to impeach Johnson when the latter stood almost alone for a decent Reconstruction program? The answer is that the readers of the *Tribune* had no reason to doubt the wisdom of these things, for the *Tribune* printed nothing other than Greeley's personal opinions. This was dangerous journalism; and a press whose freedom and whose conscience alike are conditioned by the unpredictable whims of individual men—men who *are* the papers—falls far shorter of achieving its function in a democracy than a press whose freedom and whose conscience are limited by such predictable factors as a consistent economic or political dogmatism. For these last things are more easily recognized and more easily considered in relation to editorial judgments than are the whims of a man who becomes an institution—just as they are recognized and considered by the readers of Colonel McCormick's *Tribune,* the people who read his paper all during 1948 and then went out to act in direct opposition to his advice by putting Illinois soundly in the Democratic victory column. And the present administration has very sound grounds for ignoring the McCormick press, as Lincoln did not dare ignore the blundering Greeley's *Tribune.*

Nevertheless, because the personality of such a paper as the present *Chicago Tribune* is so much the personality of its publisher, it is politically a far less desirable form of journalism than the Scripps-Howard papers, which constitute a bigger business and total more readers. The reason is that the McCormick brand of journalism is today an unnatural throwback to a phase through which the best of the American press has long since passed. Where once the personality of any newspaper was a rigid reflection of the personality of its publisher, it is now a composite personality, almost in some cases a complicated one, reflecting the personalities of many editorial forces: the columnists, the Washington and foreign correspondents, the news analysts, and the political commentators. This tendency towards a many-sided, broader personality in place of the rigid, narrow view, from which sometimes not even the letters column of a paper ever departed, is noteworthy because it better equips the journal to achieve its informative and critical ends and better equips the reader to judge the issues and candidates of the campaign on their merits.

Supplementing this present diversity of opinion in the press due to the rise of syndicated columns is the increased role of radio, particularly as it is put to use directly by the political parties. Even the largest rally could accommodate only a few thousand people and those who got to them usually heard a candidate only once. The radio made a rally of fifty million a reality, and the same people could hear a candidate over and over again. Speeches no longer passed through the filtering process of the press; remote towns and villages no longer had to be content with third and fourth-rate speakers; the Presidential candidates talked directly to the voters everywhere. Above all else, this made for direct appeal by the candidates and direct appraisal by the voters, and it made the myth element once familiar in the log-cabin days of campaigning utterly useless. A man who talks in the living room of the citizen is hard to misrepresent.

VII

The mechanics of politics have confounded good men for centuries, and have caused some completely to despair of democracy. For ultimately the conclusion of a political campaign is strictly mathematical: a standard of muchness and not of merit decides its outcome, and a good cause can be lost when numbers are against it. For this reason political managers can possess the least ample political intellects and yet be eminently successful in political management. Not called on to appraise issues, to construct policies or to examine social and historical forces, they deal primarily in the mobilization of the vote, which is to say the delivery of a larger number of votes on election day than the opposition gets. When they get beyond this, they are apt to flounder badly; and anyone who has read James A. Farley's political autobiography must marvel at what can tempt a man of such conspicuously high talent in political management to throw it all overboard in a pitiable effort to be the subject rather than the agent of that management. One gets the feeling all along that he is reading the testimony of an artist's former agent who decided to be an artist himself even though he had never before painted a picture.

The object and the limit of Mr. Farley's political career, up until his 1940 ambitions, were the construction of a party organization that in a hard mathematical contest would win. There are no qualifications about the ballot, and there are no comments. There is only room for a check mark, and the acquisition of the largest number of those marks is what wins an election. The job of the campaign manager is to build an organization that will get enough ballots marked opposite the right name. The final purpose of the party organization in the campaign is that simple—although the means is somewhat more complex. And there is no more chance, in the practical workings of a democratic society larger than the village, of an *unorganized* group winning a campaign than there is of a party without candidates.

Organizing the party is, on the higher level, a constant effort

in diplomacy and, on its lower levels, a kind of military recruit-
ment. Bad party organization in the former sense may have
cost Hughes the election in 1916, when he alienated California
during the campaign by snubbing its favorite son, Hiram Johnson; on election night Charles Evans Hughes went to bed under
the impression that he was President-elect, until California's
vote came in for Wilson. Good party organization takes care
of such disasters before they happen: the candidate visits the
right places and is seen with the right people, and preferably
photographed with them, when he gets there; it allows no party
spokesman to insult a geographic area however gently (Mr.
Farley said that he was rebuked by Roosevelt in 1936 for calling
Alf Landon the governor of a "typical prairie state"—"one of
those splendid prairie states" was the way Roosevelt wanted to
put it); it decides who can safely appear in a campaign and who
should be kept out of the limelight; it decides what pressure
group such as the C.I.O. or the N.A.M. deserves what level of
speaker.

Equally important as this higher-level diplomacy is the forg-
ing of a chain of command in the party organization that can
be counted on until election day. The supreme commander is,
of course, the candidate, but the ranking field commander is
the national chairman and campaign manager. It is necessary
for him to have a flow of intelligence reports coming in to him
every day, stemming from the precinct worker, who tells the
ward leader, who tells the city leader, who tells the county
leader, who tells the state leader. The state leaders tell the national chairman, who thus follows the political drift of the
entire nation as the campaign progresses and can break it down
into precincts if he has to. If he sees a state slipping two weeks
before election, he can concentrate his fire on it, sending in
trouble-shooting speakers or juggling potential patronage. He
must also be certain of the absolute reliance of the party work-

ers through election day. The canvasser must push doorbells, asking for support and finding out why when it is withheld. He must distribute tokens—calendars or pencils or blotters—which have room on them to advise the citizen how to vote. He organizes clubs for everyone—men, women, children, business-men, workers, veterans, old people. He drives the old to the polls and baby-sits for mothers. He watches the voting lists, checking off those who have voted and calling in a car for those who have not. If he is part of a machine, he even provides substitutes for those who have not voted, usually unknown to them, and he sometimes extends this courtesy to the grave. Many a departed Republican has voted a straight Democratic ticket, and many a lamented Democrat has found political revolution in death. In Chicago, during the thirties, Election Day was called Resurrection Day. And the dead do not split tickets. All this is the concern of the party worker in the field; but just as a battle is the joint concern of the private and the general, it is the concern also of the top command of the party organization.

VIII

The party worker who makes a career of it and who does nothing else eventually becomes a cog in a machine, which is a political force devoted mainly to self-preservation and self-per-petuation. Machines are not interested in political issues but only in political power, although they sometimes give the ap-pearance of taking a stand. To them the means of politics are an end in themselves, and they figure prominently in every campaign. Machines can be successful on the ward, municipal, county or state level; but they do not succeed on a national level, except insofar as they contribute to the victory in a national election. But since urbanization has favored the growth of machines, those contributions have become increasingly important and can account for the electoral vote in pivotal states. Properly, however, their interests stop with themselves, and loyalty to the machine is prior to any partisan loyalties. Thus, the Southern machines, most entrenched in the land, bolted Truman in 1948, and the Tammany machine bolted Tilden, Cleveland and Bryan when they were Democratic candidates. Boss Hague was loyal to whoever he thought would win, and in 1948 he was first for Truman and then for Eisenhower and then for Truman again. The McCormick machine of Illinois and the Pew machine of Pennsylvania are, however, more insidious, because their objective is to influence national policy and to control national affairs, while such disturbing elements as a Hague or Curley are content to be kingpins in their local spheres.

Nevertheless, all political machines remain local in character because only part of their operations are acquisitive, the remaining part being a constant process of covering up their sins. This covering-up involves controlling police forces, legislatures and prosecuting officials, and it would be imprudent indeed to attempt it on a national scale. But the machines must maintain a party affiliation in order to control the dispensation of Federal patronage in their own areas. They will, therefore, attach themselves to national parties even though they are ignored or insulted. Curley of Boston, one of the least efficient of machine bosses, thus attached himself to Roosevelt, and no amount of Presidential rebuffs could shake him loose. Of course, in the case of a winning national ticket, the local boss always hopes for a coattail ride to victory himself, but his real purpose is to use Federal patronage to consolidate his local position.

During every campaign the Republicans call righteously on the Democratic candidates to repudiate machines like Frank Hague's and Edward Kelly's and fail to mention the machines of Joseph Pew or Joseph Grundy in Pennsylvania or Lloyd

Marsh in New Jersey, all of whom are allied with the Republican Party. The Democrats, of course, reverse the process. Actually both parties know that they cannot repudiate the machines respectively attached to them without disrupting party unity, and neither can afford it in an election year. Moreover, the politician who has been in practice very long knows that such repudiation would be only a moral gesture, so far as the life of machines goes. The simple fact is that municipal governments in modern times in the great cities are not policy-making but service-rendering organizations, and they are concerned with awarding contracts and jobs to perform those services. And that is what interests machines and bosses—not policy or politics. Reform administrations are bound to be the exception rather than the rule, for the nature of the municipal organism is such that if a reform administration stayed too long in power it would itself become a machine, though it might be employed in less cynical pursuits.

The only outright attempt to create a national machine was staged by Huey Long in the nineteen thirties, and it came to an end with Long's assassination in 1935. But Long lived long enough to show that it might be possible. He had reached beyond the state limits to engineer the election of Hattie Caraway as Senator from Arkansas, and his Share-the-Wealth slogan had sharp implications to minds baffled by the Depression. Farley said that a secret survey made by the Democrats in 1935 indicated that the movement might have won as many as four million votes, and by holding the balance of power a national political machine could thus dictate the outcome of a national campaign. Such an eventuality represents perhaps the only threat of the machine on the national level, but it is one that will have to be watched carefully in times of distress, when any political monstrosity has the best chances. For then political campaigns have a great content of emotion and a lesser one of

reason, and the boss—a shrewdly reasoning animal himself—
counts heavily on an abdication of reasoning by the voters.

IX

From time to time tired citizens have wondered what the
practical values of a campaign were, and why it might not be
prudent to abolish campaigns, since it seems impossible to ignore
them. They have their answers in the histories of campaigns.
In 1948, for example, there was very little doubt that during the
campaign the sentiments of the majority who had elected a
Republican Congress in 1946 changed sharply and by November had changed enough to reject Republicanism in the Presidency, the Congress and several state governorships. Yet there
were no major events during that period to account for the shift,
and it must be ascribed to the thinking stimulated by the campaign.

For the function of the campaign is stimulative, though its
method seeks to be persuasive. It is highly questionable indeed
that Mr. Truman or his colleagues were sufficiently forceful
orators to convert voters right and left during the fall of 1948.
But they were provocative and persistent enough to give the
people pause, and the people began to wonder what the 1946
Congressional upset had wrought and what it portended. Similarly, Mr. Dewey's evasions and polished equivocations were not
perhaps sufficiently obvious to turn people away by throngs, but
they were weak and doubtful enough to make them wonder
what Republicanism stood for or whether it was for anything
at all. The election of 1948 was won in the campaign of 1948.

The practical effect of a Presidential campaign, no matter
how mythical the personalities created out of the candidates,
how roaring the oratory or how ringing the slogans, is to give
the voters a quadrennial period for collecting their political

thoughts. They become aware of their ballots and aware of the function of the ballot. And the important thing is not that they merely listen to speeches or read editorials, but that they think in political terms and appreciate that they rule Presidents and Senators and Congressmen. More than anything else, democracy needs this renewal of the self-realization of the source of its powers, and if campaigns served no other purpose they would be well worth the time, the money and the effort that go into them. Conversely, democracy has nothing more to fear than the voter who casts his ballot automatically, and enduring a political campaign is slim enough punishment for his crime.

Chapter Eleven

Elections

I

ACCORDING to the laws of the United States, only 531 people are eligible to vote for President of the United States and 266 of these can choose the President. According to law, they may reverse the opinion of a majority of voting citizens, and on more than one occasion they have. According to law, 18,000 popular votes in Nevada are equal to 130,000 popular votes in New York, and a Nevada voter casts seven votes for President for the one that a New York voter casts. All these political oddities are the product of an archaic institution called the Electoral College. The Electoral College is made up of delegations from each state equal to the combined number of Senators and Representatives from each state. Thus, if a state's population is too small for it to have more than one Representative in Congress, it nevertheless has three electoral delegates, because all states are entitled, for geographic and not population reasons, to two Senators and at least one Representative.

The function of the Electoral College is to allow the best minds to choose the President, and it was originally designed to safeguard the office from control by the masses and to avoid a choice based on hearsay about the candidates reaching the citizens rather than on the reliable information to which the electors were believed to have access. The electors were to meet in December and write two names down on a piece of paper. The man who got the most votes would be President, and the one who got the next largest number would be Vice-President—providing in each case it was over a majority. If it was not, then the House of Representatives, with each state casting one vote, would choose the President from the top three on the electors' list.

Alexander Hamilton, who was devoted to the idea that the few should rule in the interests of the many, thought that if this system was "not perfect, it was at least excellent." And it worked very well for the first two elections, since there was virtually no opposition to Washington. Madison took a less optimistic view of the Electoral College, holding that, in nineteen cases out of twenty, it would fail to award a majority to any one candidate, since there would be not two nominees but any number of aspirants, and that consequently the House would be electing Presidents. In practical effect, therefore, the electors would simply be nominating three men, from whom the House would be choosing the President. Hamilton was wrong, and Madison was right.

In practice as it was conceived, the Electoral College lasted for exactly eight years and elected one man, Washington. It collapsed on the third Presidential election, when Washington had withdrawn, and party organizations began to emerge. The people were reluctant simply to select respected citizens and let them choose a President. They selected the citizens to be electors but told them how they wanted them to vote. In 1796 the constituencies of seventy-one electors wanted them to vote for Jefferson, and those of sixty-eight electors wanted them to vote for Adams. But electors are legally unpledged even today and can vote for anyone Constitutionally eligible for the Presidency. And in 1796 three of Jefferson's electors changed their minds and voted for Adams, who won by three electoral votes.

In the immediately following election, in 1800, the Electoral College behaved even less successfully. Electors were required to vote for two men, but they were not allowed to specify which one was for President and which one Vice-President. With partisan processes a reality in 1800 and with the Electoral College having been designed for nonpartisan politics, the electoral system became enmeshed in its own machinery. The Democratic electors had agreed that they would vote for Jefferson for President and Aaron Burr for Vice-President. Accordingly seventy-three electors (a majority of eight) wrote Jefferson's and Burr's names down. But since they could not specify the Presidential choice as distinguished from the Vice-Presidential choice, the votes were necessarily interpreted to be for the Presidency and the result was a tie. The election was thrown into the House, where it took thirty-five ballots and a good deal of intrigue to get Jefferson elected.

In the wake of the 1800 election, the Twelfth Amendment was passed, requiring the electors to specify their choices for President and Vice-President, who were to be voted for separately. But the winners still had to have a majority and not merely a plurality of the electoral vote, so that it was still possible for the election to be thrown into the House. In October 1948 Kermit Roosevelt did some figuring on what could happen in the 1948 election; at midnight on Election Day, it looked very much as though he had ventured a prophecy rather than a possibility: "It might develop that Dewey had won 265 electoral votes, which would be one less than a majority. Truman might have 211 votes, and the Dixiecrat candidate, Governor Thurmond of South Carolina, having carried Alabama, Louisiana, Mississippi, South Carolina and Virginia, would have 55. The election would have to be referred to the House of Representatives. The House would make its choice from the *three* leading candidates, each state having one vote regardless of size. Now, let us go one step further and assume, as is perfectly possible, that while the Republicans have won a majority in the House, they have done so by carrying the biggest states, and that the Democrats actually represent more states. Then, as Dixiecrat spokesmen have already pointed out, they will hold the balance of power. They could say to the Truman supporters, 'You vote for our man or we'll vote for Dewey. Your man can't win. You have to choose between a Democrat and a Republican.' It is then perfectly possible that Governor Thurmond would find himself President, although he would have received only a fraction of the electoral votes and an even smaller fraction of the popular vote."

Although many a citizen retired on the night of November 2, 1948, believing that there would be no President-elect until the new House convened the following January, the almost solid Far West vote for Truman gave him a safe electoral majority.

A much more constant defect in the electoral system is how, even in undisputed elections, its mechanics can overthrow the popular majority. This has happened three times in our history. In 1824 Andrew Jackson had 50,000 more popular votes than John Quincy Adams. He had also ninety-nine electoral votes to Adams' eighty-four, but the electoral vote was divided four ways with 131 necessary for a choice. Clay, who had had thirty-seven electoral votes, threw his support to Adams when the contest got to the House, where Adams won in the state roll call of unit votes. In 1876 Tilden, the Democratic candidate, received 4,300,590 votes, by the Democratic count, and Hayes, the Republican, received 4,036,298. Even by the Republican count Hayes received only 4,033,768 to Tilden's 4,285,992. When the electoral vote was counted, Tilden had 184 votes and Hayes 165, with 185 votes necessary for a decision and twenty votes from Florida, Louisiana, South Carolina and Oregon claimed by both sides. Congress, after much argument about this dilemma unanticipated by the Constitution, appointed an Electoral Commission, made up of fifteen Senators, Congressmen and judges, eight of whom were Republicans and seven Democrats. In each of the four contested states, the Commission decided by an eight-to-seven vote that the Republicans were entitled to the disputed electoral votes, and Hayes therefore won by 185 to 184, despite Tilden's quarter million popular majority, about 3 per cent of the total for both men. In 1888 Benjamin Harrison got 100,000 popular votes fewer than Grover Cleveland, but won by an electoral vote of 233 to Cleveland's 168.

These are not cases merely of minority Presidents (of which there have been twelve) but of plurality candidates losing—men who had more votes than their competitors who won. And this can happen whenever the electoral votes of some states are won by small pluralities and the other candidate wins other states by large pluralities. For example, the Republicans carried New York in 1948, where Dewey got 2,828,764 votes to Truman's 2,781,599 and captured the state's forty-seven electoral votes. In Massachusetts Truman got 1,151,788 popular votes and Dewey 909,370, and thus won Massachusetts' sixteen electoral votes. Now, combining the two states, Truman won 3,933,387 popular votes to Dewey's 3,738,134—a majority of 195,253; but in the Electoral College Truman got only sixteen votes for his performance in both states and Dewey got forty-seven—a Dewey majority of thirty-one. In other words, Truman got over 50 per cent of the combined popular vote and yet Dewey got 76½ per cent of the combined electoral vote. It is this kind of distortion that can defeat the majority.

The basic flaw in the Electoral College is that it was designed to avoid popular voting and we are attempting to use it to reflect popular voting. Even if the amendment proposed by Henry Cabot Lodge, Junior, which would require the casting of a state's electoral vote proportionately to its popular vote rather than as a unit, were adopted, it would still not cure the situation. Under the electoral plan Delaware, Nevada, Vermont and Wyoming have a total of twelve electoral votes. The State of Wisconsin alone has twelve electoral votes. Yet in the last election, there were a total of only 425,997 cast in the first four states, while in Wisconsin there were 1,276,800 voters. Thus, whether electoral votes are cast as a unit or proportionately, the voters in the four small states are going to have one electoral vote for every 35,499 popular votes; and Wisconsin is going to have one electoral vote for every 106,400 popular votes. Consequently, even under the Lodge amendment, if a candidate won 638,400 votes in Wisconsin, which is half the popular vote, he would get six, or half of the electoral vote; but if his opponent won all 425,997 popular votes in the other four states, or 212,403 less than the other candidate won in Wisconsin, he would get 12 electoral votes, or twice as much as the other candidate. In variations of such cases as this the Lodge reform would destroy the equalizing effect that even the present incongruities between popular and electoral votes have.

Indeed, the only cure for the electoral system is to abolish it; any effort to improve it is like trying to improve the vermiform appendix. Moreover, the electoral system preserves inequities in voter eligibility, because the electoral vote is based on population and voter qualifications are based on state requirements.

Mississippi, for example, has a population of 2,183,796 and cast 192,190 votes (167,538 of them for Thurmond) in 1948. The 192,190 votes represented nine electoral votes. The State of Washington has a population of only 1,736,191, and therefore only eight electoral votes. But Washington cast 878,875 votes in the 1948 election. An electoral vote in Mississippi, a no-toriously backward state, therefore came with every 21,354 bal-lots, while in Washington there had to be 109,860 to earn one electoral vote. This rewarded Mississippi for its reactionary voting laws with a five-to-one influence over Washington in the Electoral College. It also rewards states many of whose citizens may be too indifferent to vote, for New York has forty-seven electoral votes whether 90 per cent or 10 per cent of the voters cast a ballot.

Yet the electoral system can be eschewed only if less than seventeen states object to an amendment, and this possibility is very remote. Nine states in the United States have nearly half of the entire population, or 65,239,378 and a total of 234 electoral votes. The other half of the nation has the remaining 297 elec-toral votes. Any resident in any one of the nine large states, therefore, counts 27 per cent less in electoral votes than those of the remainder of the nation. By an amendment, therefore, nine states would gain and thirty-nine would lose in their electoral strength, and in the face of this—coupled with the traditional jealousy of the South—certainly at least seventeen states would object. And so the Electoral College remains, largely merely to distort, although three times to reverse, the popular will.

II

A dramatic effect of the electoral system is to give the impres-sion that elections in the United States have been characterized by sweeps and landslides. Shaded maps are a popular way of illustrating election results, and they are invariably based on electoral votes. Thus, in 1936, when Roosevelt won the electoral votes of forty-six states and Landon of two, the map looked as if there were not a dissenting vote outside of Maine and Vermont.

Similarly, after 1928, the election maps indicated that for all practical purposes the Democratic Party had ceased to exist. Actually, unless the term is defined much more severely than its implications suggest, the landslide does not happen in American politics. No victorious candidate has ever won as much as two thirds of the popular vote; and only Harding in 1920 and Roosevelt in 1936 got more than 58 per cent, each of them getting only three fifths. Moreover, the greatest margin by which anyone has won the Presidency was only some 25 per cent, which was approached only twice, in the Republican victories of 1920 and 1924. This means that any election could have been reversed by a shift of one in four votes.

Twelve Presidential elections have been won with less than 50 per cent of the popular vote, beginning with Polk in 1844 and including Truman in 1948. In 1860 Lincoln won with 39.9 per cent of the popular vote, and both Grover Cleveland and Wilson served two terms though neither ever got as many as half the people to vote for him in either of his winning elections. The least that the leading losing candidate ever got was 28 per cent, which Davis got in 1920, but twenty-two losing candidates have got more than 40 per cent of the popular vote in the last thirty-one elections, and only nineteen of the winners have got more than 50 per cent. One losing candidate, Tilden in 1876, got 51 per cent, which was higher than the winners got in the next five elections. Harding won by the greatest percentage, and Lincoln by the least. Tilden lost by the smallest percentage and John W. Davis by the greatest, unless one considers that Taft, and not Theodore Roosevelt, was the leading contender in 1912, in which case Taft lost by the greatest percentage. The average with which Presidents have won since 1828 is 51½ per cent, which means that on the average less than two voters in a hundred decide the election. The average with which candidates have lost is 46 per cent, which means that with a one-tenth increase they could have won. Thus, the first great lesson to be derived from the mathematics of American politics is that, not only have there been no election landslides, but the rule is that they are very close, the average difference between winning and losing candidates being 5½ per cent.

Because of this closeness in popular votes, it would be very hard to derive any long-range meanings from Presidential elections simply by looking at each result by itself. Since Jackson's first élection, the Democrats have gone over the 50 per cent mark only nine times, while the Republicans have gone over it eleven times; and eleven times neither party has received a majority. In the eleven elections where there was no majority, however, the Democrats received a plurality nine times, and the Republicans only twice. This would suggest, although the Democrats have won only fifteen of the thirty-one elections and the Republicans sixteen, that the Democrats have the greater popular support. Since 1900 the Democrats have had a majority of the two-party vote seven out of thirteen times, but it has had a majority of the two-party vote for the Senate only eleven out of twenty-five times and for the House only the same number. However, its two-party majority vote for the Senate four times exceeded 70 per cent and for the House three times—a tremendous majority, while the Republicans never reached 70 per cent even in their best years. These combined figures show an unquestionable strength on the part of the Democrats that is both constant and upward in general level.

It is, however, precarious and not invulnerable to third-party invasions. President Truman, in 1948, got just under half the total popular vote, 24,104,836 out of 48,680,416. Wallace and Thurmond, both of whom siphoned away votes largely from the President and certainly not from Mr. Dewey, got a total of 2,326,412. If these were added to Mr. Truman's vote, he would have received 26,431,248, or about 54 per cent of the total vote,

compared to Roosevelt's 53.3 per cent in 1944. These figures confirmed what the most brilliant of political statisticians, Louis H.
Bean, graphically charted a year earlier: that the Democratic
trend was only temporarily halted in 1946 and that it will
probably continue throughout the 1950's. If this is true, it means
that the Republicans will have been out of power for nearly
three whole decades and seven elections, compared with the
last dominance of the Republicans, from Lincoln through
Arthur, which covered only twenty-four years and six elections,
in three of which the Republicans did not win a majority. It
means also that even a war and the subsequent reactions to it
could not shake the Democrats out of power, as they did in
1920. It means that the biggest third-party movement since
1912 could not interrupt their ascendancy, as one did the Republicans' in 1912. It means that the loss of the party leader
and of a whole administration could not scatter what was left,
as it did, again, in 1920. In fact 1948 was a year of political decisions, and the mathematics show that the Democratic tide is
far from beginning to ebb.

III

The Republican who can accomplish a shift of some four out
of a hundred Presidential votes can stem the Democratic tide
and send it ebbing back to the twenties. To do that, he has first
to know what gives the Democrat that precious one twenty-fifth
of margin. An election map of popular votes will tell him: the
Western farmer, the men of the prairies, the plains and the cattle
range. Labor cannot be made the scapegoat, for the three greatest labor states, New York, Pennsylvania and Michigan, with
their giant industrial cities, went Republican. But those traditionally conservative figures, the farmers and those who turned
to the West, have committed themselves against privileged

conservatism, and until a new popular conservatism evolves on the American political scene they will keep with the Democrats. And the political division will remain one-sided. One feels that such a division was accomplished for another decade when the only Republican who showed any signs of understanding it was repudiated by his party in 1944—Wendell Willkie; and that it was sealed when Harry Truman was regarded patronizingly as a mild ineffective who did not know what it was all about in 1948.

In retrospect it appears that the great political need of our times is a popular conservatism that will serve as a realistic and enlightened balance to what will soon be a twenty-year-old progressivism. But if this conservatism is made only the vehicle of fear and complaints and alarms, feeding on other compulsions of other ages and unappreciative of the present, then we stand in danger of a one-party government, not through any usurpations of the party in power but by default of the party out of power. And that is an eventuality which our present political processes could not survive.

BIBLIOGRAPHY

All that mankind has done, thought, gained or been: it is lying as in magic preservation in the pages of books.—THOMAS CARLYLE

For Those Who Want to Go Deeper

THE practical effect of a bibliography is usually its service as a statement of credentials, and sometimes an author will even file a bill of particulars, in the form of footnotes, in which the reader can find out on what grounds he makes his statements. This gesture is ordinarily less a concession to the curious than a kind of a priori answer to the querulous.

The following bibliographical notes are designed to call the attention of the curious to some titles which may satisfy his curiosity or—even better—arouse it further. It also seeks, for the sake of the querulous reader, to indicate where, if he has enjoyed disagreeing with the conclusions of the present volume, he can find confirmation of the facts that led to them. He probably will not find the conclusions themselves, but at least he will know that, although the evidence has necessarily been subjected to a manipulative and eclectic process, it nevertheless exists. And consulting the evidence, he can reappraise it to suit himself and come to his own conclusions. Indeed, it would be far more gratifying to know that this book had launched a few readers on such a rewarding project than it would be simply to have them drop the matter with the end of this very general survey.

This bibliography then is an invitation rather than a catalogue of credentials or a bill of defense. It is for those, curious or querulous, who want to go deeper into the whole matter with which these pages have been concerned. It has shoulder heads by chapters and the subject of chapters, so that those, for example, who are primarily intent on probing farther into the Republican Party won't first have to go through a series of titles on the Supreme Court; but it is to be hoped that an interest in one subject will lead to an interest in another. Yet the order doesn't make too much difference, and sometimes the best thing about bibliographical notes is that you can skip around in them and don't have to stay with any one subject.

Chapter One—THE ORIGIN AND DEVELOPMENT OF THE STATE

It is sufficiently obvious that my view of the origin of the state is teleological, and I cannot ascribe it to any one influence. But I should think, to come to his own view, the reader would want to renew his acquaintance with some of the philosophers and then to supplement this with reading one good commentary on them. He would want to read certainly Plato's *Republic* and Aristotle's *Politics* and, probably, E. Barker's *Political Thought of Plato and Aristotle*. The German philosophers, Kant and Hegel, might also be sampled, but not with as much comfort and pleasure as the Greeks; and in between their premises and conclusions, particularly in the case of Hegel, there is a great wad of attitudes ascribable only to the Teutonic mentality, and maybe this, with the persistent intrusion of theological dogma, explains a good deal of Hegel. I would think that any of the textbook editions of selections from Kant and those of selections from Hegel would be better for the purpose than reading the entire works. The effect of Hegel will probably be to show that the philosophy of the state often went as awry as its function did. I believe that we are indebted to Kant's philosophy for much to relate ethics to politics, and Kant's *Perpetual Peace* should be looked into by those concerned with high-riding national sovereignty. The earlier *Idea for a Universal History from a Cosmopolitan Point of View* has interest, too. I would be inclined to read Hegel for the purpose of stimulating the critical faculties and Kant for bolstering faith in political processes. I do not mean merely that Hegel should be a horrible example and Kant a reassuring light. But if you want to know how the state in organization and function is subject to such changes in practice, it is not irrelevant to find out how philosophies of the state have changed, too, although it is no more pleasant sometimes to contemplate than many of the organizational and functional changes.

John Locke put a pretty low ceiling on philosophy; but, as the text says, we owe much to his political thinking. A reading of *Two Treatises on Government*, when it is remembered that they appeared in 1685, is revealing in the light of subsequent political history. Eight years before *The Social Contract*, Rousseau published the less widely read *Discourse on the Origin of Inequality;* both should be read and Rousseau's extremism should be related to the political evils that he saw. Not profound and a commentator rather than a philosopher, he was significant; and those overly in love with order have tried in vain to destroy his historic position, in an understandable effort to correct his excesses.

By way of general commentary on the philosophy of the state, I would prefer the readable and wise *Man and the State* by William Ernest Hocking to most of the others, for Hocking is a mature thinker and draws on a tremendous erudition. His judgments are balanced, and he knows what he's talking about.

On the Constitutional Convention the best thing to do is to read *The Federalist* of Alexander Hamilton, James Madison and John Jay, available in many editions. *The Making of the*

Constitution by Charles Warren is the most complete account of the proceedings of the convention itself. One should supplement this with the biographies of the major participants: W. G. Sumner's *Hamilton,* Gilbert Chinard's *Jefferson, Apostle of Americanism,* and E. M. Burns' *James Madison, Philosopher of the Constitution.* Madison was very important at the convention, and consequently the third volume of Irving Brant's sound definitive biography, which covers this phase of Madison's career, has great value. It is published at about the same time as this book. Charles A. Beard's *Economic Interpretation of the Constitution* is provocative but must be balanced by A. C. Mc-Laughlin's *Constitutional History of the United States,* which finds some weak spots in the Beard study.

Chapter Two—THE PRESIDENCY

In general there are two ways of going about the study of the American Presidency. One is to read about it as an institution, and the other—more in the manner of Carlyle—to read the lives of those who have held the office. There are several institutional studies of the Presidency. E. S. Corwin, *The Removal Power of the President* and *The President: Office and Powers,* are very closely documented and scholarly performances, but they tend to look at the Presidency in a legalistic vacuum, and I do not think that they take into adequate consideration the problems of the office and especially the challenges that differ with each term. Similarly more concerned with the limitations of the office than with its actual role in our history is C. P. Patterson's no less scholarly *Presidential Government in the United States: The Unwritten Constitution.* As is probably apparent, I have inclined much more to the method of appraisal that can be found in George Fort Milton's *The Use of Presidential Power,*

1789-1943, which is one of the best studies of the Presidency that we have. W. E. Binkley's *The Powers of the President* has been reissued in revised form under the title, *President and Congress,* and is a useful, informed and comprehending study. Two Presidents, Grover Cleveland and William Howard Taft, have written books on the office, *Presidential Problems* and *Our Chief Magistrate and His Powers* respectively, but they do not seem to me particularly useful except in their application to studies of their own terms. There are several books on specific aspects of the Presidency, but I would not regard them as of interest to the general student of our political institutions, although five of them are listed for readers who may want to pursue the line of inquiry indicated by the titles: H. C. Black, *The Relation of the Executive Power to Legislation;* L. H. Chamberlain, *The President, Congress and Legislation;* L. W. Koenig, *The Presidency and the Crisis;* J. E. Pollard, *The Presidents and the Press;* and B. M. Rich, *The Presidents and Civil Disorder.* Of these the most broadly interesting is the Pollard title.

To appraise the historical development of the Presidency as distinguished from its Constitutional establishment, there are several volumes of varying merit. Herbert Agar wrote a partisan study, *The People's Choice,* which brings severe standards to bear against the occupants of the office but is provocative and well-informed. Mr. Agar, I think, is inclined to undue pessimism and does not seem reconciled to relate the office to the times consistently, so that the thesis of there being very good early Presidents and very bad later ones is too easily arrived at and not too conclusive, and I think also that he rather overrates some of the early incumbents and does not sufficiently explain the later ones. But Mr. Agar's impatience is due to his own highly civilized view of the public service, and it can be very useful in making the reader conscious of the dangers of political mediocrities. Harold Laski's *The American Presidency* is a liberal interpretation, but Mr. Laski has the habit of judging the past on the terms of his own philosophic conclusions of today and does not recognize fully the standards that were contemporary to the Presidents of the past. Some of the informal books have great value if you read between the lines, like Merriman Smith's *A President Is Many Men,* and the reminiscences of Ike Hoover, chief usher of the White House, to which can now be added the recollections of the head mail clerk, Ira R. T. Smith, in *Dear Mr. President.* Though the chief interest of such books is anecdotal, their chief value lies in the light they throw on the personalities of their subjects; for example, you can learn a good deal about Coolidge's theory of the Presidency by reading Ike Hoover on how he spent his day.

Those who have read Professor Arthur M. Schlesinger, Sr.'s essays in *Paths to the Present,* which is an urbane and knowledgeable exploration of bypaths in our history, will probably note that in some particulars I depart from the consensus of leading historians in the measuring of our Presidents. The most conspicuous variation is probably the inclusion of James K. Polk among the great Presidents. I simply subscribe to Bancroft's verdict cited in the text, and I add to it the consideration that he came to the office when it was at a low ebb. I also include Buchanan among the failures, because I believe the evidence available proves that he abrogated the responsibility of the office under conditions that could have meant the permanent wrecking of the Union—which seems to me to constitute failure. There are some other variations, too, but they are explained even if not justified in the text.

I can only suggest that you—if you are interested in making your own list—read the best biographies of individual Presidents and relate them to the history of their times. To understand Lincoln's greatness, the best work is J. G. Randall's two-volume

Lincoln the President and the same authority's *Lincoln the Liberal Statesman.* Randall is by far the most competent and thorough of the students of Lincoln's leadership, although Carl Sandburg's well-known biography explores the Lincoln personality at greater length. One should also read Lincoln's own works, and there is no satisfactory alternative to the Nicolay and Hay *Abraham Lincoln's Complete Works.* There is still no really first-rate biography of Washington, the best thus far being Worthington Ford's, Shelby Little's and John C. Fitzpatrick's; but for the achievement of Washington in the launching of the Presidential office, James Hart's *The American Presidency in Action, 1789,* is careful and useful. The void in the Washington bibliography promises to be filled more than adequately by the long biography on which Douglas Southall Freeman is now working. The bibliography on Franklin Roosevelt is growing with amazing speed, but two titles come to mind as most clearly indicating his concept of the office and his theory of its use: Robert E. Sherwood's *Roosevelt and Hopkins* and Frances Perkins' *The Roosevelt I Knew.* The Wilson bibliography is also immense and still growing, but W. E. Dodd's *Woodrow Wilson and His Work,* Ray Stannard Baker's *Woodrow Wilson, Life and Letters,* and R. Burlingame and A. Stevens' *Victory without Peace* are all good for the White House years. Like Lincoln, Wilson also should be read in his own works, the most convenient collection being A. B. Tourtellot, *Woodrow Wilson: Selections for Today.* Jefferson's works are extremely catholic in substance and extensive in range, but an adequate sampling can be made from the Modern Library collection, *Life and Writings of Thomas Jefferson,* and Saul Padover's misnamed but well-edited *The Complete Jefferson.* On Jackson there are several excellent works: J. S. Bassett's *Life of Andrew Jackson;* Marquis James's *Andrew Jackson: Portrait of a President;* C. G. Bowers' *Party*

Battles of the Jackson Period; and Arthur M. Schlesinger, Jr.'s
The Age of Jackson. James K. Polk has been greatly undervalued,
and there is only E. I. McCormac's biography that comes near
to adequacy, although this can be supplemented with the
Diary of James K. Polk, of which Allan Nevins edited a one-
volume edition. These cover the Presidents whom I have called
great.

For most of the others, *The Dictionary of American Biography* is almost uniformly excellent, but special mention should
be made of some individual longer works: Allan Nevins'
Grover Cleveland: a Study in Courage; H. J. Eckenrode's *R. B.
Hayes, Statesman of Reunion;* and Henry Pringle's biographies
of Theodore Roosevelt and Taft. William Allen White's *Masks
in a Pageant* is a sparkling commentary on the period from
Hanna through Hoover. On the whole, however, the history of
the Presidency must really be very closely related to the general
history of the United States. For this purpose, the most convenient and best of the short general histories is S. E. Morison
and H. S. Commager's *The Growth of the American Republic,*
which is in two volumes and sometimes called *The Oxford
History.*

Chapter Three—THE CONGRESS

The sources already cited for the Constitutional Convention
are necessary to discover the hopes which the Founding Fathers
put in the Congress, but to trace its development the best
method is to concentrate on the period histories of the nation
and a handful of biographies. Edward Channing's *History of
the United States* in six volumes is excellent for the period
through the Civil War. Allan Nevins' *Ordeal of the Union* is
a work of first quality for the period before the Civil War. Carl

Schurz's *Henry Clay*, C. M. Wiltse's *John C. Calhoun* and C. M. Fuess' *Daniel Webster* are necessary to an understanding of the Congress at its best. C. G. Bowers' *Tragic Era*, G. F. Milton's *Age of Hate* and H. K. Beale's *Critical Year* will show it at its worst. In general biographic studies of individual members of both houses are lacking or inadequate, and consequently the entries in *The Dictionary of American Biography* are the most reliable sources.

The institutional bibliography on the Congress has grown in the past few years, most of the titles being rightfully concerned with reform. *Congress at the Crossroads* was written by G. B. Galloway, an able political diagnostician who was staff director of the Congress' own Joint Committee on the Organization of Congress. It seemed to me that the Galloway reforms were the most moderate and realistic, but the Congress adopted only some of them in the Legislative Reorganization Act of 1946. Thomas K. Finletter, a highly informed observer, urged more extensive reforms in *Can Representative Government Do the Job?*, which I would be hesitant to consider a suitable solution. James M. Burns in *Congress on Trial* puts up an excellently written case for increased party responsibility to the extent of outright party government, but that also seems to me almost more hazardous than the present dilemma. Everyone should read Woodrow Wilson's *Congressional Government* and *Constitutional Government in the United States*, published twenty years and four years respectively before he was elected President. G. H. Haynes's *The Senate of the United States: Its History and Practice*, is useful, as are also L. Rogers' *The American Senate*, V. Torrey's *You and Your Congress* and W. F. Willoughby's *Principles of Legislative Organization and Administration*. For investigations there is M. E. Dimock's *Congressional Investigating Committees*, but that is now twenty years old, and should be updated by reference to the files of the *New York Times* and the *Washington Post,* which seem to me to have the best accounts of the investigatory activities of the Congress. M. N. McGeary's *The Development of Congressional Investigative Power* can also be brought up to date by such journals. On the Senate's treaty power there are Samuel B. Crandall's *Treaties: Their Making and Enforcement,* which was written before Versailles, and the later work of D. F. Fleming, *The Treaty Veto of the American Senate,* to which should be added W. S. Holt's *Treaties Defeated by the Senate* and the continuing series by Hunter Miller. Franklin L. Burdette's *Filibustering in the Senate* is valuable.

The best commentary on the Congress in operation is, of course, the *Congressional Record* and the publications of the several committees, but you have to be prepared to put up with a good deal of outright nonsense. Nevertheless, it is all there.

Chapter Four—THE SUPREME COURT

The definitive work on the Supreme Court is Charles Warren's *The Supreme Court in United States History,* but this ends with the Taft Court, and probably is best supplemented by C. H. Pritchett's *The Roosevelt Court: A Study in Judicial Politics.* It does not need to be pointed out that the history of the Court in effect is the history of the theory and application of judicial review. *The Life of John Marshall* by A. J. Beveridge is a good beginning for the establishment of judicial review, but to go back further there is C. Haines's *The American Doctrines of Judicial Supremacy* and, for the very early period, *The Role of the Supreme Court in American Government and Politics* by the same author. C. B. Swisher has written the only good biography of Roger B. Taney. For more on judicial review, L. Boudin's *Government by Judiciary,* R. K. Carr's *The Supreme*

Court and Judicial Review and E. S. Corwin's *The Doctrine of Judicial Review* are all good. Charles Evans Hughes's *The Supreme Court of the United States: Its Foundations, Methods and Achievements* can be related to his own position in the Court's history as a moderate.

The 1930's, of course, brought the struggle over the Court and with it a variety of books that served to bring the Court out of the law school and into the popular library. These books continued into the forties, and the two best are, I think, Charles P. Curtis' *Lions under the Throne*, written with both authority and charm, and Robert Jackson's *The Struggle for Judicial Supremacy*, which supports the idea of judicial reform with consummate ability. E. S. Corwin's *The Twilight of the Supreme Court* is entitled to careful reading, but there is room for disagreement. C. A. Ewing's *The Judges of the Supreme Court* goes through 1937 and is useful in many respects. W. S. Carpenter's *Judicial Tenure in the United States*, though over thirty years old, is helpful, and so is the collaboration of F. Frankfurter and J. M. Landis, *The Business of the Supreme Court.*

Decisions of the Court are available, so far as major issues are concerned, in H. S. Commager's *Documents of American History*, the reading of which can be profitably augmented by reference to specific Justices in *The Dictionary of American Biography*, and by such individual biographies as Henry Pringle's life of Taft, on which I drew for the material evidencing Taft's activities in judicial politics.

Chapter Five—THE BASIC CONFLICT

The chapter is derived mainly from a general survey of the history of the United States, and you can come to your own conclusions by reading Channing and Morison and Commager, already cited, and Allan Nevins and also, perhaps, Henry Adams, in their general histories.

Chapter Six—THE DEMOCRATS

Democracy seems to me to have had three major phases: Jeffersonianism, Jacksonianism and the twentieth-century era of Wilson and Roosevelt, which were different stages of the same phase interrupted by the negativist period of Harding, Coolidge and Hoover.

For the period and achievement of Jefferson, a partisan history but one of continued interest is Claude G. Bowers' *Jefferson and Hamilton*. Dumas Malone, the best of present Jefferson scholars, has published *Jefferson the Virginian,* and more of his volumes are looked forward to with eagerness by historians. Of great promise also is Marie Kimball's work, of which *Jefferson, the Road to Glory* and *Jefferson, War and Peace* have already appeared and fully justified that promise. Henry Adams' *History of the United States* is good for this period, although not especially sympathetic to Jefferson. Adams' history is a brilliant and beautifully written work and deserves wider reading. C. M. Wiltse's *The Jeffersonian Tradition in American Politics* is extremely important and should not be missed. Bowers continued his work in *Jefferson in Power,* and although he maintains the partisan view he presents an excellent case. Charles A. Beard inquired into the economic and social background of the infant republic to write *Economic Origins of Jeffersonian Democracy,* but some modification of his views may be called for; and the same is true of V. L. Parrington's treatment in *Main Currents of American Thought.* For both the origins of the Democratic Party and the founding of the later Republican Party, W. E. Binkley's *American Political Parties: Their Natural Growth* is a useful and concise commentary. Richard Hofstadter's *The American Political Tradition and the Men Who Made It* is a sophisticated and assured commentary on Jefferson and other molders of the major political traditions and is highly rewarding reading.

To supplement the works on Jackson suggested in the bibliography on the Presidency and to understand the Jacksonian movement, one should turn to William Macdonald's *Jacksonian Democracy* for a critical treatment and then to F. J. Turner's well-known *Rise of the New West* and *The United States, 1830 to 1850,* and also to his *The Frontier in American History.* E. C. Smith's *The Blair Family in Politics* shows the workings of the Jacksonian party from the point of view of some of its most active operatives. A. O. Craven's *Democracy in American Life* may with Turner be balanced against B. F. Wright's "Political Institutions and the Frontier" in D. R. Fox's *Sources of Culture in the Middle West,* and with the younger Schlesinger in *The Age of Jackson,* to weigh the Eastern and Western influences in Jacksonian Democracy.

Cleveland has to be considered apart from the main current of the history of the Democratic Party, and in general Allan Nevins' biography already mentioned covers the Cleveland interludes. For the Populist uprising under Bryan, two biographies should be read: M. Werner's *Bryan* and Paxton Hibben's *The Peerless Leader,* the critical tone of which one feels to be just. John D. Hicks's *The Populist Revolt* should be read for an understanding of what Bryan signified. Mark Sullivan's *Our Times* also becomes useful at this point and up through the 1920's.

Woodrow Wilson's New Freedom, prototype of the New Deal, is impartially surveyed in *The Pre-War Years, 1914-1917,* by F. L. Paxson, and most of the biographies of Wilson previously noted also are useful. Barck and Blake's *Since 1900* is a good broad survey. The Roosevelt era is still too close for any sound objective survey, but Charles and Mary Beard's *America in Mid-Passage* and Louis Hacker's *Short History of the New Deal* can serve temporarily, and other good contemporary accounts are in E. K. Lindley's *The Roosevelt Revolution* and *Half Way with Roosevelt.*

Chapter Seven—THE REPUBLICANS

For the precursors of the Republican Party you have to go back to Federalism, but the latter must not be confused with Republicanism. J. S. Bassett's *The Federalist System* and *The Completion of Independence* by J. A. Krout and D. R. Fox should furnish enough material on the major aspects of Federalism, but *The Works of Hamilton* also should be consulted, although there is no convenient and adequate abridged selection and you have to go to H. C. Lodge's twelve-volume collection. The more immediate ancestors of Republicanism, the Whigs, are discussed in D. R. Fox's *The Decline of Aristocracy in the Politics of New York,* A. C. Cole's *The Whig Party in the South* and T. C. Smith's *Parties and Slavery, 1850-1859;* and the works of Clay are also relevant. *Dictionary of American Biography* entries on the Whig Presidents are useful and on the whole better than any full-length biographies of them. Allan Nevins' *Ordeal of the Union,* mentioned before, is extremely important. A. C. Cole's *The Irrepressible Conflict* should also be read for an understanding of the political drifting. For the rise of Republicanism, Randall, previously cited, should be read, and so should G. F. Milton's *Eve of Conflict* and E. D. Fite's excellent *Presidential Campaign of 1860.* W. A. Dunning's *Essays on the Civil War and Reconstruction* are necessary, and so is his *Reconstruction, Political and Economic.* D. M. Dewitt's *The Impeachment of Andrew Johnson* is important for the Republicans in the Congress, and Allan Nevins' *Hamilton Fish and the Grant Administration* for the spoilsman era. E. D. Ross deals competently with the enlightened forces of the party in *The Liberal Republican Movement*. P. L. Haworth handles judiciously the Hayes-Tilden election in *The Disputed Election of 1876*. Allan Nevins' *Emergence of Modern America* is an intelligent and rewarding account of the nation during the Republican heyday. M. Josephson's *The Politicos* is an able indictment of the political errand boys. The Hanna-McKinley period is understandingly reviewed in W. A. White's *Masks in a Pageant*. There is no good biography of McKinley. H. C. Croly's *Marcus Alonzo Hanna* has some value. The confused period of Theodore Roosevelt is best clarified by the Pringle biography mentioned earlier, and his *Autobiography* is revealing—more so than that of any other President. Lewis Einstein's *Roosevelt, his Mind in Action* is an interpretation of more than routine value. Pringle is also excellent on the Taft era. Republicanism as negativism in the 1920's is competently handled in *Postwar Years, Normalcy,* by F. L. Paxson, and *This Was Normalcy* by K. Schriftgiesser. *Only Yesterday* by F. L. Allen is more informal, and S. H. Adams' *Incredible Era* is journalistic but sound. B. Mitchell's *Depression Decade* and D. Wector's *Great Depression* recount the impotence of the Republicans in the face of crisis. Ex-President Hoover's earnest plea, *The Challenge to Liberty,* shows his inability to relate theory to fact, and the campaign speeches of Alf M. Landon exhibit a similar incomprehension.

Chapter Eight—THIRD PARTIES

In order satisfactorily to examine third-party movements, it is necessary to go to the individual parties, most of which were swallowed up by the major parties. On the agrarian movements there are several useful titles: *Third Party Movements Since the Civil War* by F. E. Haynes, *Labor and Farmer Parties in the U. S.* by Nathan Fine, and *The Agrarian Crusade* by S. J. Buck. For Antimasonic movements, J. C. Palmer's *The Morgan Affair and Anti-Masonry* is helpful, and more inclusive is C. McCarthy's *The Anti-Masonic Party*. For Know-Nothingism, the most useful are the *Protestant Crusade* by R. A. Billington and *The Know-Nothing Party* by J. J. Desmond. The Socialist Party is treated adequately in M. Hillquit's *History of Socialism in the U. S.* and the much older *History of American Socialisms* by J. H. Noyes. Earl Browder's *Communism in the United States* needs allowances made for it, and perhaps *American Communism* by J. Oneal and G. A. Werner is more satisfactory. The Wallace third-party movement has not yet been properly examined, but Russell Lord's *Wallaces of Iowa* explains much, although the files of the *New York Times* are the only source so far for evidence. Third parties have usually reflected some transitory aspect of national affairs and are better explained by relating them to the general history of the nation than by isolating them and looking at them in a test tube.

Chapter Nine—CONVENTIONS

The best sources on the conventions are the proceedings published in official reports after each convention, but they should be supplemented by general political histories. There are some special studies: K. H. Porter's *National Party Platforms* and H. L. Stoddard's *Presidential Sweepstakes*. Politicians have sometimes told all: James A. Farley in *Behind the Ballots* and *Jim Farley's Story*, and Charles Michelson in *The Ghost Talks*. The Republican convention of 1920 is narrated in Mark Sullivan's *Our Times*; and, on Lodge, Karl Schriftgiesser's *The*

Gentleman from Massachusetts presents the verdict of posterity. In retrospect the contemporary press is always revealing.

Chapter Ten—CAMPAIGNS

Reference should be made to the works on the several candidates for the Presidency. R. Peel and T. C. Donnelly have analyzed two campaigns effectively in *The 1928 Campaign* and *The 1932 Campaign,* but I depended on the records in the contemporary press of what the candidates said and how their supporters whooped it up for them. S. L. Cook attempted, without complete success, to write a history of campaigns in *Torchlight Parade.* But there seems to be no satisfactory alternative to going back through history and determining the issues for yourself and then referring to the works by and about the candidates to discover how they were handled.

Chapter Eleven—ELECTIONS

The sources suggested for the Constitutional Convention above are necessary to understand the purpose behind the Electoral College. On elections all that you need is the returns in terms of both popular and electoral vote. L. H. Bean's *Ballot Behavior* and *How to Predict Elections* are exercises in the mathematics of politics by the most skilled and, I think, the most penetrating of political statisticians. C. A. M. Ewing's *Presidential Elections* and E. E. Robinson's *The Presidential Vote, 1896-1932* and *They Voted for Roosevelt,* which continues the study through the 1944 election, are exceptionally useful. *The World Almanac* has most of the necessary figures.

I should emphasize that I question seriously the value of reading any of the above specialized works or any others without first refreshing the mind completely on the social, economic and political history of the nation. It is easy to isolate political institutions and habits and to get bogged down in theories. Politics are meaningless unless related to the whole fabric of the national life, and frequently you can make more out of political trends or methods by rereading a good general history than by concentrating on the fine legalistic points of some political particular.

INDEX

INDEX

Mellon, Andrew, 273
Mexican War, 54
Michigan, 315
Miller, Justice S. F., 103, 104, 107
Mississippi, 265, 308, 311, 312
Missouri, 245
Missouri Compromise, 123
Mitchell, Charles, 101, 104
Monarchies, 20-21
Monroe, James, 35, 52, 65, 258
Monroe Doctrine, 45, 52
Morgan, J. P., and Company, 203
Morris, Gouverneur, 40, 46
Morse, Wayne, 253

National Labor Relations Board, 61, 95, 105
National Labor Union, 248
National Republican Party, 212
Native American Party, 238
Navy, Department of the, 54-55
Nebraska, 51, 79
Neolithic Man, 16-17
Neutrality Act of 1794, 41
Nevada, 51, 79, 306
New Deal, 72, 136, 139, 164, 207
New England, 43, 164, 165, 213
New Freedom, 72, 205
New Hampshire, 51, 79
New Jersey, 99, 204, 303
New Mexico, 51, 79
New Orleans, 191
New Stone Age, 16-17
New York (state), 79, 245, 268, 306, 310, 315
New York Daily News, 293
New York Mirror, 295

New York Sun, 296
New York Times, 272
New York Tribune, 296-297
New York World, 296
Norris, George W., 183
North Dakota, 51, 79

Ohio, 142
Oregon, 51, 79
Oregon boundary dispute, 44

Palestine, 265
Panama Canal, 69, 229
Parliament (British), 98
Participation Act of 1945, 50
Parties, see Political parties
Party platforms, 259-260, 263-267
Payne-Aldrich tariff, 231
Pearson, Drew, 295, 296
Pecora, Ferdinand, 104
Pennsylvania, 142, 302, 315
Pew, Joseph, 302
Pierce, Franklin, 36, 63, 64, 77, 82, 214
Political Action Committee (C.I.O.), 292
Political parties, origin, 158; functions, 159, 171-182; characteristics, 159-163; basic conflict, 160-165; economic factors, 162-163; and traditions, 163-164; social factors, 164-165; religious factors, 165; in Congress, 179, 180-184; responsibility, 180-184; conventions of, 257-276; in campaigns, 277-305. See also Democratic, Whig, Republican, etc.

Waite, Chief Justice M. R., 131

Wallace, Henry, 186, 240, 251, 252, 314

Walsh, Thomas, 182

War of 1812, 46, 54, 189

War Powers Act, 61

Washington, George, 30-31, 34, 39-42, 46, 131, 167, 258, 307

Washington (state), 79, 311-312

Webster, Daniel, 77, 141, 192, 214

Whig Party, 170, 197, 212-215, 226

White, Chief Justice E. D., 95, 131, 133-134

White Slave Act, 128

Wiggin, Albert, 101

William III of England, 27

Williams, George Henry, 131

Willkie, Wendell, 163, 180, 205, 264, 268, 270, 278, 283, 291, 293, 316

Wilson, Woodrow, 33, 34, 35, 40, 43, 45, 46, 47, 53, 54, 57-58, 70, 71-73, 87, 133, 139, 140, 186, 198, 203-205, 246, 273, 276, 282, 300, 313

Winchell, Walter, 295, 296

Wirt, William, 141, 259

Wisconsin, 245

Wood, Leonard, 272, 273, 275

World War I, 50, 54, 57, 58, 73, 205

World War II, 54, 57, 58, 72

Wyoming, 51, 79